The
Complete Book
of MODEL
FUND-RAISING
LETTERS

ROLAND KUNIHOLM

PRENTICE HALL
Englewood Cliffs, New Jersey 07632

Prentice-Hall International (UK) Limited, *London*
Prentice-Hall of Australia Pty, Limited, *Sydney*
Prentice-Hall Canada, Inc., *Toronto*
Prentice-Hall Hispanoamericana, S.A., *Mexico*
Prentice-Hall of India Private Limited, *New Delhi*
Prentice-Hall of Japan, Inc., *Tokyo*
Simon & Schuster Asia Pte. Ltd., *Singapore*
Editora Prentice-Hall do Brasil, Ltda., *Rio de Janerio*

10 9 8 7 6 5 4 3 2 1

Library of Congress Cataloging-in-Publication Data

Kuniholm, Roland
    The complete book of model fund-raising letters / Roland Kuniholm.
        p.   cm.
    Includes index.
    ISBN 0-13-334202-6
    1. Fundraising. 2. Form letters. 3. Nonprofit organizations–
–Finance.   I. Title
    HG177.K86   1995
    808`.066361—dc20
                                                    94-40556
                                                    CIP

ISBN 0-13-334202-6

PRENTICE HALL
Career and Personal Development
Englewood Cliffs, NJ 07632
Simon & Schuster, A Paramount Communications Company

Printed in the United States of America

Whitney, Jason, Andrew, Myra
Our living letters . . .

Acknowledgments

A book containing hundreds of models, samples, and excerpts of fund-raising letters is by its very nature authored by a great number of writers. I want to thank all the organizations that have permitted their sample letters to be included in this book. These samples have been written by a host of talented people—staffers, agency writers, and freelancers—and they are here for all of us to learn from. But I have had specific help from certain individuals that I want to acknowledge. First, my partner at Frederiksen & Kuniholm, Lee Frederiksen, that with his usual keen copy perception made some excellent suggestions on the organization and format of the manuscript. Writer Jim Perry also provided invaluable assistance in writing many of the model letters that appear throughout this book. Finally, I want to thank Bob Reekie of Media Associates International, Inc., for his input and assistance in regard to Chapter 15—Obtaining Substantial Financial Support with the Foundation and Corporate Request Letter. Writing winning fund-raising copy is a continuing learning process. I'm always on the lookout in my mailbox for a new type of letter or variation of one of the old standards. I hope this book provides you with the stimulus you need to craft many outstanding fund-raising letters for your work. It has always been a source of encouragement for me to know that writing letters to solicit contributions helps many worthwhile nonprofit organizations in our society today. This is the ultimate bottom line of our writing endeavors and makes it all worthwhile.

How to Use This Book

The roof of your local public library leaks, and each time it rains additional volumes in its collection are damaged.

The high school band members have been asked to compete in a state competition and need transportation to the event.

The county shelter for the homeless is running out of blankets and bedding.

Half of the Earth's tropical rain forests have been destroyed, and the rest are being wiped out at the rate of 27 million acres a year.

What do these local and global situations have in common? Each needs financial support to reach its goal—and to reach that goal, each must make its problem known to the community through a fund-raising direct mail campaign.

The Complete Book of Model Fund-Raising Letters provides you with every possible type of fund-raising letter you will ever need. You'll find a comprehensive collection of letters covering the gamut from asking for a first-time gift . . . to special appeals letters . . . to renewal letters . . . to reactivation of lapsed donor letters.

There are samples of excerpts and letters from small groups—such as the local volunteer fire department—as well as large organizations—such as World Wildlife Fund. You'll find letters that can be done on a simple budget and others that can be put to work immediately.

To help you with your particular fund-raising needs, you'll find 350 examples of letter samples, models, excerpts, teaser lines, opening lines, and tips for asking for monetary gifts.

The **model letters** can be picked up and used as is with whatever variation you need to personalize them for your organization.

The **sample letters** illustrate how other organizations (large and small) write this type of letter.

The **excerpts** allow you to see how the most critical sections of your letter should be written.

The **teaser lines, opening lines,** and **tips,** presented throughout the book, help you get the most from your fund-raising efforts.

In short, you have everything you need right at your fingertips to quickly produce all the various types of fund-raising letters you will ever be called upon to write.

In addition to letters that raise funds directly, you will also find other letters that you will need from time to time. These are the support letters that help you recruit volunteers, acquire gifts from board members, solicit contributions-in-kind, answer complaint letters, and acknowledge contributions from your donors.

A special feature of this book are the four telemarketing scripts you can use to solicit funds. We have all received phone calls from organizations asking for our financial support. Sometimes we're receptive to the call—other times, we're not. The difference is usually based on several factors: familiarity with the organization, the timing of the call, and the caller's presentation. There is a right way and a wrong way to make fund-raising calls; the scripts included here will show you how to get the most out of your fund-raising phone calls.

How to Use This Book

A good way to start is by scanning the contents to select the type of letter you need. In Part One, you'll find examples of new donor acquisition letters, including:

- straight contribution
- nomination-to-membership
- front-end premium
- back-end premium
- survey
- special events
- protest/petition

Part Two's letters solicit repeat gifts from your existing donors. These letters include:

- special appeal
- renewal series
- major donor
- telemarketing
- sustainer or regular monthly donor
- lapsed donor reactivation

In Part Three, you'll find the following specialty letters that are very important in any fund-raising operation:

- referral
- foundation and corporate request
- volunteer/activist solicitation
- contribution acknowledgment
- to a board member
- to an employee
- gift-in-kind request
- complaint answer

Each chapter in these three parts indicates which organizations use this particular type of letter, gives suggestions for when to write it, and show you how it's done. In addition each chapter provides model letters that you can use as is or that you can easily modify to suit your organization's particular needs. The model letters are followed by actual sample letters from other organizations to give you further help on how this particular type of letter is used by other organizations.

Before you mail your letter, you will want to take a careful look at Part Four. In this concluding part, you will see how to write all the other components of a fund-raising package so your letter's message will have the highest possibility of being acted upon. These components include:

- getting your envelope opened
- writing strong opening copy
- asking for the right gift amount
- structuring the fund-raising offer
- designing your direct mail package
- producing cost-effective mailings
- testing

A Final Word

The Complete Book of Model Fund-Raising Letters is a source book you'll want to keep at your desk. Within its pages are the letter-writing secrets that will unlock thousands of dollars of extra contributions for your organization. Familiarize yourself with the book's contents. Before you know it, you will have accumulated all the letters you need to raise funds by direct mail. Good luck!

Roland Kuniholm

Contents

Chapter 2

Eliciting Funds with the Nomination-to-Membership Letter 35

Chapter 3

Raising Funds with the Front-End Premium Letter 51

Chapter 4

Using the Back-End Premium Letter to Improve Response 66

Chapter 5

Obtaining Information—and Funds—with a Survey Letter 79

Chapter 6

Boosting Participation in Sweepstakes, Raffles, and Bazaars, Through Special Event Letters 91

Chapter 7

Making Your Voice Heard Through the Protest/Petition Letter 114

Part II

Letters for Soliciting Repeat Gifts from Your Donors 127

Chapter 8

Requesting Additional Funds Through the Special Appeal Letter 130

Chapter 9
Getting the Most from Renewal Series Letters 155

Chapter 10
Reaping Substantial Funds with the Major Donor Letter 182

Chapter 11
"Calling In" Funds with the Telemarketing Script and Follow-up Letters 195

Chapter 12

Acquiring Regular Monthly Donors with the Sustainer Letter   215

Chapter 13

Reactivating Donors with the Lapsed Donor Letter   226

Part III

Letters That Accomplish Special Purposes 237

Chapter 14

Adding to Your Donor/Member List with the Referral Letter 240

Chapter 15

Obtaining Financial Support with the Foundation and Corporate Request Letter 253

Chapter 16

Chapter 17

Part IV

Easy-to-Use Tips to Make Your Letters Work 303

Chapter 18

Getting Your Envelope Opened 306

Chapter 19
Writing Strong Opening Copy 313

Chapter 20
Asking for the Right Gift Amount 320

Chapter 21
Structuring the Fund-Raising Offer 329

Chapter 22
Designing Your Direct Mail Package 337

Chapter 23
Producing Cost-Effective Mailings 353

Chapter 24
Testing: Learning from Your Own Winners and Losers 359

Part I

*Letters for Acquiring
New Donors*

PART ONE illustrates all the different types of fund-raising letters that you can use to acquire new donors. Each chapter in the first section covers a special type of letter to acquire a new donor.

How to Determine What Kind of Letter to Write

The first step in writing a letter to acquire a new donor to your cause is to determine the type of letter that is appropriate. In this section you will see a variety of approaches—from letters that ask for a contribution without utilizing any special inducement whatever—to letters that organize the fund-raising appeal around techniques such as surveys, petitions, and premium offers, to name just a few.

So the first step is to decide the kind of letter you want to write. Here is a list of questions to guide you in selecting the right type of letter to use for acquiring a first-time donor.

1. Is your work primarily social service? You will probably want to look first at the Straight Contribution letter (Chapter 1) and then consider some of the Front-End premium offers (Chapter 3).

2. Do you offer substantial membership benefits? Look carefully at the Nomination-to-Membership letter (Chapter 2).

3. Do you appeal to a highly select audience? This also would lead you to utilize the Nomination-to-Membership Letter (Chapter 2).

4. Is your organization merchandise-oriented? If you offer a variety of merchandise items through a catalog or through your publications, then a Front-End Premium Letter (Chapter 3) or a Back-End Premium Letter (Chapter 4) would be appropriate. The Sweepstakes Letter in the "special events letter" chapter (Chapter 6) would also be effective in this case.

5. Are you an issue-oriented, activist organization? If you are involved in an issue that is a cause with your prospective donors, consider mailing the Survey Letter (Chapter 5) or Protest/Petition Letter (Chapter 7).

6. Does your message have broad general appeal? If you don't target a specific segment of the population, consider a Front-End Premium Letter (Chapter 3) or a Sweepstakes Letter (Chapter 6).

7. *Does your work involve a highly-emotional, simple-to-explain need?* Here, the Straight Contribution Letter (Chapter 1) might be best. Or, you might consider an up-front premium or a paperback book (Chapter 3).

The optimum conditions for using each of the following types of letters are summarized at the beginning of each section. Consider these factors to get a better fix on whether or not that is the type of letter you want. After you've decided which type of letter to write, you will see a number of writing tips along with model letters that you can use and samples illustrating just how other mailers follow the particular technique.

These tips and copy suggestions — along with complete model letters or letter structures in each section — will provide you with all you need to put together a winning letter. Just include the specifics on your particular organization and need for funds and you're ready to mail. It's as easy as that!

Before finalizing your copy, take a quick look at the material in PART FOUR. There you'll see some of the general components of a good fundraising letter plus suggestions on how to write the copy for all the other elements in a complete fund-raising mailing package. By following these suggestions, you'll have a direct mail fund-raising effort that presents your need for funds in the strongest possible manner.

One final tip before you begin writing: Study your competitors. There's a reason why fund-raising organizations adopt particular approaches in their letters to raise funds. The ones you see used over and over again are the ones that are working . . . that are raising significant amounts of funds. If other mailers in your field have spent their budgets finding out what works — and what doesn't — it makes a lot of sense for you to follow their lead. This doesn't limit your creativity. It simply helps get you on the right track to begin with.

That's why I urge fund-raisers to get on as many fund-raising lists as possible and collect as many samples as they can from similar types of organizations. Study the new donor letters *and* the appeal and other followup letters to donors. Note which ones are mailed regularly. Use these as your jumping-off point in a brain-storming session to think through just how you would adapt this approach to your appeal. Every now and again you will see mailings that are a total departure from the standard way of reaching your market. Don't emulate these until you see them mailed regularly and by other mailers as well.

Now, let's take a look at all the different types of letters you can use to acquire that all-important first-time donor.

1

Using the Straight Contribution Letter to Raise Funds

In this first chapter youre going to look at the oldest and most basic of all the types of fund-raising letters used to solicit new donors—the straight contribution letter. I call it that because it relies on no other technique than the simple approach of a written message to ask for a gift for a particular need.

The straight contribution letter is the purest form of a fund-raising letter that exists. A need is described. A solution is offered. A gift request is made to the prospect to put the described solution to work. Other than the good feeling the donor will have by contributing, no special inducements are offered. It is simply one concerned person (the letter-writer) inviting a second person (the prospective direct mail donor) to send a gift so help can be given to a third person (someone who represents many others in need).

We lead off with this most fundamental of all the types of fund-raising letters because it—more than any other type of letter—relies on effective writing techniques to get a response. These writing suggestions are not limited to the straight contribution letter and can be incorporated in most any type of letter you have to write. Now let's see when you should write such a letter and how to write it.

When to Use the Straight Contribution Letter

Typically social service agencies that alleviate human suffering or provide for an urgent physical need—whether it be for food, clothing, or medical help—utilize the straight fund-raising letter. The described needs in these cases are emotionally compelling and are usually ones that people can immediately identify with: starving children needing food or medical aid, homeless people needing a place to sleep, fleeing refugees needing a safe place of protection. Letters asking for gifts to alleviate these types of urgent human needs do not require elaborate presentations to make the case. That's why a simple, direct asking for a gift in cases like these works. Let's see how to do it.

How to Write the Straight Contribution Letter

In this section you're going to see 15 writing tips that will help you write a strong straight contribution letter. Each of the tips is followed by an example to show you how it's done. Not all 15 tips apply to each and every letter you send, of course, but they do provide a helpful checklist. Review them as you prepare a letter asking for a contribution for your work. You'll be surprised to see how easily and effectively they fit into the approach to ask for a contribution.

At the conclusion of this chapter you'll also see a number of *model letters* that show you how to combine these tips in a complete letter. In addition you'll see samples of actual letters by different organizations that exemplify the writing techniques that work for the straight contribution letter. Here are the 15 tips for writing the straight contribution letter.

1. CATCH ATTENTION WITH A PROVOCATIVE OPENING.

Your letter is coming unsolicited. The opening phrases and sentences should be provocative and so intriguing that the prospect is hooked into reading more . . . and more. As a thousand-mile journey starts with the first step, your direct mail letter starts with the first word . . . then phrase . . . then sentence, and so on. These opening "steps" or words are critical to the success of your mailing. Here are some examples of strong openings to fund-raising letters:

- How faithful would *your* church attendance be if you could be arrested for attending?

- This is a very difficult letter for me to write. But if telling you my story could help find my missing son, or prevent another child's abduction, I will gladly accept the heartache it brings me. I cannot adequately express in writing

the pain I feel when I look into my son's empty
bedroom . . .

- I'm writing to offer you a job. It's not a permanent job, you understand. It's not a paying job.
On the contrary, it will cost you money . . .

2. USE COMPELLING INDIVIDUAL STORIES.

Emotional, compelling stories that speak to the need are essential.
They take the message out of the realm of the abstract into the concrete real
world where people live. Get good examples from your case files and write
them as dramatically as you can. Prospects relate to feelings first. They
understand a clear example of one needy person. Here are some case
examples that speak to the heart:

- She stood on the curb looking scared and lonely
in a skimpy halter top and bright red lipstick.
It was two in the morning. A chilly breeze
whipped up the street and seemed to make her
shiver. She was a child . . . just a child.

- I know a little boy who isn't scared of monsters,
dragons, or ghosts. What frightens seven-year-old
Matthew is much more terrifying—and it's not
make-believe. Matthew is afraid of the crack
addicts and gangs who hang out on his block. And
he gets real scared when his mother, the only
parent he's ever known, has to work late and
leave him in the apartment alone . . . no child
should ever be so afraid.

3. ASK FOR THE GIFT EARLY AND OFTEN.

A good fund-raising letter will make the first "ask" or request for a gift
very early—usually by the middle of the first page. And repeat "asks" will
appear throughout the letter. The order in which direct mail letters are read
is spotty at best. That's why you should make frequent pitches for a gift
response throughout the letter. Remember, there's no tomorrow for a first-
time prospect after your direct mail letter has been pitched. The letter should
make it abundantly clear throughout that you are looking for a gift response.

- I urge you to consider making a tax-deductible gift ($25, $35, $50, $100, or more if at all possible) for _____'s _____ project that is helping so many youngsters today.

- Please translate your gratitude into a gift that perhaps represents a bit of a sacrifice.

- A gift of $15 from you right now would be a great boost. And if you could send <u>an extremely generous gift of $400</u>, your gift could help provide a new well for a village that now relies on dirty disease-ridden water. This well will help bring good health to all the children of the village for generations to come. Whatever you can send, please send it <u>today</u>.

For more ways to specifically ask for the gift, refer to Chapter 20. There you'll find a list of 51 different ways to make the gift request.

4. TELL WHAT THE GIFT WILL ACCOMPLISH.

Donors can understand one specific example of how their gift will be put to work. Describe in concrete terms exactly what you can accomplish with a single gift. This way you help the prospective donor visualize being right there on the action line and seeing what a gift will do. Here's how to do it.

- $19 will feed ten from our mobile canteen. $37 will buy a large food basket for a family of five. $62 will cover the costs of a senior citizen's overdue electricity bills. $110 will help support our after-school programs.

- Could you provide a New Testament in Russian for a believer who has probably never even seen one before? They cost $5.00. How many books on "The Life of Jesus" can you furnish? They are only $1.00 each. (Perhaps you can supply a whole class of 25 students eager for God's Word?)

- Your tax-deductible gift of $20 will provide two dairy cows for farmers in rural India. $50 will enable a Cambodian village to erect an irrigation dam to improve rice production. And a gift of $100 will help ten village cooperatives in Bolivia purchase and plant enough seed corn for an entire growing season.

5. BE PERSONAL.

The prospects who receive your letter are a little suspicious at first. They want to know who you are. Is the person signing the letter a real flesh-and-blood person? Can you be trusted? Do you represent a reputable organization? It puts the recipient at ease when you share some little personal things about yourself that he or she can identify with. Prospects want to know your connection with the organization asking for a gift. Be direct and personal.

- I founded _____ myself. I got the idea during World War II. I was a Navy medical officer, and I simply couldn't get the people of the South Pacific, where I served, out of my mind. Sickness and disease ran rampant among them! So in 19XX I began _____. Two years later, we launched the first peacetime hospital ship ever . . . (Project Hope)
- It's 11:30 P.M. on a Tuesday night and I'm tired, I need a shower, and I want to go to bed. But I can't sleep . . . not until I finish this letter and pray that God will fill your heart with compassion for the poor of Appalachia—as he did mine in 1957. That's when I started—in the back room of a small church—to help the poor help themselves. (Christian Appalachian Project)

6. WRITE WITH A SENSE OF URGENCY.

Your direct mail fund-raising letter comes in the daily mail along with other communications that require a response (e.g., bills and personal letters). Select a need for your letter that is a true emergency and indicate you are looking for an immediate response. Here are some examples of writers who knew they had an urgent need and stated it.

- They desperately need the support that only <u>YOU</u> can provide.

- The sooner we hear from you, the sooner we can put your contribution to work—and keep another child alive and well.

- The situation is desperate, even life-threatening.

- Our need for your support is so terribly urgent because, even as I write this letter to you, someplace in the world . . . innocent victims of government abuse are imprisoned, suffering unspeakable physical and mental agonies.

7. HIGHLIGHT THE VOLUNTEER ASPECTS OF YOUR WORK.

People like to feel they're giving to a popular movement. It helps to know that a number of nonpaid volunteers are also involved. A potential donor reasons this way: "If other people care so much about the need by volunteering, the least I can do is give." A volunteer movement shows wide public support, worthy of supporting.

- This movement we call _____ consists of those who care—over 50,000 trained volunteers who carry the good news to prisoners like the ones I spoke to in _____ that night.

- A network of more than 100,000 committed volunteer workers across this country and around the world has been developed to build and remodel modest homes.

- And a critical tool in _____ fight against torture is our <u>Urgent Action Network</u>. This extraordinary international network is a highly organized system of concerned people who agree to be on call to send immediate Urgent Action letters on behalf of tortured prisoners of conscience.

If your organization is short on volunteers, take a look at Chapter 16. Specific letters to encourage volunteer participation are found in that chapter.

8. GIVE YOUR PROSPECT "PERMISSION TO BELIEVE."

People want to believe what you have to say—but before they make a gift—they are looking for some clues that tell them the requesting organization can be trusted. They want to feel that your organization is reputable and will use the gift wisely. A prospect may be turned on emotionally to the need you describe, but before writing out a check, a prospect wants to be assured he or she is not being taken in. Make sure you tell your readers things that allow them to believe you are reputable. Here is how some fund-raisers get this across.

- As a former U.S. president, I have been asked . . .

(Note: The fact that a former President signs this letter quickly communicates validity).

- I urge you to add your name to the roster of members of the only organization of its kind in history to have won the <u>Nobel Prize for Peace</u>.

(Note: See how you can convey credibility by referring to this prestigious prize.)

9. DESCRIBE NEEDS YET TO BE MET.

People want to feel like they are helping alleviate a pressing problem. They are not excited about contributing to a large fund or paying for your overhead. What is the urgent challenge before you that requires special funding? If the donor doesn't respond will this need will go unfulfilled? It's also important that the need or goal of your fund-raising letter sounds attainable. If it's too great an objective, people may reason, "If they need that much, my small gift won't make any difference."

- As you read this letter, there are 300,000 homeless kids on America's streets . . . kids who are alone, hungry, tired, and scared.

10. OFFER HOPE.

People don't want to give to an insoluble problem. They do like to give to a project that is going to succeed. What is the light at the end of the tunnel that will happen if the prospect responds to your appeal?

- The impact on society could be tremendous. Prison violence drastically reduced. Lower crime rates. Hundreds of millions of dollars that you, the taxpayer, would have to spend to build new prisons could be saved.

- And what's even more exciting—because each community volunteer is responsible for the health of many families in the village, your gift to _____ multiplies. In _____, a single $21 gift enables a community volunteer to treat 40 families, so <u>your gift to ( ) is multiplied 40 times</u>!

- But there <u>is</u> hope. And it's so incredibly simple. The solution is water. Clean, pure drinking water.

11. SHOW APPRECIATION.

Even though you write with urgency about a genuine need, take time to thank your donors. Thank them for even considering the appeal. Thank them for the care they have shown in the past. I don't like to think of this as a "technique." Genuine appreciation is always in good taste.

- For all you do, please know that you have my deep heartfelt thanks.

- But any gift you give will be appreciated. And used. Thank you and God bless you.

12. INFORM PROSPECT.

An informed donor will be a better long-term donor. While emotions are essential in getting attention and involvement, it is also important that your donor begins to realize some key facts about your work. The best fund-raising letters contain lots of new factual information for the prospect.

- I want to share two facts with you. * Our planet produces more than enough food to feed the world's population. *Today, 60,000 people died of hunger.

- Do you realize that in many developing countries 4 children out of 10 succumb to one of these diseases before they reach their fifth birthday.

- To keep pace with the current rate of incarceration will require the construction of 250 new cells a day at a daily cost of $17.5 million. It costs $20,000 a year to take care of one prisoner and it costs $80,000 to build one new cell!

13. PROMISE SATISFYING FEELING OF GIVING.

The act of giving is a gratifying personal feeling. People like to do it. People feel good about doing the right thing. Giving, in a very real sense, gives the donor a sense of personal worth and identification. It doesn't hurt to refer to this feeling in your copy.

- And what a warm feeling of satisfaction that will give you.

- I assure you, the tremendous feeling of satisfaction you'll gain from taking part is beyond compare.

14. BASE THE APPEAL ON PAST SUCCESS.

People like to give to winners . . . to causes that have a demonstrated track record of success. Explain how you have been successful in the past and how a current gift will achieve similar results.

- . . . past donations have enabled us to: Serve over 500,000 meals to the hungry and homeless in 1994. 100,000 of those through our mobile feeding program.

- I am pleased to tell you that during our history we have sent more than 12,000 doctors, nurses, and other highly trained health professionals to teach modern medical skills to the people of over 60 developing nations.

- With the help of caring friends like you, _____ has set up more than 445 revolving loan funds to build housing for the poor.

15. PRESENT A PERMANENT SOLUTION.

People don't want to give to a project that will be in constant need of additional funds. They like to feel that your solution is a long-lasting one, one that is a real solution to the problem.

- The good news is that this is not just a handout. Interest-free, nonprofit home loans are offered to poor people so they can pay back into the revolving loan funds to help someone else in need.

MODEL LETTER
STRAIGHT CONTRIBUTION—HOMELESS SHELTER

Dear Friend,

CATCH ATTENTION WITH A PROVOCATIVE OPENING (POINT 1)

Food, clothing, shelter, and love. Every child deserves them. Every child needs them.

But I know eleven children desperately short of all four.

INFORM PROSPECT (POINT 12)

They, and their mothers (and some fathers), are temporary residents of the Safe Haven Homeless Shelter here in _____. And I can tell you that, by the time they reach us, they have very little with them. The clothes on their backs. One suitcase for a whole family. Meals have been missed. And certainly proper nutrition has gone by the boards.

And the stress on their parents cuts the love short, too.

So when they get to the homeless shelter here on Main Street, they have very little.

ASK FOR THE GIFT EARLY AND OFTEN (POINT 3)

I am asking you to help these children with a special gift of $10, $15, $25 . . . or more, if possible.

Or you may want to make a gift-in-kind. I hope you can find some clean, well-repaired hand-me-downs for children of all ages. I especially need jeans, T-shirts, sweaters, raincoats, winter coats, shoes of all kinds.

BE PERSONAL (POINT 5)

If your home is like mine, you have clothing that hasn't been used for a long time.

USE COMPELLING INDIVIDUAL STORIES (POINT 2)

Denise, 15, is a good student in school, but she doesn't have a winter coat to wear to get to the school bus. Billy, who just turned 6, is outgrowing his only pair of jeans. We have five children under six who need clothing of all kinds.

ASK FOR THE GIFT EARLY AND OFTEN (POINT 3)

And when you contribute I will put it toward our "socks and underwear" fund.

PROMISE SATISFYING FEELING OF GIVING (POINT 13)

We can give these children shelter, food, love . . . and you can give them what they need to make a new start in life. What a satisfying feeling you will have knowing you have helped some deserving children right here in our own community.

ASK FOR THE GIFT EARLY AND OFTEN (POINT 3)

Can I count on you for a gift of $15? Or a gift of some clothing or other items you no longer need? Your contribution is tax deductible.

SHOW APPRECIATION (POINT 11)

Thanks for opening up your heart . . . and caring. It means a lot.

Sincerely,

HIGHLIGHT THE VOLUNTEER ASPECTS OF YOUR WORK (POINT 7)

P.S. Over 100 of your neighbors in _____ help us in the food preparation and other services. Your gift will allow their efforts to be so much more productive. Thanks.

MODEL LETTER
STRAIGHT CONTRIBUTION—VOLUNTEER FIRE DEPARTMENT

BE PERSONAL (POINT 5)

Dear Greater Falls Resident,

CATCH ATTENTION WITH A PROVOCATIVE OPENING (POINT 1)
GIVE YOUR PROSPECT "PERMISSION TO BELIEVE" (POINT 8)

This is an unusual letter. It is signed by 37 citizens who have a message for you:

"Support your local volunteer fire department—it's worth every penny."

Now why should you believe us?

BASE THE APPEAL ON PAST SUCCESS (POINT 14)

Simply because each of us faced an emergency in the past year—in every case the Greater Falls Volunteer Fire Department responded—and in every case a situation was made safe. A fire was put out. And in some cases lives were saved!

And in every case, the citizen volunteers performed professionally, courteously, and—when needed—heroically.

ASK FOR THE GIFT EARLY AND OFTEN (POINT 3)

Now, we hope you never have a visit from the Fire Department. But we do hope you will make a contribution—$15, $25, $50, or more, if possible—to the Volunteer Fire Department Annual Fund Drive.

So that—if you <u>do</u> get a visit from these "volunteer professionals"—their equipment and training will be up-to-date.

INFORM PROSPECT (POINT 12)
TELL WHAT THE GIFT WILL ACCOMPLISH (POINT 4)

So often, the margin of safety for firefighters, and the margin of <u>saving people</u> is very slim. Seconds count. That's why the annual fund pays for new radios, overhauls on engines, advanced training, the latest in lifesaving equipment.

We know we never expected a visit from the fire department. But we're glad they came! And we're proud that our community has these men and women who give their time and risk their lives for you and me.

And we were—each of us—very glad of the high level of training we saw.

BE PERSONAL (POINT 5)

Each of us has contributed to the Annual Fund. We strongly urge you to do it too. Do it for the safety of the courageous volunteers—and for the safety of everyone's family in our community.

Thank you

Signed, (37 Citizens)

BE PERSONAL (POINT 5)
ASK FOR THE GIFT EARLY AND OFTEN (POINT 3)

(Script note): You might be surprised at who is a volunteer firefighter. Doctors, lawyers, carpenters, students, housewives and secretaries. You probably know some of the letter-signers, but may not know that their "second profession" is saving lives in our community. I look forward to receiving your tax-deductible gift to help in their dedicated efforts. Thanks.

Signed, John Doe,
President.

MODEL LETTER
STRAIGHT CONTRIBUTION—HOSPICE

Dear Friend,

USE COMPELLING INDIVIDUAL STORIES (POINT 2)

Marie is 98 years old. She doesn't have too many more years to live. But the other day she told me one of her fondest dreams. It wasn't all that major but it was heartfelt. She really would like to have a table lamp beside her bed and a rug on her bedroom floor.

ASK FOR THE GIFT EARLY AND OFTEN (POINT 3)

That's why I am writing you today . . . to ask you for a special love gift of only $15 to help a lonely senior citizen like Marie. Our budget simply can't pay for such "luxuries." But they are the type of things that give joy and peace to some very wonderful people we work with here at the _____ Hospice.

TELL WHAT THE GIFT WILL ACCOMPLISH (POINT 4)

Each of the residents at _____ Hospice has a similar modest request for clothing, a radio, a mirror, an electric blanket . . . small personal things like that.

But I can't afford to give them these things. I would like to have a separate refrigerator for medicines and another microwave . . . but the hard fact is I can't afford that either.

ASK FOR THE GIFT EARLY AND OFTEN (POINT 3)

And so I am writing to ask you for a special tax-deductible gift so we can provide a household item or two for the residents of _____ Hospice.

INFORM PROSPECT (POINT 12)

You see, the cost of dying, even at a hospice, is very high. And to give each of our 50 residents the comfort and dignity he or she deserves, we invest our small budget in people, not things.

And more than half our residents have no health insurance—it's run out, or they aren't eligible. Many others have no family.

We do not turn them away. Every person deserves to spend their last days in comfort and dignity, and so we serve them.

It is exhausting, but deeply satisfying work—but I would like to give these people I have grown to love and admire a few of the little amenities of life.

ASK FOR THE GIFT EARLY AND OFTEN (POINT 3)

Will you help? We could put your gift to good use today . . . whether it's $5 or $100. Gifts of $20 or more are especially needed. Your support will help us provide exactly what one of our residents needs: a lamp, a small television or radio, a tape player.

PROMISE SATISFYING FEELING OF GIVING (POINT 13)

Think of the smile you can bring to an older friend . . . someone who has been faithful and caring all of her or his life. I can't think of a greater blessing to know I have touched the life of a fellow-citizen in a time of need.

ASK FOR THE GIFT EARLY AND OFTEN (POINT 3)

To donate an item, simply call XXX-XXXX. I will probably answer the phone, but if the answering machine is on, just say what you have to contribute and leave your phone number. A volunteer will get back to you quickly.

Or, if you have no item to give, you can send a
tax-deductible check in the enclosed return envelope.

Thank you. You have no idea how much the little
things count.

Sincerely,

BE PERSONAL (POINT 5)

P.S. I'd love to show you our facility. I think
you'll be impressed. Just give me a call before you
drop by, and I'll be sure to be on the lookout for
you. Thanks for caring.

STRAIGHT CONTRIBUTION LETTER
COVENANT HOUSE

Thursday, 4:00 P.M.

Dear Friend,

She stood on the curb looking scared and lonely in a skimpy halter top and bright red lipstick.

It was two in the morning. A chilly breeze whipped up the street and seemed to make her shiver. She was a child . . . just a child.

We pulled our Covenant House van up to the curb and rolled down the window.

"Hi, what's your name?"

"Janice," she said hesitantly, as if she really had to think about her answer.

"Why don't you hop in, Janice? We've got some hot chocolate and sandwiches. We can talk. You hungry?"

"Yeah, kind of. But not really. I mean, like, I really gotta go. I can't talk now. Maybe later. Will you be back around in a couple hours?"

She glanced nervously up and down the street at the passing cars. We could tell she was dying to jump in, but she was scared. Really scared.

"OK," she finally said. "But only for a minute or two then I gotta go. My boyfriend is gonna be really mad if he finds out I'm doin' this." She climbed in and sat down stiffly across from me. "Your boyfriend?"

"Yeah, he told me he doesn't want me talking to you guys. So I can't stay long. Can I have a sandwich, too? I'm really hungry."

"Sure, but why do you call him your boyfriend if he lets you walk the street at night? Do you mean your pimp?"

"Oh, no, he's not a pimp, he's my boyfriend," she insisted with intensity. "He loves me. He really does. He buys me lots of nice things."

Reprinted with permission, Covenant House

After a few weeks on our Crisis Van, you know when a homeless kid is telling you something to convince you . . . or telling you something to convince herself. This year we'll help rescue 28,000 kids from the street, and we know how to spot them when they're in serious trouble. In Janice's case, her fingers gave her away . . . (Additional copy on Janice)

"I'm scared, I'm really scared. Do you think you can help me? My boyfriend beats me up sometimes if I don't do what he tells me. I think . . . I think I'm pregnant. Oh God, what am I gonna do?"

We sat there for twenty minutes as Janice's story tumbled out in a torrent of confusion and tears . . . (Additional copy on Janice)

I know Janice's story sounds incredible—almost too incredible to be true. But it's only the tip of the iceberg!

As you read this letter, there are 300,000 homeless kids on America's streets . . . kids who are alone, hungry, tired, and scared.

Please. Will you help us rescue another innocent kid tonight?

You see, by donating what you can to Covenant House today, you can give homeless kids like Janice a new life. Thanks to you our Covenant House vans will be able to search America's streets for homeless kids in trouble . . .

Please pray for them. They need it. And if you can send a gift to help them, I'd really appreciate it. It's been tough lately making ends meet. A gift from you right now would be a wonderful answer to our prayers.

Thank you. May God bless you.

In God's Love,

Sister Mary Rose McGeady
President

As many times as I have read the story of Janice, I still get teary-eyed. This compelling and interesting example tells the whole story. A lot of dialogue is used. It just flows and keeps your attention as it tells you exactly what Covenant House does to rescue young kids on the inner-city streets. Note the short sentences and paragraphs. If you are fortunate enough to have a powerful case example like this, here's the way to use it in a winsome way.

STRAIGHT CONTRIBUTION LETTER
MISSIONARY FOR SCRIPTURE UNION OF PERU,
MARTY CLARK

CHRISTMAS 19__ IS ALMOST HERE

A lovely custom here in Peru is to give and/or receive a large basket filled with exciting food surprises that you would not normally have during the year . . . for example: canned fruit, potato chips, chocolates, imported cookies in a tin, and cocoa. Normally, the bottom is filled up with daily necessities like oil, beans, rice, sugar, and tinned milk. Right on top is placed the ever-present Peruvian Christmas cake, "Paneton."

Paul (note: Paul is Marty's husband and co-worker on the mission field in Peru. He grew up in Peru), as a child, always saw the big baskets wrapped in cellophane (so that you could see what was in it) in the store window to be bought or raffled off nearer the 24th of December. He always "wished" for one, but never had one until we were married. One Christmas the children and I had so much fun fixing one up for him.

Two years ago, Paul decided to use money that had come for "whatever you want to do" to prepare a basket for each of the Scripture Union staff . . . larger ones for those with families. It became a family project as we shopped for, divided the purchases, bought the baskets and covered them with Christmas paper, filled them, and then covered them with the yellow cellophane.

Such excitement as we made two trips in the car to the office to put them in strategic places to be found when the staff arrived at work. One of our oldest members told Paul later how much he appreciated it, that he had always seen them (like Paul had) and never thought he would EVER have one. He was overwhelmed!

Reprinted with permission, Scripture Union of Peru

After two years, there is no money. We decided that we would just not be able to give them. Paul shared with one of the staff that there would be no baskets this year—seemed only fair to let him know ahead of time. Carlos, a hard-working man and father of 2, couldn't believe what he was hearing. Paul told me that at least 3 times he questioned, "We aren't going to have baskets this year?"

Evidently, these past two years had meant much more to him than we had even realized. Another staff member always packed up the contents of his basket and had gone north of the city to his parents and shared what he had received. Now, this would not be possible . . . and he would not be able to provide this for them.

Staff salaries in Peru are not high. They allow for daily living at a modest level . . . certainly nothing EXTRA—not even for Christmas.

I suggested to Paul that I would send out a few letters to selected people in case we might be able to change the decision we took.

Any chance of your helping?

We will understand if you can't, but at least we are letting you know. Each basket requires approximately $40 to prepare, and we need 18 baskets if we are to continue this custom!

We would see that each staff worker out of Lima receives one as well. If you are able to help in this project, mark your gift "Basket-Peru" and send to Scripture Union (U.S. address) or send a check directly to us in Peru made out to Union Biblica del Peru.

Thanks for any ideas you might have on the subject!

/Signed/
Marty Clark

Would love to hear all about your family!!

This letter, written by a missionary in Peru, does all the right things to be effective. It's intensely interesting. It has a lot of emotion. It makes a simple but very strong case for a need. It asks for a specific size gift and tells exactly how the gift will be used. It went to a select list of supporters. Study this letter carefully. It should encourage any writer of fund-raising letters to know that if you are right on the basic principles the copy will excel. This one does. And it succeeded in raising money for the Christmas gift baskets.

NEW DONOR ACQUISITION LETTER
MEMORIAL SLOAN-KETTERING CANCER CENTER

Note: A little yellow stick-it note was affixed to the top of page 1 of this letter with this personalized copy: Mr. _____, The cancer research we are doing right now may someday benefit you. Please read this important letter and see how. Thank you. M.C.

Dear Mr. (Name Fill-in),

You may never need us . . . but right now we need you.

Here at Memorial Sloan-Kettering we are making significant advances in the fight against cancer. Our scientists have:

- Armed monoclonal antibodies with cancer-killing drugs to seek out and destroy cancer cells.

- Pioneered new methods of breast reconstruction that minimize disfigurement.

- Developed a new chemotherapy protocol called M-VAC that represents a significant advance in the treatment of bladder cancer.

- (Four more cancer research advances cited)

Advances like these are enabling thousands of Americans to survive cancer—people who would have been lost just a few years ago.

That's why I am urgently seeking your help.

Memorial Sloan-Kettering Cancer Center is the oldest and largest non-profit cancer research center in the country.

Right now we must find new friends and contributors like you to help us continue our intensive cancer research program.

Reprinted with permission, Memorial Sloan-Kettering Cancer Center

For the fact is, 3,000 new cases of cancer are diagnosed each day. At that rate, cancer will strike in 3 out of 4 families.

That is why I say, you may never need us . . . but right now we need you. Even a gift of $10 will help make a difference.

Please send the most generous cancer research gift that you can today.

The advances we make in research today may save your life or the life of a loved one tomorrow.

Thank you so much for your help.

Sincerely,

Mortimer H. Chute, Jr.
Vice President for
Development

P.S. While even $10 will help, gifts of $25, $50, $100, $500 or more are urgently needed and deeply appreciated.

But please send what you can—<u>any</u> amount. Every gift is important.

When you're raising funds for cancer research, you know that a great majority of the people on your lists will have a personal interest. This letter keys in on this personal concern and does an outstanding job of telling how the funds raised are used in breakthrough research. The letter also excels in making a strong ask for a gift. It stresses a minimal gift of $10 in the text, but in the P.S. it increases the range of need. This is an easy-to-read letter that makes a compelling case for a gift.

NEW MEMBER ACQUISITION LETTER
RAILS TO TRAILS CONSERVANCY

>   Pioneers built it.
>   Abe Lincoln worked for it.
>   Jesse James robbed it.
>   And America grew great on it.

But now, the magnificent railroad system criss-crossing America is being abandoned at a shocking rate. Already 115,000 miles of line are out of service!

These abandoned rail corridors can be turned into the world's greatest trail network for you and me to enjoy . . . if <u>you</u> step in to help.

<u>Accept our special invitation to join the Rails-to-Trails Conservancy now at reduced rates and receive a FREE handsome commemorative patch, FREE one-year (six issues) subscription to The Walking Magazine, and other benefits of membership</u>.

Dear Friend,

Picture an emerald necklace . . . or what the President's Commission on Americans Outdoors calls "a greenway of trails" . . . linking America.

Where hikers and cyclists, joggers and strollers, people in wheelchairs, young or old, active or physically impaired, can enjoy . . . in cities and rural communities across the country . . . some of America's most beautiful natural scenery.

This fantasy can come true . . . simply by converting abandoned rail corridors into trails for public use.

If they're not converted, some of America's most precious and unique resources will simply go to waste.

During the past 15 years, U.S. railroads have abandoned thousands of linear miles of land—leaving

Reprinted with permission, Rails to Trails Conservancy

it chopped up for development or even used as dumping
grounds for trash.

Bankruptcies . . . mergers . . . changing transportation needs have led private railroad companies
to abandon 3,000-4,000 miles of track each year—over
12 miles each day.

Much of this million-acre land resource was
donated to the railroads by the American public in
the first place . . . but is now being lost forever
to public use.

It's time that stopped.

And that's why the Rails-to-Trails Conservancy was
created . . .

Today, we have members across the country. And
we're slowly building our dream of an emerald necklace of trails strung across America . . . working
with local, state and federal agencies to create
usable, enjoyable trails out of corridors abandoned
by private rail companies.

Most of these corridors are located in beautiful
spots . . .

And because all are carefully graded on gentle
terrain, they're perfect for linear sports like
running . . . bicycling . . . walking . . .
horseback riding . . . cross-country skiing. . .

—and for less active senior citizens, parents
with small children, and the physically handicapped
as well.

But once the corridors are broken up, just like
Humpty Dumpty, they can't be put together again!

Over 100 rail corridors have already been successfully converted into parks and trails in 23 states. And
at least 90 more rail-trail conversions are underway.

Congress recognized the value of preserving railroad corridors . . . (information on favorable legislation follows here).

But . . . despite their overwhelming benefits,
there are major hurdles to rail-trail conversions—

hurdles the Rails-to-Trails Conservancy can help overcome. (paragraphs on work with state and local agencies cited in this section)

So if you share our dream . . . and want to enjoy the ribbons of land we all once owned . . . join us!

<u>WE</u> <u>need</u> <u>your</u> <u>help</u>.

With your membership support . . . (listing of projects that can take place with membership support)

When you join the Rails-to-Trails Conservancy, one of your many benefits of membership will be discounts on all our workshops, conferences, and publications like the Citizen's Manual and Legal Manual.

Right now, we have 80 new projects in progress . . . and each week we hear from communities across the country who need help creating rail-trails in their areas.

Won't you help us help them?

We can bring about more successful conversions . . . but only with your support behind us.

Eventually, your membership could help realize the dream of connecting a network of national trails . . . an emerald necklace stringing from Manhattan to Missouri to the West Coast.

Please . . . join the Rails-to-Trails Conservancy before these unique and irreplaceable corridors disappear for good.

Because of very real time pressures on this issue, we must have national membership support as quickly as possible.

So if you join the Conservancy now—in response to this letter—you can join at specially-reduced membership rates.

Return the enclosed membership acceptance card with your check in the postpaid envelope provided.

Help create rail-trails for Americans to enjoy for
years and generations to come.

                              Sincerely,

                              David Burwell
                              President

    P.S. As a member, you'll receive a FREE one-year
subscription to <u>The Walking Magazine</u>, a FREE Rails-
to-Trails commemorative patch, and a FREE subscription to our own quarterly newsletter TRAILBLAZER, as
well as discounts on all publications and conferences.
    Return the enclosed Charter Membership Form
today.

    Here's an organization with a unique mission—converting abandoned
rail corridors to trails for the public enjoyment. Notice how a "Johnson Box"
opening paragraph is used (see Chapter 19 for a discussion of how to begin
your letter). This opening is provocative, but in very short order it makes the
case for the organization and it includes the offer of the letter. You don't
have to read too far in this excellent letter to catch the vision and dream of
the organization. The copy combines some wonderful allusions (e.g., "emerald necklace"), but it forcefully makes the case for the organization . . . outlines a strong offer . . . and features benefits. In its original form this is a
five-page letter . . . teaching us that long well-written copy is the way to go.
This letter has been used by Rails-to-Trails Conservancy to establish a very
solid membership base.

2

Eliciting Funds with the Nomination-to-Membership Letter

As its name implies, the nomination-to-membership letter is a letter to a prospect advising that he or she has been "nominated" or "selected" for membership in the nonprofit organization. We all like to be singled out...or chosen. And when the choosing comes from an organization whose goals we value, this type of letter packs a strong punch. The type of membership offered in such direct mail letters generally does not accord full voting privileges in the inviting group. Even so, the word "membership" is a wonderful selling word that quickly communicates identification. Membership in groups we admire is the way we like to identify ourselves. It is a shorthand way of telling others who we are and what we stand for. It's the sense of personal identification that is the magic here.

Many times donors to organizations that don't officially promote membership as such consider themselves members anyway. So if the conditions are at all right for you to send a nomination-to-membership letter, you should do so. The results can be phenomenal.

When to Use the Nomination-to-Membership Letter

If supporters of your organization possess a strong affinity with your goals—and if your organization provides good membership benefits—then a nomination-to-membership letter is an excellent way to acquire new members. There is a believable sense of flattery in this approach. The letter-writer adopts the attitude that "you are one of us . . . that's why we've decided to nominate you for membership." The secret is to mail to lists of logical prospects. A person who does, in fact, share your outlook and many of your concerns will respond favorably to the invitation.

How to Write the Nomination-to-Membership Letter

The nomination-to-membership letter works best when these writing guidelines are followed.

1. INFORM THE PROSPECT OF SELECTION.

It's essential to tell early on exactly why the recipient was selected for the nomination. From the very outset, note that the person receiving the letter has been specially selected for the honor. There is a tendency for insiders of a nonprofit group to feel that a "nomination" really isn't valid when you're sending a mailing to a large number of direct mail recipients. In actuality the nominating organization has selected special lists that represent just a fraction of the total mailable universe. So it's appropriate and effective to approach such carefully selected recipients with the nominations-style mailing.

- We put a great deal of care and thought into the selection process. While the decision to accept is entirely yours, I would be delighted to welcome you as a valuable new Associate Member of _____ should you decide to join our ranks . . .

- I am delighted to inform you of a special honor! A <u>Charter Membership</u> in _____ has been reserved in your name.

- The Officers and Board of Trustees Cordially Invite You to Enjoy the Benefits of MEMBERSHIP in _____.

- I am pleased to inform you that <u>you have been nominated for Charter membership</u> in the _____. This honor is being extended to a carefully selected group of American citizens. <u>I'd like to congratulate you for being among those chosen</u>.

- It is my pleasure to inform you that you have been selected as an Associate Member of _____.

2. HIGHLIGHT MEMBERSHIP BENEFITS.

Consider every benefit of membership the nominee will receive and describe them in special insider terms to the prospective member. You may have some "routine" benefits or services that you feel aren't all that glamorous. It's a mistake not to mention them. When a person joins a new organization, their excitement level is at a peak. This prospective new member will enjoy reading about every benefit that their membership offers.

- And—if you join today—you'll receive all our valuable Charter Membership benefits, including: **<u>Free Subscription</u> to our quarterly newsletter . . . **<u>Substantial discounts</u> on art books, publications, very attractive jewelry, and other items . . . **<u>Advance Notice</u> and discounts for our many stimulating art-study tours, seminars, lectures, concerts, and other special events . . . **<u>Special discounts</u> on parking **<u>Personal recognition</u> . . . your name will be inscribed in our permanent "Honor Roll of Charter Members."

- And I think you will be pleasantly surprised by the special benefits accorded to Members of the National Advisory Council. First, you're entitled to <u>two free tickets</u> to our breathtaking movie, *At Sea*. Then there are special discounts at our Ship's Store. Plus you'll receive a specially designed decal and colorful calendar. The benefits list goes on. Just look at all your new membership privileges in the enclosed brochure.

- WHAT ARE THE BENEFITS OF BEING AN ASSOCIATE? You will discover, as a new Associate, that there are many very fine perquisites that come with election. <u>Most important, you will receive (_____) magazine</u> . . . In addition to (_____), you will <u>also receive free admission to the Museum</u>, its

library, and field station. <u>Should you visit the
Museum</u>, you will be welcomed in the elegant,
wood-paneled Associates' study and library. You
will be eligible for Museum-sponsored trips and
expeditions with scientists to the far reaches of
the globe. You will also receive discounts on
items bought through the Museum's catalogs—
including large discounts in the Museum's famous
book catalog. <u>You will receive discounts</u> off
Nature shows, lectures, films, special programs,
and other Museum benefits.

- Membership means invitations to splendid Museum
  events such as the _____. What's more, you
  are kept-up-to-date on happenings at _____—
  between visits—through a subscription to
  _____. Still other benefits await you,
  which I haven't ample space to describe here . . .
  including tours, a generous 15% discount on purchases in the Gift Shop, and discounts on reproductions
  of select objects from the _____ Museum.

3. DOWNPLAY RESPONSIBILITIES OF MEMBERSHIP.

A prospective member may be turned off if he or she feels that membership will take time and effort beyond the simple act of contributing. On
the one hand, it's effective to flatter the person as being one who very likely will do more than an average citizen. Emphasize that any involvement is
voluntary and that no additional time will be required.

- Even though <u>membership will require little on
  your part, it will mean a lot to us</u>. It is good
  to know that you, along with a loyal group of
  citizens from all around the country—and from
  many different backgrounds—actively support the
  _____.

4. ENCLOSE AN INTERIM MEMBERSHIP CARD.

People who identify with a particular cause are proud to carry and
show their membership card. It's best if the interim card is good for some

benefits. But people primarily want to "show their colors" and let others know where they stand on an issue of importance to them. That's why the enclosure of an interim card that immediately supplies this psychic and tangible reward is effective. Generally the card will be given a 30-day time period for usage. It also shows that you have such confidence in the recipient's interest that you're willing to extend immediate privileges of membership.

- A courtesy card, numbered and registered in your name and good for the next 30 days, is enclosed. When you return the enclosed reservation form accepting membership, your permanent card will be forwarded. We extend this invitation because we believe you're the sort of person who values

  _____ .

- Your temporary Associate identification card is enclosed. You may sign it and begin using it immediately.

- In the meantime, please feel free to begin taking advantage of your Complimentary Guest Membership. Keep the enclosed Guest Card handy for any _____ activity that may appeal to you.

5. ASK FOR A "YES" OR "NO" DECISION.

To get action on the nomination, it helps to ask the recipient to let you know with a "yes" or "no" decision. This implies that you are waiting for an answer (which, in fact, you are) and that you need to hear from the nominee soon.

- We would request that you return the enclosed invitation as soon as possible, indicating whether or not you will be accepting this election. (If you wish to decline election, please return the election form marked Decline. This will allow us to keep our records up to date.)

- Even if you can't become a member at this time, we would appreciate knowing your decision so we can complete issuing nominations to other Americans chosen for this honor.

6. STRESS QUALITY OF MEMBERSHIP.

There's a nice feeling in knowing that you are associating with people having interests similar to yours. Joining a membership group appeals to that gregarious instinct in all of us. We do feel that we are known by the "company we keep." Let potential members know what kind of "company they will be keeping."

- Associate members of _____ form one of the largest and most powerful groups of scientists and informed laypeople in the world. When we look for new Associates, we look for people who care about this planet and its breathtaking diversity of life. We look for avid readers, people who have a lifelong love of learning.

- This honor is being extended to a carefully selected group of American citizens. <u>I'd like to congratulate you for being among those chosen</u>. We need people like you . . . patriotic people from all walks of life. People to uphold the memory of the brave men and women who proudly served our country in the United States Navy.

- By accepting this invitation, you become part of a special group of people all over the globe whose enthusiasm and curiosity about their world is enriched by belonging to _____.

7. TELL HOW MEMBERSHIP FUNDS WILL BE USED.

While a membership-type appeal doesn't carry the urgent-need-for-funds message that other types of mailings do, it is still important to let members know that a portion of their dues will be used for projects and activities they believe in.

- With your support as a Charter Member, this mag-nificent new museum in our nation's capital will bring long-awaited honor and acclaim to history's most neglected body of art—<u>the work of women artists</u>! . . . Now . . . you and I have the chance to rescue the masterworks of women artists from

oblivion. To build the widespread public visibility, awareness and appreciation they so richly
deserve.

- What's more, you can take pride in knowing that a
  portion of your dues will help underwrite the
  costs of our research, exploration, and educational projects.

MODEL LETTER
NOMINATION TO MEMBERSHIP—GENERIC

Dear Member-Elect,

INFORM THE PROSPECT OF SELECTION (POINT 1)

I am pleased to inform you that you have been selected for membership in _____.

STRESS QUALITY OF MEMBERSHIP (POINT 6)

This honor is accorded only to a select group of individuals each year . . . people who appreciate the value of _____.

Let me congratulate you on your nomination. I look forward to your joining our ranks and to meeting you personally at one of our membership gatherings.

ENCLOSE AN INTERIM MEMBERSHIP CARD (POINT 4)

I have enclosed an Interim Membership Card—made out in your name and specially numbered—so you might start enjoying our membership benefits right away.

As soon as we receive your Membership Acceptance Form (enclosed) we will put your permanent card in the mail to you. You'll also receive your first issue of our members-only newsletter and other materials for new members only.

It's not necessary to include payment with your acceptance. You may elect to be billed later . . . or, if you prefer, you may charge your new membership to one of your credit cards.

But it's important we have your decision as soon as possible. If you can't accept your nomination, please advise us immediately. We issue a limited number of new memberships each year and we need to know whether you will be joining with us or not.

I want to tell you about the special privileges and benefits you are now entitled to. But first let me say why this is such an important time for you to join.

TELL HOW MEMBERSHIP FUNDS WILL BE USED (POINT 7)

A growing membership in _____ accomplishes a number of things. Our members actively participate in many activities that give visibility to our work. Whether it's _____ or _____ citizens all around our country see that our movement is strong and growing.

Also when we testify in _____ hearings for such issues as _____, legislators take notice that we are a vibrant and growing organization.

We are really proud of the fact that due to our efforts Congress passed the _____ Act which _____.

It never would have happened without the broad-based membership support from _____.

And part of the membership dues goes directly to support _____. This project has been one of our most successful endeavors to advance the cause of _____.

Through these efforts members give substance to our mission.

HIGHLIGHT MEMBERSHIP BENEFITS (POINT 2)

Now, let me tell you what is in store for you as a member.

First, as I mentioned, you will receive our newsletter. In it you will be kept up-to-date on all the membership activities as well as the latest news from headquarters.

You will be invited to participate in our special meetings and seminars. And you will receive invitations to join in special tours throughout the year.

One benefit that is popular with our members is the opportunity to buy books and gift items at special members' discount prices. And late in the year be on the lookout for a specially designed colorful calendar sent free of charge to all members.

DOWNPLAY RESPONSIBILITIES OF MEMBERSHIP (POINT 3)

Membership will require very little on your part. You can involve yourself as much as you wish, but essentially you are lending your name and voice to a movement that is critical to _____.

ASK FOR A "YES" OR "NO" DECISION (POINT 5)

Please take just a moment now—while my invitation is before you—to confirm your election to membership. Your permanent card and special new membership materials will be put in the mail to you as soon as we receive your acceptance. If for any reason you can't accept now, please advise us so we can keep our records up-to-date.

I look forward to welcoming you as the newest member of _____.

Sincerely yours,

ENCLOSE AN INTERIM MEMBERSHIP CARD (POINT 4)

P.S. Don't forget to detach and keep your Interim Membership Card while waiting for your permanent card to arrive. With the Interim Card you can _____ . . . so make sure to hold on to it and use it. Thanks for your support.

NOMINATION-TO-MEMBERSHIP LETTER
U.S. NAVY MEMORIAL FOUNDATION

Dear Fellow American,

I am pleased to inform you that <u>you have been nominated for Charter Membership</u> in the National Advisory Council of the U.S. Navy Memorial Foundation.

This honor is being extended to a carefully selected group of American citizens. <u>I'd like to congratulate you for being among those chosen</u>.

Please give this nomination your careful consideration. The reason is simple.

<u>We need people like you</u>.

Patriotic people from all walks of life. People to uphold the memory of the brave men and women who proudly served our country in the United States Navy.

The National Advisory Council has an important role to play in the success of the U.S. Navy Memorial. First, we want a growing, vibrant Council made up of people from all across America.

The Council will be available to provide support, advice and visibility as we develop a fitting Memorial right here in our Nation's Capital . . .

<u>The Memorial honors the men and women of the U.S. Navy who have served our country well in war and peace</u>. We remember those who have "stood in harm's way" from our earliest days as a nation right up to the turbulent, ever-changing world we live in today.

As an American and a Council Member it will very much be <u>your</u> Memorial . . . a living, growing tribute.

Even though <u>membership will require little on your part, it will mean a lot to us</u>. It is good to know that you, along with a loyal group of citizens from all around the country—and from many different backgrounds—actively support the U.S. Navy Memorial.

    <u>Your involvement will mean more than you real-
ize</u>.

    And I think you will be pleasantly surprised by
the special benefits accorded to Members of the
National Advisory Committee.

    First, you're entitled to <u>two free tickets</u> to our
breathtaking movie, *At Sea*. Then there are special
discounts at our Ship's Store . . .

    The benefit list goes on. Just look at all your
new membership privileges in the enclosed brochure.

    So you won't have to wait to take advantage of
what's in store for you, I've enclosed your specially
numbered Interim Membership Card.

    <u>You can use this card immediately</u>—before your
permanent card arrives—to get an early preview.

    I suggest you detach your interim card and carry
it with you. Then...

    <u>Return your Advisory Council Membership Acceptance
form today</u>.

    You can join the Advisory Council for as little
as $25.

    Or, if you prefer to help even more at the out-
set, you can be a Sustaining Member of the Advisory
Council when you contribute $100 or more to support
our mission.

    Sustaining Members receive a special complimentary
edition of <u>SEA BATTLES IN CLOSE-UP: WORLD WAR II</u> as
our special way of saying "Thank You..."

    As a Member of the National Advisory Council, <u>you
uphold a proud tradition</u>. It's an honor I hope you
will accept.

               Sincerely,

               Alan Shephard
               Rear Admiral
               U.S. Navy (Ret.)

Here's a nomination-to-membership letter that features the honor of being selected. You'll also note that the responsibilities of participating are downplayed. Any person with a Navy background or with relatives who served in the Navy would appreciate this patriotic copy approach. Note especially the upgrade book premium for a higher-level joining gift. Because of this logical offer of a book on naval sea battles, the average gift is higher than what most nonprofit organizations get from new members.

NOMINATION-TO-MEMBERSHIP LETTER
THE NATIONAL MUSEUM OF WOMEN IN THE ARTS

Dear Friend,

I am delighted to inform you of a special honor!

An <u>Associate Membership</u> in the National Museum of Women in the Arts has been reserved in your name. Yes, an <u>Associate Membership</u> in the first—and <u>only</u>—major museum in the world dedicated to celebrating the stunning achievements of women artists, past, present, and future.

With your support as an Associate Member, this magnificent new museum in our nation's capital will bring long-awaited honor and acclaim to history's most neglected body of art—<u>the work of women artists</u>!

As you may know, the great achievements of women in the arts—as in so many other fields—have been tragically ignored for too long.

For centuries, women artists have struggled against opposition from family, blind prejudice from society, and even public scorn. They've been forbidden proper training by the art schools of their day . . . prevented from exhibiting at the best galleries . . . and over-shadowed by better-known fathers, husbands, and brothers.

Still, they persevered!

Now . . . you and I have the chance to rescue the works of women artists from oblivion. To build the widespread public visibility, awareness and appreciation they so richly deserve.

But . . . I must ask for your favorable reply immediately.

The Board of Directors of the Museum has authorized the acceptance of new Associate Members for a limited time only—so that I may invite you to join us today, with full Associate Membership benefits.

And believe me, your help is needed urgently! Already our Museum is recognized as one of the most important, innovative new art institutions in the nation—indeed, in the world.

But we've just barely begun. There are still so many spectacular artists whose work simply languishes in attics and dusty storehouses. Unseen. Unappreciated. Unknown!

Women who have created magnificent works in painting, sculpture, drawing, and all forms of fine art. Women like . . . (Specific artist cited here)

Despite the progress we've made since 1987—and it is considerable!—women artists are STILL largely ignored and their artistic talents unappreciated in most museums.

For example, although nearly 50% of all practicing artists in the United States today are women . . . 95% to 98% of the works in our nation's art museums are by men.

That's why the development and growth of The National Museum of Women in the Arts is so critically important—<u>and why I'm so eager to have you accept your invitation to Associate Membership immediately</u>.

You see, at this critical, still early stage in our development, it is more vital than ever for friends like you to demonstrate your support. The more Associate Members we can attract, the stronger will be our voice of recognition of history's great women artists.

With your generous help, we will be much more than a structure that houses paintings and sculpture by women.

The example you and I set—through our exhibitions, educational programs and research facilities—will awaken the entire world to a new appreciation of women artists.

And—if you join today—you'll receive all of our valuable Associate membership benefits, including:

**<u>Free Subscription to</u> . . . (Benefits described at this point)

And, if that isn't enough . . .

Your Associate Membership will give you the satisfaction of knowing that you've made possible a world landmark in the history of art.

Isn't it about time you and I finally had the chance to see and appreciate the great works of history's most neglected artists?

So, <u>please join our historic mission today</u>.

                    Sincerely,

                    Rebecca Phillips Abbott
                    Director, Administration

Even though the nomination-to-membership letter typically takes an upscale tone, this doesn't mean that it has to be without strong emotions. This letter shows how to raise the battle-cry and to keep the focus on the urgent need for funds. At the same time it does all those things this chapter recommends as essential to a nomination-to-membership letter.

3

Raising Funds with the Front-End Premium Letter

The offer of a special inducement to give in the form of a free gift provides a powerful motivation. There are two types of premiums offered in fund-raising mailings. The first is the *front-end premium*, in which the gift item (be it a decal, name and address stickers, a paperback book, a religious medal, note cards, or some other small item of value) is enclosed in the mailing asking for the gift. The second type of premium offer is a *back-end premium*, in which the premium or gift item is sent—as an inducement to give—*after* the contribution to the cause has been made. Back-end premiums are generally of a higher value and are used to solicit larger than average gifts. In this chapter we're going to look at the front-end premium letter, and in the chapter that follows you'll see how to utilize the back-end premium letter.

When to Use the Front-End Premium Letter

The use of a front-end premium in a fund-raising letter is something that should be tested to see if the additional cost of the premium generates enough additional members and income to pay for the cost of the premium plus a little extra. Actually, if you just trade dollars (get enough additional income to pay for the added cost of the premium), it would be worthwhile. That's because you are most likely getting more members who will send additional gifts from your subsequent mailings to them.

If you have a mailing that is borderline in results, consider the inclusion of a front-end premium. The improved results due to including a front-end premium may give the letter just enough new life to bring it into profitability. Smart promotion people are always on the lookout for up-front premium possibilities that they can acquire for their mailings at a reasonable cost. Use of a front-end premium is an excellent way to give a different look and feel to your mailing package.

How to Write Front-End Premium Letters

Premiums that are enclosed with the initial request for a gift should be low cost and have some type of immediate perceived value (e.g., name and address stickers, note cards). The objective is to instill some sense of obligation and appreciation for the premium item to the extent that the prospect will respond with a contribution for the need specified. There's another category of a front-end premium that is more issue or cause related (e.g., bumper stickers, decals, certificates). In these cases it is the hope of the fund-raiser that the recipient who receives and displays the cause-oriented item will also feel a sense of obligation to give to the organization he or she is promoting. Here are six guidelines to follow in writing copy referring to a front-end premium:

1. PREMIUM SHOULD HAVE SOME CONNECTION WITH THE LETTER TEXT.

Some years ago a direct mail package that made an offer of gardening equipment enclosed a rubber washer. The letter-writer referred to the washer saying something along the following lines: "Pretty soon, as Spring approaches, you'll be out in your garden and turning on the water again. And, if you're like me you'll find that you need a washer to keep the hose from leaking. So here it is . . . ." This was a clever and very tasteful tie-in to the main copy message of the letter. Here are some other examples.

Page 1 of a religious organization's letter asking for a gift for Scripture distribution at Christmas opens as follows:

- The enclosed Christmas Scripture ornament is for you! I send it with my warmest Christmas greetings, and with one very special wish . . . that you will help us share God's Word with people around the world who desperately want a Bible this Christmas.

A museum found that a little enclosure of a bookmark-sized reproduction from its collection outpulled an expensive four-color brochure in a comparative test mailing. Here is the way the museum referred to this front-end premium in the P.S. of its letter:

- The enclosed reproduction Fraktur is sent with our thanks for taking the time to read this letter from _____. Fraktur was a medieval German art form that was practiced in Pennsylvania until the middle of the 19th century. The original Fraktur bookmark is displayed at the _____ Museum.

2. EMPHASIZE THAT THE PREMIUM IS A GIFT.

Whenever a list of the magic words in direct mail appear, the word, FREE, is almost always at the top of the list. Consumers have been conditioned over years and years of advertising to react positively to *free* gifts. So, clearly tell the prospect that the enclosed premium item is a free gift or comes with your compliments. For example, two packs of name and address stickers were enclosed in a mailing from a disease organization's mailing. Here's how the copy was worded:

- Please accept this gift . . . and help put an end to _____! These stickers are our gift to you. Use them to help speed up your mail . . . and as a reminder that there is hope for the thousands of children suffering from _____.

3. DON'T IMPLY THAT A GIFT IS REQUIRED BECAUSE OF THE PREMIUM.

This is not considered ethical in direct marketing. The recipient didn't ask for the item so, in fact, it is a gift. Don't imply otherwise.

- We hope you will enjoy and use (describe enclosed item) enclosed with this mailing. While you are under no obligation, we do hope you will give the serious message of this letter your attention . . .

4. IF POSSIBLE, SELECT A THREE-DIMENSIONAL PREMIUM.

The rubber washer mentioned earlier gave the mailing a three-dimensional feel. In Chapter 18 you'll see why three-dimensional enclosures are effective in getting the envelope opened in the first place. A front-end premium with some bulk to it (be it a rubber washer, a pack of address labels, or a paperback book) can serve double-duty: help get the envelope opened and improve response to the mailing.

A university's annual fund appeal enclosed a packet of flower seeds and utilized a "growth" copy theme. The seed packet added bulk to the mailing package. It also provided a rattling sound, which intrigued the prospect to open the envelope and find out what was inside.

- Growth! Surpassing the $1,000,000 mark is an important milestone for _____ Alumni Fund and is compelling testimony to the commitment of all _____ alumni. Your support not only provides direct financial resources, it is also a sign of your commitment and serves as seed money to garner funds from a variety of other sources. The overall growth in resources is vital to the University's continued success in meeting the challenges facing private education.

5. USE PREMIUMS THAT HAVE A LONGER LIFE THAN THE MAILING.

If the free front-end premium is an item the recipient wants to retain (e.g., calendar, bookmark), you have an opportunity to keep your organization's name before the prospect for a longer period of time. The adage "out-of-sight, out-of-mind" applies. It's good to be in the prospect's mind for a longer period with an item he or she values and uses.

A letter from an organization promoting the welfare of animals enclosed name and address labels and referred to them in the copy this way:

- I hope you will use the complimentary name labels I've enclosed on your holiday greetings because I want everyone to know about your concern for animals.

```
    Your  name—and  the  name  of  _____—are
vitally  important  to  the  well-being  of  all  ani-
mals  because  we  both  care  about  them  very  much.

    I  wish  I  could  tell  you  that  everyone  is  con-
cerned  about  protecting  dogs,  cats,  farm  animals,
and  wildlife,  but  the  sad  truth  is  animal  abuse
continues  at  an  alarming  rate.
```

6. A CAUSE-ORIENTED PREMIUM WORKS.

You'll find that the desire to advertise one's convictions is an innate tendency on the part of most donors. Bumper stickers allow your prospects to do this effectively. Donors are people of conviction. And they like to show it. They want others to know something important about them. And if there's a clever twist to it, so much the better.

A letter from an international children's relief organization referred to enclosed note cards this way:

```
• Perhaps  you're  wondering  why  _____  is  sending
  you  these  beautiful  note  cards.  They're  unique.
  They're  eye-catching.  They're  great  ways  to  write
  to  your  friends.  But  there's  an  even  more  impor-
  tant  reason.  _____  is  not  in  the  greeting
  card  business.  We're  in  the  compassion  business.
  We  lovingly  provide  food,  clothing,  education,
  and  health  care  to  the  desperately  needy  children
  of  our  world.  But  we  felt  that  a  great  way  to
  introduce  you  to  our  children  would  be  through
  the  colorful  pictures  on  these  cards.  Each  pic-
  ture  was  drawn  and  colored  by  a  _____  child.
```

A veterans group referred to its enclosed note cards this way:

```
• When  we  started  mailing  these  cards,  people  said
  we  were  nuts!  We  began  sending  out  our  own  pack-
  ages  of  beautiful  holiday  greeting  cards
  absolutely  free  to  good  people  like  you.

    You'll  lose  your  shirts,  doubters  said.  Folks
  will  use  the  cards  (as  they  have  the  right  to  do)
  and  you'll  never  hear  a  word  from  them!
```

But listen to what really happened! It's a
heartwarming story in which thousands of people just
like you have chosen to help _____.
        We are the _____ . . .

MODEL LETTER
FRONT-END PREMIUM—ARTS ORGANIZATION

Dear Friend of the Arts,

Local artist Jean Wilson—a product of Francis Taylor High School in our area—created the distinctive arts bumper sticker I have enclosed.

PREMIUM SHOULD HAVE SOME CONNECTION WITH THE LETTER TEXT (POINT 1)
A CAUSE-ORIENTED PREMIUM WORKS (POINT 6)

Please accept it as a gift from one arts lover to another. I hope you will display it proudly—it conveys a message that I trust you and I share: THE ARTS IN OUR ELEMENTARY AND HIGH SCHOOLS ARE A NECESSITY, NOT A LUXURY TO BE CUT OUT AT THE SLIGHTEST BUDGET CRUNCH!

Did you know that the arts budgets for our region's schools have been cut 15% over the past five years—and are only 1/3 the budget for sports?

EMPHASIZE THAT THE PREMIUM IS A GIFT (POINT 2)

So while this bumper sticker is a gift for you—the important thing is that you display it so others can see it. And learn about the arts and the Arts-In-Schools Foundation. It would be wonderful if you could help us with a financial contribution so we can get more bumper stickers on more cars—so we can prepare factual information for school boards—advertise—send speakers to PTA meetings and country and city council meetings.

Our goal is to convince parents and educators and politicians that the arts are vital to making good students, good citizens, and a decent society.

It's sad but true that the people who organize best for special programs in schools are the sports parents! And sports are great, but when it comes to fighting for the school programs we love, we are in danger of being shouted down, make no mistake about it.

USE PREMIUMS THAT HAVE A LONGER LIFE THAN THE MAILING (POINT 5)

That's why we need you to display your bumper sticker—and why we need your financial support today.

A gift of $25 will enable us to send out nearly 100 more bumper stickers—or help pay an artist to lay out an informational brochure. Answering phone calls, writing letters of protest, attending meetings—all cost money.

In short, we can turn the tide against the movement that says arts are a frill, but only if all concerned are willing to pitch in and help.

Please display your bumper sticker. And, if you can, please return your gift to me today. Help us spread the word that arts are part of an education.

Thank you.

Sylvia Proctor
Executive Director

P.S. In the short year we have been in existence, we have saved the school band at _____ school, paid for a great books course at _____ , and stopped the _____ school board from eliminating music lessons at _____. Help us continue!

FRONT-END PREMIUM LETTER
SLAVIC GOSPEL ASSOCIATION

I want to tell you why the bookplates I've enclosed for you to sign are so important.

P.D., Jr.

Dear Friend:

I'd like to tell you the most amazing, most thrilling news to come out of the Soviet Union in more than 70 years . . .

THE IRON CURTAIN HAS OPENED TO THE GOSPEL! SOVIET AUTHORITIES ARE LETTING BIBLES IN! RUSSIAN BELIEVERS ARE OPENLY SHARING THEIR FAITH!

Yes, it's true. President Gorbachev's "glasnost" is giving Soviet Christians more religious freedom than they've had at any time since the Communists came to power.

This is a miraculous answer to generations of prayer by Christians all over the world. My own father, who died in 1987, began praying for this day years before I was born. <u>And now it has happened</u>.

Yet in the middle of this moment of rejoicing, there is a problem . . .

For the first time in 70 years, evangelical church-es in the Soviet Union are allowed to teach Sunday School. <u>Yet they have no children's Bibles. NONE</u>.

In all of history, there has never been a com-plete children's Bible in the Russian language. We have been able to send in <u>just a few copies</u> of a new children's Bible, and the response was beyond our greatest hopes.

There is such an incredible hunger among children for the Word. One little Russian girl wrote a letter to Jesus. It came to us. I'd like you to read it:

Dear Jesus,

Please send me a Children's Picture Bible. The same kind you sent to my Aunt Masha. I'm going to read it and show it to my classmates. They don't know you, but I do because my grandfather told me about you.

I love you, Jesus.

Anna

Anna and millions of other children and their parents who love the Lord want Bibles. They want to read those precious, comforting words. They want to share Jesus with others.

I don't know about you, but with all my heart I want Anna and millions of boys and girls like her all over the Soviet Union to have their own children's Bibles.

That's why I'm so excited to tell you that we have a thrilling opportunity—right now. After months of prayer and hard work, we're ready to print a fully illustrated children's Bible and distribute it to children in the Soviet Union.

Think of it . . . the first ever printing in the Russian language of a picture Bible for children.

Picture a child like Anna learning Bible truths for the first time. Picture mothers and fathers and grandparents using the Children's Picture Bible to teach their little ones about God. This Bible could introduce an entire generation of Soviet children to Jesus Christ.

The need for this Bible is overwhelming. We receive thousands of requests every month from all over the Soviet Union. I hope and pray we can answer each one. Because I know just how much it will mean to the children and their parents.

The cost to print and mail one copy of the Children's Picture Bible to a child like Anna is just $10.

If you could make it possible to send just one Bible, you will help a child learn about Jesus. And that child will begin growing into the strong Christian witness that the Soviet Union needs so much.

I've enclosed six special Bible bookplates with this letter. Each one has a place for you to sign your name, a promise to pray, and a Scripture verse. Each one is printed in both Russian and English.

I'm hoping you will sign as many as you can and send them back to me with your gift. Then we'll place one bookplate in each Children's Picture Bible you provide before we send it on to a child in the Soviet Union. If you'd like to send more than six Bibles, let us know, and we'll rush you more bookplates to sign.

Each family that receives a children's Bible will be able to thank the Lord for you by name. They'll be able to pray for you. And each bookplate will be a lasting remembrance of your prayers and your love.

We have been praying so long for the chance to reach Russian children. It has finally happened. Now we can reach children like Anna . . . a whole generation who might otherwise never know the Bible. Now is our chance. NOW IS THE TIME.

God has placed an incredible opportunity before us. Let's do everything possible to give children's Bibles to Russian children while the doors are still open. Would you make a gift today? A child is waiting.

Thank you for doing whatever you can.

For the children,

Peter Deyneka, Jr.
President

P.S. My father, who founded the Slavic Gospel Association more than 50 years ago, told me about a short time in the 1920s when the doors were open to the gospel in the Soviet Union. He worked hard to challenge believers in the West to send in Bibles. Few responded. Very few Bibles got in.

Then the doors closed. The opportunity was gone. We haven't had another chance like that until today.

WE CANNOT LET IT SLIP AWAY AGAIN! Please—sign as many bookplates as you can and send your gift today.

This letter does a lot of things well. In this mailing the up-front premiums of six bookplates were utilized as involvement devices by requesting that the donor sign them so they could be placed in gift Bibles. Note how the script copy on page one and at the end of the letter keys in on the premiums and the need to sign and return with a gift. The early paragraphs talk about a new opportunity that has created a new need. This literary construction is a good way to get attention. This letter also has a nice sense of urgency. It gives a very convincing reason for acting now. Note particularly the all-important P.S. in this regard. The reason this letter is so effective is that excellent writing and promotional techniques are utilized in a quickly grasped, immediate need.

FRONT-END PREMIUM LETTER
WORLD VISION

Dear Friend,

Perhaps you're wondering why World Vision is sending you these beautiful note cards.

They're unique. They're eye-catching. They're a great way to write to your friends.

But there's an even more important reason.

World Vision is not in the greeting card business. We're in the compassion business. Through Child Sponsorship, we lovingly provide food, clothing, education and health care to over one million children around the world.

But we felt that a great way to introduce you to "our children" would be through the colorful pictures on these cards. Each picture was drawn and colored by a World Vision child who has been sponsored by a caring friend like you.

In reality, the world of these children was at one time darkened by disease, hunger, and despair. For most of them, there was little hope for the future.

But today, they paint a brighter picture because their world has become a brighter place.

Today, because of Child Sponsorship, these children are receiving food, clothing, medical care and an education. Their families and communities are given a chance to become strong and self-reliant.

Most importantly, each of these children have seen God's love through the compassionate touch of one World Vision sponsor. As one child wrote, "All of us should be smiling because God loves us."

These children have a new life today—and hope for the future—because one friend like you cared enough to make a difference.

Reprinted with permission, World Vision.

But while World Vision Sponsors are changing the lives of children and communities around the world, there are 50,000 children in Africa, Asia and Latin America who are still waiting to be sponsored. Each child has urgent needs. Each one needs a caring friend to make a world of difference in their lives.

You can help change the future of one of these children by becoming a Child Sponsor today.

Your gift of only $20 every month will be enough to make sure one little girl or boy has a nutritious diet, adequate clothing, proper medical care and the opportunity to go to school.

And your gifts can help transform his or her community with things like pure water, a medical clinic or a school classroom.

Your sponsorship for $20 a month will make all the difference in the world to one waiting child.

And one little girl or boy is waiting for you to say yes today.

To become a Child Sponsor, simply fill out the card I've enclosed and tell us the age and country of the little boy or girl you want to sponsor. You'll receive a photograph and information about your child and learn how to develop a friendship a world away.

You'll begin a relationship that will change your life and the life of a child forever!

Thank you for saying yes today.

Gratefully,

Robert A. Seiple
President

P.S. You can begin to change the life of one waiting child today. Just call 000-000-0000 right now and tell us about the child you want to sponsor. And please, keep the enclosed cards as our gift to you from our children.

This child sponsorship offer very tastefully incorporates a front-end premium of a set of cards. The letter acknowledges that World Vision is not in the "greeting card business" but in the "compassion business." This makes for an excellent transition to the main message of the letter—an invitation to the prospect to become a sponsor for $20 a month to support a needy girl or boy. Note that the pictures on the cards were done by World Vision children. Whenever you can pick a useful front-end premium of value that is closely related to your mission like this, you are much better off. The copy flows beautifully because of this connection.

4

Using the Back-End Premium Letter to Improve Response

In this chapter we turn our attention to the back-end premium letter. A back-end premium is defined as a gift of some type (e.g., book, a reproduction) that is promised to the prospect for taking a specified type of action. It is promised to influence the prospect to give by a stated time deadline, or it can be offered in connection with a particular size gift that you are asking for. To be effective, back-end premiums should have a high perceived value. And if the premium itself is an exclusive with the fund-raising organization, so much the better. A major four-way parallel version of the New Testament for *Christianity Today* Magazine (see sample letter at the end of this chapter) was instrumental in converting an almost totally free circulation list of 200,000 recipients to fully paid. This Bible premium was extremely popular with the ministerial and lay leader market that the magazine reached, and more important, it was an exclusive offer with the magazine. In addition, it was related to the ongoing content of the regular publication. That's why it was so effective. It was featured prominently in all the mailings using this offer.

When to Use the Back-End Premium Letter

A back-end premium is a good option to consider when the tangible benefits of the underlying offer need to be enhanced. A back-end premium offer is an effective way to "beef up" the offer and get an improved response. Or, if the mailer has available to it a major item such as a book or some other gift item that has a relationship to the work, it's a good idea to offer it as a test. But here again you need to measure if the increased response more than pays for the cost of the back-end premium. Consider this, too: It's important not to overshadow the underlying offer with the back-end premium offer. If this happens, members or contributors will be conditioned to expect a similar back-end premium offer on all future mailings. So, there's a need to strike a fine balance . . . have a back-premium offer of obvious value but not so overpowering that it sets up future promotion obstacles.

How to Write the Back-End Premium Letter

Back-end premiums are typically more substantial in value than front-end premiums. That's why it's important to give more copy emphasis to the value of the back-end premium. Here are the guidelines to follow in writing back-end premium copy:

1. MENTION THE PREMIUM OFFER EARLY ON IN THE LETTER.

The point here is to put your best foot forward. If you have selected some special item of obvious value and you're offering it in connection with a gift, you should highlight this point in the copy. It's a great way to get attention to the basic message of your letter. You build up desire for the premium and then tell how it can be received with a gift.

The lead paragraph to an environmental group's letter soliciting new contributions starts this way:

- ```
  This letter deals with today's most critical
  environmental problem . . . your support will
  entitle you to a FREE tote bag . . . the exclu-
  sive symbol of _____ membership . . .
  ```

2. SELECT A PREMIUM THAT IS CLOSELY RELATED TO YOUR CAUSE.

If this guideline was true of the front-end premium, it is much more the case with a back-end premium. You are trying to gain logical new members or contributors to your cause . . . people who will make repeat gifts to your organization over subsequent years. If the subject of the premium is unrelated to your cause, it will be difficult to solicit repeat gifts from the unrelated premium-sold donors.
  ```

The U.S. Navy Memorial Foundation—dedicated to remembering the service of Naval personnel—offers a special World War II book on naval battles that was right on target with its core market.

- Because I am so hopeful you will want to accept this invitation, I have reserved in your name a special complimentary edition of <u>SEA BATTLES IN CLOSE-UP: WORLD WAR II</u> . . . this special edition, reserved for you, will be limited to Sustaining Members of our World War II 50th Anniversary Advisory Council and is not available to the general public. Your copy will be clearly marked as a Sustaining Member edition.

Another fund-raiser came up with a perfect back-end premium in acknowledgment of contributions to its theater support group, two free tickets to a performance.

- . . . you will be eligible to receive a pair of complimentary tickets to an upcoming performance when you complete and mail the enclosed membership form. You will be contacted when tickets are available. Many people join _____as Associates for this benefit alone . . .

3. EXCLUSIVE BACK-END PREMIUMS ARE DESIRABLE.

If the premium you're offering in connection with a contribution is readily available at retail or other sources, it is not as attractive. If you publish a magazine, consider putting together a reprint of a number of articles from the magazine (aka self-premium) and offering the reprinted booklet as an exclusive premium only by contributing to your organization. The less generally available an item is, the more appealing it can be made to sound.

One museum offered an exclusive reproduction item right out of their collection.

- When you return the accompanying Guild Application Form, your permanent card will be forwarded, along with a special welcoming gift, <u>The Delaware Cup</u>. The Delaware Cup is just one of 50,000 objects in the collection . . . but it's

```
also a visitor favorite. Hence our decision to
reproduce it for you. The reproduction of this
19th century English original earthenware cup
features a cerulean blue design as well as the
legend . . . A Present From Delaware. The intent
behind our sending you this reproduction, I hope,
is clear: To welcome you to membership in the
Guild.
```

4. DESCRIBE THE END BENEFITS OF HAVING THE PREMIUM.

When you select an appropriate premium for your cause, you can inject some honest flattery in the copy describing the premium. "For someone like yourself who appreciates . . . this book will be of great value . . . ." Build desire by telling all the good things that will happen by possessing the premium.

5. SELECT A BACK-END PREMIUM THAT IS EASY TO FULFILL.

Occasionally a fund-raiser will come up with an attractive back-end premium only to find out later that the costs of fulfillment are too high . . . or worse, it is a difficult item to package and ship. The last thing a fund-raiser wants is returned merchandise due to breakage. So, when you consider the appeal of a back-end premium, also think through how it will be packaged and shipped. If there are some glitches on the fulfillment end, you're well advised to look for some other item that's easier to ship.

6. STATE THAT THE BACK-END PREMIUM IS FREE.

While there is usually a condition with a back-end premium—obligation to send a gift—it's effective to mention the word "FREE" in connection with the gift stipulation.

- ```
  Join _____ Today . . . and We'll Send You FREE,
  Your Members-Only Tote Bag! The Perfect Way to
  Show Your Support. This tote bag is yours
  absolutely free when you become a member of
  _____ . Your tote bag, displaying the
  _____ logo, was designed especially for
  _____ members.
  ```
  ```

MODEL LETTER—BACK-END PREMIUM LETTER "CITIZENS AGAINST WASTE"

Dear fellow enemy of government waste,

MENTION THE PREMIUM OFFER EARLY ON IN THE LETTER (POINT 1)

If you want to see city managers, county council members, and high-priced municipal consultants scamper out of the room, just hold up a copy of the free book I want to send you, and tell them you're going to read aloud from it.

SELECT A PREMIUM THAT IS CLOSELY RELATED TO YOUR CAUSE (POINT 2)

This book, an exclusive publication from Citizens Against Waste, is yours FREE for joining our organizations—and it reprints 50 BIG TAX-SAVING SUCCESS STORIES FROM ACROSS OUR NATION—CULLED FROM THE NATIONAL PRESS.

Stories like the town that FIRED EVERYONE ON THE TOWN PAYROLL—the county that MADE RECYCLING ACTUALLY MAKE MONEY—and the city that CUT STAFF WHILE IMPROVING SERVICES.

And this fascinating book is yours when you join Citizens Against Waste, the watchdog organization that is spreading the word that local government doesn't have to bankrupt citizens to keep from going bankrupt itself.

Join today at a reduced membership rate of just $20 for the next year, and you will receive—six hard-hitting issues of Waste-Line, the whistle-blowing exposé of government waste across the country—and which includes tips and ideas on how you can cut your local taxes yourself.

EXCLUSIVE BACK-END PREMIUMS ARE DESIRABLE (POINT 3)

These stories, reprinted in full with permission from national magazines and newspapers, are exclusive because NO ONE ELSE HAS THE GUTS OR THE FORESIGHT TO BRING ALL THESE "GOOD NEWS TO TAXPAYER" STORIES TOGETHER.

But that is what Citizens Against Waste is all about.

Stopping bloated government—sounding the alarm over inefficiency, waste, and sloth. And if you are willing to spend just $20 to join CAW for a year, you can be a part of stopping local government waste.

(Add additional benefits of organization here.)

DESCRIBE THE END BENEFITS OF HAVING THE PREMIUM (POINT 4)

Quite frankly, this same book that causes government officials to blanch will cause you to smile. Because it shows that there is hope—common sense—and real action across the country when the chips are down and citizens are willing to act. It shows you ways your town or city can save money and reduce taxes. And it gives tips on how you can get this book to the right people!

STATE THAT THE BACK-END PREMIUM IS FREE (POINT 6)

Would you like to receive a FREE copy of this little book?

DESCRIBE THE END BENEFITS OF HAVING THE PREMIUM (POINT 4)

It's yours for joining Citizens Against Waste today. You'll see how people across the country are "reinventing government" for real, and saving taxpayers money in the bargain. And your membership will help stop that waste, and make you part of the most important grassroots movement today.

Join us. You'll be glad you did, and your grandchildren will appreciate it, too!

Sincerely,

Wilson Smith
Director

**EXCLUSIVE BACK-END PREMIUMS ARE DESIRABLE (POINT 3)
STATE THAT THE BACK-END PREMIUM IS FREE (POINT 6)**

P.S. I want to emphasize that this FREE book is
not available anywhere else—only through Citizens
Against Waste. I hope you will accept your free copy.

BACK-END PREMIUM LETTER
CHRISTIANITY TODAY MAGAZINE

If you had lived in the 13th Century, the free gift described below would have been worth at least as much as the average workingman earned over a 15-year period.

Dear Pastor:

Back in the Middle Ages, a laborer had to spend the equivalent of 15 years' income just to purchase an ordinary copy of the Bible. While modern printing methods have reduced the price substantially, you—as a minister—must still find it rather costly to acquire the various translations, concordances, and commentaries you need in your library.

Undoubtedly that's one of the reasons for the enthusiastic reception clergymen have given "The New Testament in Four Versions" . . . which I want to send you <u>free of charge</u>. This single volume contains the complete texts for four of the most frequently used translations . . . spread out in parallel columns, on facing pages, for instant comparison.

In the first column, you'll find the King James with its majestic, classical language. Next to it, verse by verse, is the Revised Standard incorporating new knowledge of the original Greek texts. Then the Phillips, in its free-flowing contemporary style. And in the last column, the New English with a completely new rendering of the original.

No longer will you have to jump up from your work and pull down your King James to compare a passage with the Revised Standard . . . (More benefits of premium)

And remember, this handsome, 864-page hard-cover New Testament <u>costs you nothing</u>! It's yours . . . as a gift . . . simply for accepting a one-year trial subscription to CHRISTIANITY TODAY: 25 issues for $5.00.

Reprinted with permission, *Christianity Today* Magazine.

As a matter of fact, you couldn't buy a copy of
"The New Testament in Four Versions" anywhere—at any
price—even if you wished to do so. For this special
edition was printed exclusively for CHRISTIANITY
TODAY and is used solely as a means of welcoming new
subscribers.

You'll find this New Testament an appropriate
"companion gift" with the regular issues of our magazine. CHRISTIANITY TODAY is one of the outstanding
contemporary journals of Biblical theology. Every
other week you receive scholarly, thought-provoking
articles by leading Protestant spokesmen and theolo-
gians.

CHRISTIANITY TODAY is in the forefront of the
evangelical position—applying the test of
Biblical truth to the wide spectrum of modern
life . . .

(More descriptive copy of the magazine content)

You'll discover all this for yourself after you
look over but a few issues. And you may have that
opportunity by filling out and mailing the enclosed
subscription card.

The card entitles you to critically examine
CHRISTIANITY TODAY, and "The New Testament in Four
Versions" as well. If you're not completely satisfied, simply return the New Testament anytime within
two weeks of receipt, and we'll refund your full
$5.00 subscription price.

Otherwise, you may keep the New Testament—and
continue enjoying the twice-monthly visits of CHRIS-
TIANITY TODAY for a full year.

Please fill out and return the card now in the
self-addressed, postpaid envelope.

                                        Sincerely,
                                        Circulation Manager

P.S. Payment with your order enables us to ship your copy of the New Testament—free and postpaid—without delay. If it's inconvenient to enclose your check now, we will start your CHRISTIANITY TODAY subscription at once, send you a bill, then forward your free copy of the 864-page "New Testament in Four Versions" as soon as your account clears.

Even though this letter was mailed some years ago, it illustrates exactly how to write copy for a major back-end premium. If you are fortunate enough to have a major back-end premium like this, here is the way to write the copy. The benefits of the premium are emphasized. The fact the premium is an exclusive with the magazine is also stressed. And the premium benefits would appeal to individuals who also have an interest in the underlying product, the magazine. It was this premium and this type of copy that turned this magazine from almost totally free or controlled circulation to fully paid. It was a classic.

BACK-END PREMIUM LETTER
VEGETARIAN RESOURCE GROUP

FREE BOOK FREE BOOK FREE BOOK

NEW—From the Vegetarian Resource Group
<u>Simple, Lowfat & Vegetarian</u> . . . Unbelievably
Easy Ways to Reduce Fat in <u>Your</u> Meals

Whether you're a vegetarian or just trying to reduce
the fat in your diet . . . whether you're needing to
reduce the risk of heart disease or cancer or simply
wanting to look and feel better . . . you will benefit
from this <u>landmark new book</u> that's just loaded with hundreds of practical and simple eating suggestions.

<u>But here's the best news about this major new
volume</u>:

Get the <u>Vegetarian Journal</u> plus many other benefits . . . and you will receive the $15, 368-page
<u>Simple, Lowfat & Vegetarian</u> ABSOLUTELY FREE!

<u>Dear Friend</u>,

I have an exciting <u>free offer</u> for you. But first
I have a question:

"Where do you get reliable information for eating
better?

If you're like most busy people today your advice
comes from a variety of sources . . . newspaper and
magazine articles . . . talk shows . . . conversations with friends who are trying the latest fad diet
. . . and on and on.

Little tid-bits of information that may work for a
while. But in the end you're right back to square one.

Let me suggest a better idea . . .

<u>Go directly to the source—The Vegetarian Resource
Group</u>! Learn how to eat better from professionals who
"practice what they preach" in the pages of <u>Vegetar-
ian Journal</u>.

That's what <u>Parade, The Washington Post, The Los Angeles Times, The Detroit News, New York Newsday, and many others do</u>. Articles appearing in these publications were based on information from VRG's highly respected dietitians and writers.

The media seeks our advice because we're an impartial professional group interested in providing the latest and best information on the vegetarian diet. Our mission? Provide people with easy-to-follow changes in their regular eating habits that will help them improve their health . . . <u>clear, concise, authoritative . . . and fun</u>!

In a moment I want to tell you what you will gain from your FREE book, <u>Simple, Lowfat & Vegetarian</u> and your regular bi-monthly copies of <u>Vegetarian Journal</u>.

But first let me describe a few convictions that I think you may already share with me . . . <u>Vegetarian Journal</u> readers have been getting this wise advice for years. Here's just a sampling from recent issues . . .

By subscribing to our 36-page, bi-monthly magazine <u>Vegetarian Journal</u>, you will receive practical advice you can trust. And all of this helpful information is verified and approved by Registered Dietitians and Physicians.

You'll also get . . . (More benefits and a description of the type of reader the magazine is looking for)

To receive your FREE book, sign up for . . . <u>The Vegetarian Journal</u>—Eight Issues for Only $25.00

You may be wondering if this offer is as good as I say it is. Here's what I'd like to do to convince you to at least try our magazine.

You may cancel your subscription—and return your book—anytime within 60 days for a full refund.

I can't think of a better offer . . .

To receive your copy of <u>Simple, Lowfat & Vegetar-</u>
<u>ian</u> simply complete the enclosed subscription form
today. We'll get your book in the mail to you—free
and postpaid.

                              Sincerely,

                              Charles Stahler
                              Publisher

    P.S. (Description of one chapter from free book)

Here's the way to write copy when you offer a major premium. In this
case the book was given to those who accept the two-year subscription
offer. The free book was the lead to the letter and heavily emphasized
throughout. Because the content of the premium was similar to the content
of the magazine the copy flows from premium to magazine in a smooth
fashion. This highlights the importance of selecting a premium that is closely related to the basic product. The letter closes with a money-back guarantee . . . all in all a very strong pitch for a targeted audience.

5

Obtaining Information—and Funds—with a Survey Letter

One of the all-time-great cold prospect salesmen found that the magic phrase to use in opening new doors was, "I wonder if you might help me?" The magic behind this phrase is exactly why surveys work in direct mail fund-raising. The fund-raiser is asking for some genuine help in the form of some answered questions. Most people like to help. It puts the responder in the one-up position. To be asked for help indicates that you, the responder, have some special information or knowledge that is valuable. You are flattered to be asked. A survey response also allows for an initial involvement not requiring the gift of money. As a person answers the questions the mental pump is primed . . . a softening process has been engaged in . . . and a gift, in many instances, is a natural outflow of the answering process.

When to Use the Survey Letter

If you are fortunate enough to promote a cause that has strong emotional overtones—*and at the same time* some vocal opposition—a survey enclosure is a natural. Generally surveys work best on hotly contested issues where strong feelings run deep on both sides of the issue. A survey is a good way to open up a dialogue with your prospects. You start by asking for something relatively easy to do (e.g., answer a few questions) and then as the prospect's mind gets in gear, so to speak, you progress to the second stage of asking for a gift to accompany the answers to the survey questions. In effect, answering the questions has helped the respondent get in touch with the emotional hot buttons. And, after getting excited about the issue, they are given the opportunity to do something very practical to solve the problem. If there is some particular piece of legislation in which your organization wants to have a strong input, consider the survey. Or, if your opponents appear to be winning the day and putting you down, use the survey letter. It works. Finally, it helps to have a strong case in the form of statistics or other objective evidence that can be presented to the person answering the survey. While the framework is emotional, the content provides lots of substantive information.

How to Write the Survey Letter

A survey letter can write itself if you have in mind two things: first, the ultimate result you're looking for . . . a result the questions will help you achieve, and, second, the emotions and feelings surrounding the issue in question. Basically you write the letter giving as much information as possible to help in guiding answers to the questions. And you intersperse why you need the survey, why you are in a fighting mad mood, and why you need a gift. It's a no-holds-barred approach. The techniques you learned in the first chapter come into play here. But there are some special points in particular that you want to make sure are covered . . .

1. TELL THE RECIPIENT WHY HE OR SHE HAS BEEN SELECTED TO RECEIVE THE SURVEY.

A fund-raising survey letter is based on the assumption that the recipient has some special insights that would be valuable to the organization conducting the survey. The copy should highlight the fact that the prospect has been specially selected and why. Here are a few examples of how to phrase this important copy point.

- As an American environmentalist you have been picked to participate in the first Global Survey ever conducted on the most ominous environmental threats facing our planet today!

- You were specially selected to participate in a large national survey of American voters . . . we have carefully selected you as someone we feel we want to have take part in this important survey. Your past activities indicate to us that you are a person who actively follows national events and will be well informed on important issues.

- I could only afford to send out surveys today to a special group of key people like you who I thought would be most interested in helping us.

- You have been chosen to participate in a critical National Referendum designed to focus leadership attention on one of the most urgent problems now facing America.

2. GIVE A RATIONALE FOR THE SURVEY QUESTIONS.

A prospect needs to know what you will do with survey results. Why are they important? How will they help advance your cause? The questions should have a slant to them . . . it should be fairly obvious as to how the answers relate to the end result you are fighting for.

- We feel it's important that Congressmembers, Senators, and the press know how the people feel about limiting congressional terms. Also we'd like for the general public to know how people in your home state would vote if the election were held today.

- Your responses will help us measure local views on environmental problems, and the toll that these issues are taking on individual lives—the insights we need to help develop the most effective solutions and strategies.

- Poll results will be released to the media, and state and local governments, to show the need to protect scenic resources and clean up the visual pollution that blights our neighborhoods, degrades our countryside, and erodes the unique character of our cities and towns.

- Your response, when added to that of other women's rights supporters, will show us which issues are of major concern to many, many voters.

3. PROVIDE LOTS OF FACTS.

Most survey letters are lengthy. The reason? You need to give the recipient a lot of background data to intelligently answer the survey questions. Before answering the questions, they will need to know key facts about your issue and the fight you have on your hands. This is why a survey is so effective in communicating your position. The questions serve as a motivator for people to become acquainted with the facts of your position as presented in your letter.

- Already, around the world, you can see with frightening clarity the damage caused by overpopulation. Globally, over 800 million people suffer from starvation—<u>with 12 million children under the age of five dying each year</u>! . . . Even though Americans make up only 5% of world population, we consume 11 times the world's average in energy, 6 times the steel, and 4 times the grain. Because of such heavy consumption of resources, even a small population increase here can adversely affect countries around the world.

- Though reduced to just 6% of the earth's surface, the tropics are home to more than 60% of all life on earth . . . About 25% of the medicines now produced commercially in the United States are derived in whole or in part from tropical plants.

4. UTILIZE AN "EMOTIONAL KICKER."

Here's a writing tip before you start . . . get your own feelings in gear before you begin to write. Sit down with an associate and verbalize on how you feel about the issue. If you aren't hot under the collar, don't expect your recipients to get too excited. You are not just collecting facts to present as general research. You are forced to solicit this information because of the misstatements, half-truths, and generally false information being put out by your opponents. You want to lead your charge with the banner of truth. Disseminating the truth (in the form of the answered questions) is critical when the horrible falsehoods of the opposition are graphically described.

- . . . our battle in Congress remains an uphill fight, with many special interest groups arrayed against us. But we do have one powerful weapon our opponents lack—and that is <u>the force of public opinion on our side</u>.

- But today, fed up with 10 years of abuse and neglect, the women of America are on the move again! Anger is a powerful fuel, as the politicians found out in the recent elections <u>AND . . . are about to discover again in the months ahead</u>! Rather than just get mad, we're determined to put our issues at the very top of our country's political agenda . . . By taking action <u>right now</u> and finding out what you and millions of progressive citizens feel about the <u>priority of abortion and other women's rights issues</u>, we're determined to shape the political and legislative agenda for Congress and the country.

5. BRACKET THE SURVEY REQUEST WITH A GIFT "ASK."

This is an essential feature of the survey letter. You start by asking for the survey information, but you conclude by bracketing the survey response request with a gift request. A person who has taken the time to offer his or her opinions is mentally engaged in your issue and is receptive to the financial gift request. That's why on almost all survey letters you will see that the pitch for returning the survey is combined with an "ask" for a gift.

- Here's how you can help!

  1. <u>Fill out and mail back your ballot today</u>. Your views and vote for the most beautiful and ugliest towns will help us publicize the need to protect our scenic heritage and rekindle pride in America.

  2. <u>Send the largest contribution you can, today, to help us</u> expand our National Campaign.

- _____ can't solve this population problem alone. We need <u>your</u> help. Here's how.

<u>First, you can help</u> by completing the enclosed
National Referendum and returning it to me within
the next 10 days. Mailed to a select group of citizens, this referendum can help us approach national
news media and government officials with convincing
evidence of public views on the need for increased
action on population issues. <u>Second, you can help</u>
us do something about those issues by sending your
membership fees to support our campaign.

- Please help. Join _____ today. Send me your
  Opinion Survey, your Petition, and your most generous contribution—today!

6. MAKE THE QUESTIONS EASY BUT SUBSTANTIVE.

You tread a fine line here. You don't want the questions to be so difficult
and hard to answer that people just put it off, and eventually ignore it. But
when you oversimplify the questions you run the risk of sounding just too
obvious and not substantive. So you must come up with easy-to-answer questions that have a substantive ring to them. Generally it's a good idea to begin
with "Were you aware of the problem . . . " types of questions. And finish with
a question that asks, "Would you be willing to make a small financial sacrifice
to solve the problem?" This question leads to the gift response part of the survey. Here are some typical questions asked on fund-raising surveys:

- Before reading this mailing, were you aware of
  the gravity of the _____
  crisis?

- Would you be willing to make a small financial
  contribution today to help prevent a full-scale
  _____ crisis in the next decade?

- Which of the following _____problems do you
  feel are of serious concern to you and your community? (Check all that apply.)

- Please rank the top five issues you consider most
  important to be addressed before the upcoming
  election. "1" represents your highest priority,
  "2" your second, and so forth.

MODEL LETTER—THE SURVEY LETTER
"CITIZENS AGAINST PORNOGRAPHY"

Dear Friend,

I'm simply outraged. And I think you will be too when you hear what is happening in Happy Valley.

A recent decision by our Town Council means that pornographic bookstores will be permitted to operate anywhere they want in Happy Valley. And with just the weakest safeguards for selling their obnoxious wares to underage children.

This decision was slipped through when the Council had barely a quorum . . . and no advance notice of the pending action.

TELL THE RECIPIENT WHY HE OR SHE HAS BEEN SELECTED TO RECEIVE THE SURVEY (POINT 1)

That's why I'm writing to you and a number of your fellow-citizens in Happy Valley. I want to know what you think about this outrageous action.

Would you take just a few minutes now to answer the questions I have listed on the enclosed Family Values Survey? In meetings I have attended—and in all the discussions I have had with Happy Valley residents—I don't think the Council's action represents what citizens in our community really think.

UTILIZE AN "EMOTIONAL KICKER" (POINT 4)

Councilman Jones had the temerity to state that: "It's a nice combination . . . it promotes free speech and it's good for business." If you're like me you're sick and tired of so-called free speech proponents masking their true intentions with such platitudes.

What Councilman Jones didn't tell you is that his son operates 10 such porno shops in our state and is ready to move into Happy Valley . . . if we let him. I for one don't plan to let him without a fight.

MAKE THE QUESTIONS EASY BUT SUBSTANTIVE (POINT 6)

Please tell me what you think on the enclosed survey. There are only 6 questions. They're easy to answer. And I plan to present the response to them at an upcoming Town Council meeting, along with a resolution that will prohibit the operation of porno book shops in Happy Valley.

PROVIDE LOTS OF FACTS (POINT 3)

I've enclosed a reprint from _____ entitled "The Supreme Court, Free Speech, and Pornography." You'll learn what the recent Supreme Court decisions on pornography really mean. And you'll see what other communities have done to follow the law and to ensure that family values are preserved in their communities.

Here's something else I think you should know. Remember what happened in Unhappy Valley? Sadly that neighboring city's name is almost synonymous with degradation. It wasn't always that way. But 10 years ago they opened wide the gates to porno stores and other related businesses. It hardly helped business. Gradually, and almost imperceptibly, some businesses moved out. And people too. Their experiment with "free speech" devastated what was once one of the nicest communities in our state.

I've also prepared—and enclose with this letter—a list of other citizens of Happy Valley who agree with the upcoming resolution I plan to propose to the Town Council. Feel free to call any of them and check their views before you return your survey.

BRACKET THE SURVEY REQUEST WITH A GIFT "ASK" (POINT 5)
GIVE A RATIONALE FOR THE SURVEY QUESTIONS (POINT 2)

And when you return your completed survey, please enclose a generous tax-deductible gift. If you can send $100 it would be put to use right away. But gifts of $50, $25, and $15 are welcome too.

Here's what your gift—when combined with those from other citizens—will allow us to do. We have established an Emergency Fund to take care of the following needs:

1. Run an ad campaign in our town and county papers. We need to get all the facts before our citizens before the upcoming Town Council Meeting.

2. Tabulate the survey results and circulate to each member of the Happy Valley Town Council along with a copy of the enclosed _____ article.

3. Produce a video to show at rallies and at other local gatherings.

This is an ambitious undertaking. But I can't think of any cause closer to my heart than preserving the great family values and culture of Happy Valley. I have lived here 25 years. My kids have grown up here. And I don't want to see our community invaded by some short-term profiteers who will make their gains at our expense and then move on.

This is your chance to speak up. It's really true . . . all it takes for bad things to happen is for good people to remain silent. I urge you to send in your survey . . . and include a large tax-deductible gift.

　　　　　　　　　　　　　Sincerely,

　P.S. If you would like some additional surveys please call _____ and we'll rush you some for your friends and neighbors. Time is of the essence . . . and we need all the help we can get. Thanks for your support.

SURVEY LETTER
CAMPUS CRUSADE FOR CHRIST INTERNATIONAL

Dear Christian Friend,

You were specially selected to participate in a large national survey regarding the war against Christians now being waged on America's college campuses.

If you cannot take the time, we will understand. Or if you do not wish to state your views now, that's okay.—But we would appreciate it if you would <u>return your survey today</u> either filled out or blank.

We plan to announce the results soon, and we want to know if you will be participating.

We carefully selected you as someone we hope will take part in this important survey because your past activities tell us that you are a strong Bible-believing Christian who is well informed on important issues . . .

And we thought you would also want to know about the crisis Christians now face on America's college campuses.

You see, right now Christians are under the most ferocious and vicious attack ever on American college campuses. I will tell you more about this in a moment and how you can help fight back. But first, let me explain why this survey is so important.

You see, most polls ask only a few hundred people their opinion. And most polls do not focus on the views of Christians. <u>This poll is different</u>. We plan to poll 1,000,000 (one million) Christians across the nation.

We will then tabulate and send the results to all the boards of directors and every President of all 2,300 major colleges and universities in America. And we will release the results to the media at a major news conference.

You can be sure a massive survey like this will be seen and carefully studied by the leaders of America's universities. We will gladly send you the results as well. This poll will help us <u>send a message</u> to leaders of America's colleges and universities that Christians are very angry and upset about the anti-Christian bigotry on campuses today and <u>identify those Christians</u> who are willing to join us in the battle for the university—and the hearts, minds and souls for the next generation of American leaders . . .

You see, we are convinced that the battle for the campus is crucial to the survival of a vibrant Christian faith in America.

I am not exaggerating when I say that America's universities are waging a war against those who speak up for the Christian faith. Here are just a few examples . . .

(Note: At this point this six-page letter offers many examples, lots of "Did you know" data, statistics, and quotable material to back up the writer's position.)

Our goal is to train, equip, and motivate 32,500 Christian professors to explain the Gospel to their students. <u>This will allow us to expose all 13 million students</u> now on college campuses to the Christian faith every year!

That, in a nutshell, is our Battle Plan for taking the campus back. We have come a long way in 12 years. But we need to get many more good Christians like you involved in this battle . . . .

We need at least 1,000,000 Christians to participate if this survey is to have the impact we're looking for. So please,

1. Complete your 1992 NATIONAL SURVEY OF CHRISTIANS.

2. Rush this important document back to us . . .

3. Please include a contribution of $15, $25, .
. . . We want to release the results of this
survey very soon. <u>So please let us hear from
you in the next few days</u>. Thank you so much
for your help and participation.

Warmly, in Christ,

National Director

Here's a dramatic example of the survey letter. It argues out of an
underdog position, but with the strong hope that results of the survey and
the action plan of this organization will get a dramatic turn-around. There's
a lot of deep-felt emotion that comes through. To a list of people committed to the work of Campus Crusade for Christ, this is an extremely effective
approach. It's a call to arms. It's loaded with facts and all kinds of information relevant to the Crusade's cause. And it makes the strongest case possible for returning the survey.

6

Boosting Participation in Sweepstakes, Raffles, and Bazaars, Through Special Event Letters

Even though direct mail fund-raising is a fairly serious affair, sometimes providing a little "fun and games" in the act of giving can give a real boost to your returns. For some organizations, this means a sweepstakes that offers a number of special prizes to respondents. Other groups may run a bazaar or an auction. And for years fund-raisers have been running enticing dinners for "X dollars" a plate. All these approaches are designed to reach out and reward the contributor with something a little extra, something over and above the good feeling of helping a worthy cause. These types of letters aren't as common probably because it requires a fair amount of extra work on the part of the fund-raiser to arrange for the special benefits. But if the conditions are right, the special event letter can raise an amazing amount of money for your cause. This chapter provides you with all the information you will need to develop a special events letter. Let's see when to write such a letter . . . and how it's done.

When to Use the Special Event Letter

Because we're considering a variety of special event letters in this chapter, we'll discuss the factors for each one separately.

Sweepstakes Letter—If you can develop a list of sweepstakes prizes that relate to your overall mission, the sweepstakes letter is an excellent fund-raiser. In some cases nonprofit organizations find that they can approach companies to donate the prizes in exchange for a little publicity. The sweepstakes letter also makes sense if your organization is merchandise oriented. If, as a regular course, you offer merchandise-type benefits or publish a catalog for members to buy products at special prices, then a sweepstakes letter is a good choice. You will be acquiring donors who will respond to your subsequent merchandise offerings. Or, if you are just looking for a way to get the maximum possible response, the sweepstakes letter is a good way to go. While there is a lot of extra work involved in a sweepstakes offer, this offer almost always increases the response over standard offers.

Bazaar, Dinner, or Ball—By their very nature some nonprofit organizations are able to offer enjoyable events in connection with a gift. In this chapter you'll see a model letter for a symphony orchestra that invites donors to an evening of music, international gourmet foods, and an auction—an evening that the symphony has the resources to produce. If you can arrange a special event utilizing the facilities you already have, certainly do so.

How to Write the Special Event Letter

A letter that offers some special prizes—or other unique benefits over and above the normal—should follow the suggested writing tips mentioned in Chapter 1. But there are four special factors to stress with this type of a letter:

1. EMPHASIZE THE BENEFITS.

Whatever the added extra benefits that you have decided to offer (e.g., sweepstakes prizes, a dinner dance, a bazaar) feature these in the copy. The copy on these added extras should have lots of sizzle. It should be a great deal of fun just to respond. Everyone likes to be recognized—or rewarded—for their involvement, and that's what this type of letter does.

2. STATE WHY HELP IS NEEDED.

There's a danger of discussing only the benefit side to the exclusion of the urgent need. Take a look at the WETA sweepstakes letter at the end of this chapter. It shows you how to combine the prize descriptions with the urgent need for money. Indicate in whatever ways are appropriate that you want to reward your contributor for helping support a worthy cause.

3. MAKE IT EASY TO RESPOND.

This is one of the basic principles of writing fund-raising letters. But when it comes to special events, the offer can become complicated. That's because you are requesting a gift, *and at the same time* you are offering some special inducements to give. Think through the offer and make it as easy as possible to respond. You don't want potential contributors setting it aside because they are confused.

4. GIVE A DEADLINE.

Whether it's a sweepstakes or a special dinner, you need to have a deadline for responding. That date should always appear prominently in the copy. On other types of fund-raising mailings, you may accept gifts for months and even years after mailing. That is not the case with a special prize letter. Make sure the prospect knows what the deadline date is.

Four Unique Factors of a Sweepstakes Mailing

Before you proceed with a sweepstakes letter, be aware of these four distinctive factors:

1. Once you are out with your first mailing, *all prizes have to be awarded*. Even if you get a poor initial return you cannot decide to cancel the sweepstakes and not award the prizes. You have to select winners for every prize promoted in your mailing, no matter how small the size of the initial mailing.

This means *you can't test a sweepstakes mailing* in the traditional direct mail way. You can decide to curtail the total amount of subsequent mail drops, but you can't do a small mailing as a test to see if you want to award the prizes. After you "go public" with a mailing of any size, all prizes have to be awarded. There is a way to assess early results and how heavy you want to go in subsequent mailings (see early-bird prize offer discussion later in this chapter).

2. You have to provide an *equal chance for noncontributor responders to win the prizes*. The copy should make this point as you will see from the samples in this chapter. The response form should add a "No, I don't wish to contribute but would like to enter the sweepstakes . . ." box.

3. *You must advise recipients of the mailing how anyone who writes in can obtain a winners list.* You need to convey to recipients that there will be an above-board selection of winners. It's also required that the mailer provide a list of winners to those who request it. Before you conduct a sweepstakes mailing, have legal counsel check with state authorities to review all applicable laws.

4. *Include the rules of the contest in the mailing*. Establish the rules of the sweepstakes after you have consulted with the appropriate authorities. It's not a bad idea to have your sweepstakes run by an agency that specializes in sweepstakes. They will know exactly what rules should be adopted and other technicalities such as states that prohibit sweepstakes and must be excluded from the mailing lists. If you develop the rules yourself, remember to cover the following points:

   a. State that it is not necessary to join or contribute to win a prize.

   b. Tell how the prize winners will be selected.

   c. Give a deadline date for entering.

   d. Indicate who may not enter—employees or agents of the nonprofit organization and individuals living in specified states as noted by your legal counsel.

   e. State that sweepstakes promotion is subject to all applicable federal, state, and local laws and regulations.

   f. Give an address where anyone can write and get a list of all the winners.

Three Tips to Help Your Sweepstakes Mailing Succeed

Finally, in regard to sweepstakes keep these three important points in mind:

1. *The prize list must be compelling*. Develop an attractive list of prizes. The Grand Prize should be one with overwhelming appeal. It's also important to have a great number of prizes. Most people like to be tempted by the grand prize, but they reason, if they don't win, there's a chance they may win a lesser prize. If possible also select prizes that are related to your underlying mission. If you don't, you may get a large number of donors who have no interest in making subsequent gifts.

2. *Use a non-postage-paid return envelope*. The prospect's use of his or her own stamp is a minimal way to screen out individuals who have no interest in your work. Some recipients will send in an entry simply to find out if they have won—if they can do it at your expense. If they have to use their own stamp, marginally interested prospects will not respond.

3. *Offer an early-bird prize*. Select one special gift and offer it to people who respond by a much earlier date than the final cut-off date for the over-

all sweepstakes. There's an important reason for doing this. It allows you to get an early reading of how well the mailing is doing. In a sense it's a way of testing how well you're doing without having to wait until the final deadline. If returns are good, you can keep mailing with confidence. If not, it allows you to curtail further mailings at an early point. But remember, as stated earlier, once you are in the mail with one sweepstakes letter you have to award all the prizes.

MODEL LETTER—SWEEPSTAKES OFFER
ENVIRONMENTAL GROUP

Dear Friend,

Congratulations. You are eligible to win the Summer Fun Caribbean Cruise in _____'s new All-America Environmental Sweepstakes.

EMPHASIZE THE BENEFITS (POINT 1)

Just think of the fun you and your family will have on the Caribbean Cruise . . . all expenses paid. Fine dining. Dancing. Just relaxing in the sun. Duty free shopping trips. And the pleasure of meeting and making new friends . . .

Even if you don't win the Grand Prize, there are over 1,000 additional prizes for our lucky winners. Cameras. Binoculars. Wildlife prints. Books on nature. And more.

MAKE IT EASY TO RESPOND (POINT 3)

To enter the All-America Environmental Sweep-stakes, simply complete the enclosed entry form and mail it today. That's all there is to it.

Winners will be selected at random. And notified by registered letter.

GIVE A DEADLINE (POINT 4)

But you must enter to win. That's why I urge you to mail your entry no later than _____.

STATE WHY HELP IS NEEDED (POINT 2)

It's not necessary to join _____ when you enter. But I hope you do. _____ is conducting this major campaign in order to attract many new members to its cause.

Today, the rain forests in Brazil face imminent destruction unless we act. Every 24 hours another ___ acres of rain forest are bulldozed or burned. That's why _____ has launched this All-America Environmental Sweepstakes. Proceeds will go to our newly launched campaign to Save Our Rain Forests.

EMPHASIZE THE BENEFITS (POINT 1)

And when you join _____ each month you will receive our colorful newsletter informing you of success to reach our goal of saving 2,000,000 acres by the year 2000. We'll keep you informed through presidential update letters. All members also receive our annual gift catalogue with special members-only prices for gift cards, books, and many other items.

GIVE A DEADLINE (POINT 4)

I look forward to hearing from you and welcoming you as the newest member of _____. Don't forget we must hear from you by _____ in order for you to be eligible for the Sweepstakes prizes.

Sincerely,

President

P.S. If you return your entry by _____ you will be eligible for our early-bird prize drawing . . . a limited-edition art print of the jaguar . . . one of the species that depends on the preservation of the rain forests. It's illustrated in the enclosed brochure along with all the other attractive prizes you might win.

MODEL LETTER—RAFFLE
FRATERNAL ORGANIZATION

Dear Friend,

EMPHASIZE THE BENEFITS (POINT 1)

Would you like to win an all-expense paid trip to New Orleans?

Just think of the fun you will have with three days and nights in a first-class New Orleans hotel for you and a guest . . . round-trip air fare . . . all meals paid for . . . and $300 cash spending money to boot!

And while you're on that trip, wouldn't it make you feel good to know that the cost of your $2 winning raffle ticket helped fund research into the causes and prevention of blindness?

Your _____ Club has been funding blindness research for more than 50 years, and great strides are being made.

STATE WHY HELP IS NEEDED (POINT 2)

But since blindness has many causes, the cost of research is high, and contributions are needed from thousands of people to make the needed break-throughs.

The cost of the raffle tickets I have enclosed for you—at $2 per ticket—will add to the Blindness Research Fund and hasten the day when we find cures for blindness.

And each ticket you buy adds to your chances of winning.

Please see your enclosed tickets for the conditions—and remember that Uncle Sam may require you to pay taxes on your winnings next year.

MAKE IT EASY TO RESPOND (POINT 3)

Five tickets are enclosed. To "activate" your tickets, simply tear off the stubs, and send them back in the enclosed envelope with a check totalling $2 for each ticket. If you want more tickets, call XXX-XXXX.

GIVE A DEADLINE (POINT 4)

I must receive your tickets by June 1 for the June 15 drawing. And you do not have to be present to win.

I know you will feel good aiding the Blindness Research Fund.

And there's the chance you'll feel even better for three days on vacation in New Orleans!

Please act today. I need to hear from you by June 1 to include you in the drawing.

Sincerely,

President

MAKE IT EASY TO RESPOND (POINT 3)

P.S. You don't have to be present to win that trip to New Orleans. But I do need your "activated" raffle tickets by June 1 to include your numbers in the drawing. Good luck.

MODEL LETTER—BAZAAR HOSPITAL

Dear Mr. & Mrs. _____,

Enclosed is your invitation to the Mercy Hospital Bazaar.

I am writing you early because you are among those people who know how special Mercy Hospital is, and how caring the entire staff and volunteers are to patients and their families.

But what you may not know is that one reason for that special care is the Mercy Hospital Spring Bazaar. And I hope that this letter will convince you to attend this annual event.

Let me tell you how many glowing letters of appreciation I receive from former patients and their families about the orderlies, nurses, nurses' aides, and volunteers here at Mercy. Equal to our first-rate equipment and medical staff is a support staff that makes Mercy stand out beyond that level of excellence.

STATE WHY HELP IS NEEDED (POINT 2)

And yet we would not have that support staff if we depended only on payments from patients and insurance companies. Because we turn no one away, and keep patients' out-of-pocket expenses as low as possible, receipts from our annual Bazaar allow us to maintain the high level of support staff we have, in these ways:

- Training for volunteers
- Training for support staff
- Salary differential for superior workers so we can keep them at Mercy
- Salaries for extra staff so each patient has the attention he or she needs
- And much, much more . . .

In addition, the Bazaar, besides adding vital revenue to the Mercy budget, provides a wonderful recognition event for employees of the hospital, in the form of door prizes, recognition of employees of the month and year, and special events.

I think you will agree that Mercy Hospital is a vital contributor to our community. Not just because it provides medical services, but because it stands as a model of kindness, concern, and caring for those in need.

MAKE IT EASY TO RESPOND (POINT 3)

To participate in the Bazaar, simply call XXX-XXXX to reserve your place. We want to accommodate all levels of interest and are making three levels of involvement available to you:

EMPHASIZE THE BENEFITS (POINT 1)

Here are the benefits you will receive by choosing one of these levels:

<u>Bronze</u>—$30 per pair of tickets . . . provides entry to the Bazaar, one chance for the Bermuda vacation drawing, and two complimentary drinks.

<u>Silver</u>—$100 per pair, all of the above, plus entrance to the 4:00 P.M. reception I am hosting to honor Dr. _____.

<u>Gold</u>—$500 per pair, all of the above benefits, plus entrance to the Mercy Ball that evening.

Your ticket prices, besides bringing you a wonderful day (and night!) of entertainment, will help us provide the benefits and recognition our wonderful staff so richly deserve.

GIVE A DEADLINE (POINT 4)

I hope I will see you there. Please feel free to call my assistant, _____, if you have any questions.

Reservations for Silver and Gold tickets should be
made a week before the event.

   Thanks so much for your support of Mercy
Hospital.

                              Sincerely,

                              Director

   P.S. Your ticket prices are tax-deductible except
for value received, which we have estimated at $20
Bronze, $75 Silver, $300 Gold.

MODEL LETTER—AUCTION
SYMPHONY ASSOCIATION

Dear Friend of Music,

Please accept this invitation to join me and (name of solo performer) at the Annual _____ Symphony Auction and Luncheon, to be held from 11:30 to 3:30, April 22nd, at the _____ Hotel.

EMPHASIZE THE BENEFITS (POINT 1)

You will have a wonderful time meeting celebrities of the music world, meeting musicians from the symphony who will provide music, and bidding on exciting prizes that range from midnight gourmet picnics to "Love Boat" cruises.

And again this year, eleven gourmet shops from around the county will vie with each other in serving the most memorable food at the luncheon.

STATE WHY HELP IS NEEDED (POINT 2)

But even more important than the fun and food, you will also be part of ensuring that our own symphony enchants and pleases audiences of all ages for another year.

I can't imagine _____ County without a symphony of its own. As much as our parks and play fields and schools, it adds prestige and value to our community, putting us on a par with many cities.

Stocked with first-rate musicians from internationally acclaimed orchestras, our symphony plays summer concerts, provides school programs, teaches young musicians, and offers a full range of classical music . . . right here in _____.

Yet you may not know that the very existence of the _____ Symphony is in doubt every year. Funding is scarce. Governments are tightening their belts.

And perhaps most distressing of all, few in government really understand the great loss you and I
and our community would suffer if we lost the _____
Symphony.

If you appreciate the need for classical music
here at the "grassroots" level, and if you, along
with me, don't want to see the Symphony die, please
join me on the 22nd. (And have an elegant time in the
process.)

MAKE IT EASY TO RESPOND (POINT 3)

To attend this fun event, simply fill in and
return the enclosed response form. You may elect to
charge one of your credit cards if you prefer.

Tickets are $15 per individual or $25 per couple. Patron tickets are $75 per couple; Benefactor
tickets are $200 per couple. Patrons and Benefactors
are recognized at special receptions during the
year, and in each event's program and our Annual
Report.

GIVE A DEADLINE (POINT 4)

May I hear from you by April 15th? That way I can
make sure to include you in the special events. Space
is very limited, as I am sure you can understand. I
do hope you can join all of us on the 22nd.

                                        Sincerely,

                                        Symphony President

EMPHASIZE THE BENEFITS (POINT 1)

P.S. (Solo Performer) is eager to meet with
patrons and benefactors of the symphony. Although
he will certainly be circulating throughout the

party, I have arranged for patrons and benefactors
only to meet him personally at a brief reception at
11:30. Please let me know if you can attend by the
15th.

    Thank you.

SWEEPSTAKES LETTER
WETA (PUBLIC TELEVISION STATION)

You may already have won a 19__ Honda Prelude! And you still have a chance to win one of 341 other exciting prizes in WETA's spectacular Spring Sweepstakes.

Dear WETA Member,

It's Sweepstakes time and you may already be the Grand Prize winner in WETA's spectacular Spring Sweepstakes.

Hundreds of prizes. Hundreds of chances to win . . . including a chance to win your choice of the Early Bird Vacation Prizes just for sending your entry in today.

WETA's Sweepstakes begins with the many good people who donate the goods and services that make up our terrific prize list. They make our sweepstakes affordable. Then people like you make it work.

From experience, we know that thousands of people who respond to the sweepstakes will take the time to enclose a check in support of their favorite public television and radio programs. And thousands who are already members will send us additional contributions with their entries.

Mail your entry today. And try to enclose a contribution. The _____ family did and they drove home the Grand Prize winner of a Mercury Sable.

Everyone benefits from the WETA Sweepstakes. Every dollar of contribution expands our capacity to bring you quality programming. You're a winner every time you tune into TV 26 or FM 91.

But these are times when we badly need your support.

The effects of tax reform have been difficult on nonprofits! We have never been more dependent on viewer and listener contributions. Income from national underwriters, grants and major gifts have been hit hard by tax reform. And government funds are severely constrained due to the enforced priorities of spending limitations. Only individual gifts from people like you are growing.

We need your help today. The law says you don't need to make a contribution to enter the WETA Sweepstakes. You don't need to . . . but we need you to. We need your help now more than ever. And the WETA Sweepstakes is a great reason to give.

Send in your Sweepstakes entry today!

Good luck! And, remember, you can't help but be a winner in the WETA Sweepstakes.

Sincerely,

Susan Richmond
Vice-President

P.S. Thousands of people will enter the WETA Sweepstakes without bothering to read this letter. We have a special bonus prize for people like you who gave us a chance to plead our case for quality public broad-casting—a top of the art Macintosh SE Computer and Image Writer II printer for one lucky winner. To be eligible, just write "MAC" in the Bonus Box on your entry form. It's our way of saying thanks for hearing us out.

P.P.S. Please take a moment right now to return your entry form with your check for $20, $30, $50, or more. We'll both be glad you did.

This sweepstakes letter makes a strong case for the current need for funds. While the letter states, "you don't need to make a contribution to enter," the copy tastefully asks for a gift to accompany the entry. The P.S. on this one is particularly noteworthy. For those who read the P.S. they are offered a special added bonus prize. WETA has successfully used the sweep-stakes approach for years; this excellent letter copy is a major reason why it is so effective for them.

SWEEPSTAKES LETTER
FRIENDS OF THE KENNEDY CENTER

Accept this invitation as a new Sustainer member of the Friends of the Kennedy Center, and we will offer you a pair of complimentary tickets to an upcoming performance. PLUS: If you act now, you also have a chance to WIN any one of 1,082 Sweepstakes prizes . . . in the Friends of the Kennedy Center Sweepstakes!

Dear Friend,

I'm writing today to invite you to become a member of a unique organization called the Friends of the Kennedy Center, composed entirely of people like you.

When you join, you'll receive a wealth of benefits, each designed to help you get more pleasure and more meaning out of every visit to the Kennedy Center . . . whether it be for music, theater, film, opera, or ballet.

Membership in this unique organization is only $25. However, for a limited time, if you join the Friends at the $50 Sustainer level, I will give you a pair of complimentary tickets to an upcoming Kennedy Center performance.

But before I describe the many benefits, let me say a word or two about our nationwide Friends Sweepstakes that you are eligible for. I hope you'll join the Friends. But it's not necessary to join to have a chance to win any of these spectacular prizes:

- A Transatlantic Cruise for Two Aboard the Queen Elizabeth 2! Plus, a Pair of Invitations to the 19__ Kennedy Center Honors Gala and an Expense-Paid Weekend in Washington, D.C.

Reprinted with permission, Friends of the Kennedy Center.

- A Mediterranean Cruise for Two on the Royal Viking Line!

- A Pair of Subscription Series Tickets for the 19__ Kennedy Center Season! Deluxe Opera Glasses, Too!

- A Videotape Recording from the Kennedy Center's Collection of the World's Most Memorable Operas and Ballets!

You could win any one of 1,082 prizes in this SWEEPSTAKES . . . but when you join the Friends of the Kennedy Center at the same time, you are certain to enjoy some exciting membership benefits for the next year.

First, as I mentioned above, as a Sustainer member you will receive a pair of complimentary tickets to an upcoming performance at the Kennedy Center. For theater lovers like ourselves, there is no better reason to join, especially when you consider that <u>the value of a pair of tickets could be greater than the cost of an entire year's Sustainer membership in the Friends</u>! . . .

(Other benefits of membership follow.)

The Kennedy Center has truly developed into the National Cultural Center envisioned in the planning stages. Those who support it can be proud of helping to make this possible. In order to fulfill its role as the nation's cultural center with broad national programs (mandated by Congress) and to offer a wide range of outstanding theater, music, dance and opera year-round, the Center must rely on private contributions from the Friends of the Kennedy Center and other sources to supplement its box office receipts and other earned income.

Naturally, you aren't obliged to become a Friend of the Kennedy Center to enter our SWEEPSTAKES.

But I sincerely hope you will. Because the Kennedy Center and the performing arts are strengthened with each new Friend who joins us. I look forward to welcoming you as a member very soon.

                              Sincerely,

                              Thomas J. Mader
                              Executive Director

    P.S. To receive extra benefits, you may prefer one of the higher membership categories listed on the enclosed brochure. But whether you join or not, make sure to return your official SWEEPSTAKES Entry Form. You must enter to win any of the 1,082 prizes in our charter SWEEPSTAKES offering. And if you enter by March 31 you will also be included in a special drawing . . .

This sweepstakes letter shows that upscale organizations can use such an offer effectively. Higher than average gifts are promoted on this offering. Note especially that the sweepstakes prizes are sublimated to the regular benefits. In effect, the sweepstakes prizes are used as "added extras" to stimulate response. Also note that the prizes selected are very much on target with the underlying mission of the organization. If the recipient has any interest at all in the performing arts, this has to be an exceptionally appealing letter.

TICKET SALES/CONTRIBUTION LETTER
GARDNER HIGH SCHOOL BAND

We are planning the first (ever) band alumni concert, with proceeds going to support the Gardner High School Band program. The concert will be followed by a reception in the high school cafeteria.

In addition, former director Henry Gates, presently the New York University Band conductor, has been engaged to return to Gardner High and serve as conductor.

The concert is deliberately planned for fall, so that you can spend the summer getting your lip (chops) back and practicing your twirling and flag bearing.

Two rehearsals are planned:

August 28—to see what we have for instrumentation—and September 11—to prepare for the concert.

During the concert weekend historical band photographs, films, and memorabilia will be on display. If you have any films or photographs to donate (or lend so that we may reproduce), please contact us.

Don't be shy—come and join the fun!

Please fill out the Information Form on the next page and mail to (organization's mailing address):

Did you know that . . .

The Gardner High School Band history shows ups and downs, bumps and bruises, cheers and accolades. But the underlying GHS "spirit" has never stopped.

Did you know that . . .

- the GHS Band was formed in 1925, under the direction of Elmer Pierce
- the GHS marching band first appeared in the fall of 1929, sparked by the direction of John P. Redmond

Reprinted with permission, Gardner High School Band, GHS Alumni Concert Committee.

- there have been 9 band directors in 67 years
- twirlers made their first appearance in the early 40s
- in 1952, there were 120 members in the GHS band
- in 1927, there was one senior in the band (initials, C.W.)
- in 1993, there is one senior in the band (initials, C.W.)—history is repeating itself.

1993 brings new life and excitement to the GHS band. Help us celebrate 67 years of the Gardner High School Band's contribution to quality in our community.

Information Form

Class _____

Name _____

Address _____

Phone _____

- -

____ I will perform!

Instrument _____

____ I have my own instrument

____ I need to borrow from GHS

____ I will not be performing

____ I can't wait! Please send ____ concert tickets at $5 each.

____ I cannot attend, but would like a souvenir reunion program. (Please send $2.00 to cover postage.)

____ I would like to give a donation to the GHS band, c/o the GHS Alumni Concert Committee

My check is enclosed TOTAL $ _____

This is a very brief but very effective fund-raising piece for a high school band. This letter went to all band alumni. To someone who has played in this band (first organized in 1925), this is a powerful appeal. It is based on the strong affinity that graduates who played in the band would have for this type of a reunion. And, of course, even if the recipient doesn't plan to come, it allows for a very effective pitch for a gift. Alumni fund-raising that ties in with whatever particular interest a person had while in school is most effective. It can be a sports team, a band like this or any other extra-curricular activity.

7

Making Your Voice Heard Through the Protest/Petition Letter

Do supporters of your work possess a strong sense of moral outrage over what the opponents on the other side of your issue are doing? And is there some governmental body—or other official group—to whom you can make a legitimate protest? If these conditions exist for your cause, then the protest/petition letter is a natural for acquiring new donors. Anger—or moral outrage—is probably one of the most effective copy platforms on which to base a fund-raising appeal. But make sure the anger is bona fide and that it is directed against the forces arrayed against your cause.

When to Use the Protest/Petition Letter

The protest/petition letter is a near relative to the survey letter covered in Chapter 5. Both types of letters ask for an involvement on the part of the prospective donor. That is, an involvement other than just sending a gift. In the case of the survey letter, you are looking for answers to survey questions from informed citizens to bolster the case. In a protest/petition letter, the issue is so threatening or dangerous that you simply want the prospective donor to sign a petition to the responsible governmental agency with the desired action you want that agency to take. In other words it is patently obvious to your potential donor what the action or desired end result should be. The issue is not something a targeted prospect would take a long time to deliberate over. The focus of the protest/petition letter should be one strong overriding issue that demands immediate rectification.

The best time to write the protest/petition letter is when there is a lot of media publicity about your issue. Send it out at a time when your potential recipients are actively thinking about the issue. They will want to vent their anger and moral outrage by responding with a petition and a gift.

How to Write the Protest/Petition Letter

1. SELECT AN ISSUE THAT PRODUCES AN IMMEDIATE "OUTRAGE" RESPONSE.

It should be an issue that gets your prospective donors "hot under the collar." Simply stating the problem to them will develop an innate sense of anger. No further elaboration is needed to make your point. Such highly charged issues as the prochoice/prolife issue, the clear-cutting of ancient forests, or the drug companies' testing of new drugs and chemicals on defenseless animals are the types of issues that work best for a protest/petition letter. When you reach individuals who agree with you on the issue, you will spark an immediate emotion and response. If you have an issue like one of these, a protest/petition letter will work. Here are a few examples of issues that deal with strongly emotional issues:

- America's neglect is killing our children. In the past year, 40,000 babies like _____ died before their first birthday. Virtually no other industrial nation lets so many of its babies die. America could save thousands of babies with good prenatal care for all mothers and early medical care for infants . . . Somebody has to speak up . . .

- Your signature on the enclosed petition to the United Nations to save tropical rain forests can help prevent the most devastating environmental crisis our planet has ever experienced.

- For the first time in history a fundamental liberty and constitutional right are about to be taken away from you and other Americans.

Two months ago, a federal appeals court in Philadelphia ruled that *Roe* v. *Wade,* the landmark case that protects access to safe and legal abortion, is no longer the law of the land.

This case is being appealed to the U.S. Supreme Court where an antichoice majority is ready to act.

Within the next six months, women in America could lose all constitutional protection for their right to choose.

That is why I am writing you to ask for your signature and support for an act of Congress that is the one remaining hope to preserve a woman's right to choose in America.

2. STATE HOW YOU WILL USE THE PETITIONS YOU RECEIVE BACK . . . HOW THEY WILL HELP ACHIEVE VICTORY.

When prospects rush off their petitions to you, they like to know that a governmental body or other accountable agency that can correct the problem is actually going to see them. Citizens in a representative form of government expect that their voices will be heard and acted upon by the elected government officials. That's why a protest/petition letter works. It takes advantage of this fundamental desire to speak out and be heard by someone who is in a position to do something about the problem.

- I need your help <u>right now</u> to save the proposed International Treaty on Global Warming. For at this moment, the fate of this planet-saving Treaty may rest in the hands of concerned Americans like you and me. Why? Because our President—to our national shame—is the <u>only leader in the industrialized world who currently opposes a tough Treaty</u> that would stabilize fossil fuel use—the first step in averting catastrophic climate change.

3. TELL HOW YOU FEEL ABOUT THE ISSUE IN PERSONAL TERMS.

Write the copy in the first person singular. After you have worked up your own sense of outrage on the issue, put it down on paper. One of the popular sessions in the Dale Carnegie Course is the one where participants speak out on an issue of concern. But the speakers are given a rolled up "log" made from newspapers and are urged to slam it down on a desk as they speak. It's amazing how this gets the emotions in gear . . . and the attention of the listeners. The same is true of writing a protest/petition letter. Try this exercise as you think about the issues of your letter. It is bound to surface the right emotional stance for your letter. Your prospect will identify with your feelings if they are expressed in the strongest possible emotional terms.

- I don't know how you feel about the lies and falsehoods being put out by the _____. Well, I'll tell you how I feel . . . I'm pretty damn mad. And I'm not going to put up with it any-more. That's why I'm writing you today. Please return your petition and I'll see that it—along with thousands of others—gets put on the desk of the _____.

4. ASK FOR A GIFT AND OUTLINE HOW YOU WILL USE IT.

The big idea behind the protest/petition letter is to alarm people enough to stimulate an immediate reaction and to motivate a response of the petition. At the same time make sure to tell your prospects why you need funds to fight your opponents. Your prospects really want to know this. They will feel good about venting their anger. They will feel even bet-ter knowing that you have a program to stop the "bad guys" from doing their damage.

- It's going to cost a lot to tabulate the returned petitions. Then we need to run a full page ad in the ____ to let all the citizens know what's really happening and what those of us who are concerned about ____ really think. With your help we stop the bureaucrats and their PAC friends from their self-serving plans. With your Petition and your gift we can win this battle to get HR ____ passed in this session of Congress.

List of Key Phrases for a Protest/Petition Letter

- We cannot remain silent . . .

- It's time to stand up and be counted . . .

- I beg you to add your voice to our rising chorus . . .

- I am outraged that . . .

- I am sickened . . . fed up . . . and we're not going to take this abuse any longer . . .

- Somebody has to speak up. You and I and thousands of other Americans must demand that . . .

- It is shameful that . . .

- I protest . . . and demand that you take immediate action . . .

- I need your help right now . . .

- I am profoundly concerned about . . .

MODEL LETTER—PETITION
"SAVE OUR NEIGHBORHOOD CITIZENS' ASSOCIATION"

Dear Friend,

SELECT AN ISSUE THAT PRODUCES AN IMMEDIATE "OUTRAGE" RESPONSE (POINT 1)

I'm writing you today because the _____ Council just approved a proposal for a new sports stadium in the Morningside section of downtown _____. What a catastrophe this would be.

It would disrupt the long-established residential patterns of our neighborhood. School patterns would be in jeopardy. And traffic and pollution would escalate in the historic section of our town.

TELL HOW YOU FEEL ABOUT THE ISSUE IN PERSONAL TERMS (POINT 3)

I don't know about you but I'm outraged over this decision. I have lived in _____ for 25 years and this is the last straw. To have thousands of noisy sports "fans" drive in from the suburbs for a few hours of loud entertainment each week . . . and then leave us who live here in the dust is not what we want.

And what really gets me is this. We're being lied to. The Council—in its cozy league with the developers—thinks it can ride roughshod over our feelings. They tell us we'll get more funds for roads, schools, and public facilities. You and I know that we'll only get a few dribbles while our neighborhood goes down the tube.

I say "enough is enough." I love _____. And I don't want to see the developers ruin what has taken literally centuries to build up here. It's time we stood up and did something about it.

STATE HOW YOU WILL USE THE PETITIONS YOU RECEIVE BACK . . . HOW THEY WILL HELP ACHIEVE VICTORY (POINT 2)

That's why I am sending you—and other voting citizens of _____ the enclosed protest petition. Please

sign it today. A public hearing has been set for
April 10th. I will be there to present all the petitions we receive back from this mailing.

And we need your gift along with your petition.
Already we have set up an <u>emergency fund</u> to finance
our SAVE OUR NEIGHBORHOOD CAMPAIGN. Experts have
been contacted . . . plus officials from other
cities. We're meeting almost around the clock to
map out an alternative to this disastrous stadium
plan.

Please send as large a tax-deductible gift as you
can. It will go to immediate use in our campaign. We
can beat our anti-city foes back . . . but they need
to hear a strong voice from citizens like yourself.

We simply can't let the high-paid industry lobby-
ists to continue to spread their lies and half-
truths. I'm fed up with their maneuvering simply to
make a few quick bucks.

STATE HOW YOU WILL USE THE PETITIONS YOU RECEIVE BACK . . . HOW THEY WILL HELP ACHIEVE VICTORY (POINT 2)

In addition to our testifying at the next City
Council we are working with federal officials who
have to finance part of the stadium costs. First, we
will testify before a congressional subcommittee.
Second, we are contacting each and every member of
the _____ Committee and presenting copies of our petitions. And finally we have launched a media blitz to
let the public know how their elected officials are
distorting the truth.

We need your support today. Sign your petition
and return it with a generous gift. If you can
send $100, please do so. I don't know what is the
right amount for you. But I know the need is
urgent. So, send what you can—$25, $50, $100, or
more if possible—and I will see that you get a
full report of progress on our SAVE OUR NEIGHBOR-
HOOD CAMPAIGN.

We have no time to lose. Please let me hear from you today. Even if you can't send a gift, please sign and return your petition. Every citizen counts. Your voice will be heard.

Sincerely,

Campaign Chair

PROTEST/PETITION LETTER
COALITION TO STOP GUN VIOLENCE

Richard Haymaker
Baton Rouge, Louisiana

Dear Cathy _____,

You have probably already heard my family's story.

On October 17 of last year, the police called to tell us that Yoshi Hattori, a teenage exchange student who lived with us, and who we loved as a member of our family, had been shot to death . . . (details of murder described).

All too often, those killed are innocent children like Yoshi.

<u>That's why my wife Holley, Webb, and our daughter Elizabeth and I are sending this urgent plea to you and other members of the Coalition to Stop Gun Violence (CSGV) to ask for your assistance today</u>.

Our family is not going to allow Yoshi's death to be in vain . . .

Along with his parents in Japan, and with the help of the Coalition we're conducting a national petition drive in memory of Yoshi and the thousands of other children killed every year by gun fire. We want to collect as many petitions as possible to present to President Clinton and to Congress—demanding an end to unrestricted gun sales.

In Japan, Yoshi's parents have already collected almost <u>1.5 million signatures</u>. Unfortunately, his death hasn't produced the same outrage in America, and we've only been able to collect a fraction of that number.

<u>That's why we're sending you a copy of our petition. Since you are a member of the Coalition and an advocate for gun control, we're hoping that we can count on your support</u>.

Reprinted with permission, Coalition to Stop Gun Violence.

And we also hope that you can return your petitions along with a generous additional contribution to the Coalition, which is taking a lead in helping us to organize our petition drive.

Your contribution to CSGV is not only important to this national petition drive, but also is crucial for Coalition's other work for reasonable gun control measures.

For months, we have been trying to gather as many petitions as possible through every means available—we've given dozens of interviews to newspapers, magazines, and the networks, and we have been in contact with a multitude of organizations, both small and large.

We hope to collect at least one million signatures, but the task of collecting petitions is a tough job. We have only been able to collect 25,000 signatures so far through the efforts of our family and friends.

That's where the Coalition has stepped in. They have put their faith in our efforts and have supported us from the very beginning. They've offered us invaluable assistance in organizing our drive, and through this mailing we hope to collect thousands more signatures.

To achieve our goal, we must count on committed individuals such as you and the other supporters of the Coalition to Stop Gun Violence.

As a supporter and member of the Coalition, you've shown genuine concern about the terror guns have held over our nation—you understand the threat that firearms pose to our children and our society . . . (discusses Japanese society's repulsion about the rampant gun violence in America)

That's why we feel we must take on this campaign to enlighten the politicians in Washington and the American people to the threat posed to our children, and our society in general, by firearms.

The petitions are from the heart, not an attempt to lobby for any specific legislation. We feel the Coalition, with its more experienced staff, is better able to fight for individual gun control measures.

The value of this petition drive is as an educational initiative. The process of the drive brings people into the debate, gives them something they can do immediately, encourages activism, and gives them a sense of representation when the petitions are delivered.

These petitions ask the President, the Congress, and the whole nation to wake up and address the plight that is being caused by our country's policy of almost-unrestricted access to dangerous weapons.

Yoshi was shot by a .44 Magnum . . .

There is no viable reason why such a weapon should be available on the open market for anyone to purchase with no questions asked.

<u>That's why your signature on these petitions and your additional contribution to the Coalition are so important at this time</u>.

Along with Yoshi's parents, we will soon deliver these petitions to President Clinton and to Congress, and it is imperative that we have as many signatures as possible.

We're counting on you, as a dedicated supporter of the Coalition to Stop Gun Violence, to sign your copies and return them as soon as possible.

And it is just as imperative that the Coalition have the funds necessary to assist us in our drive and continue their lobbying efforts to ban the sale and ownership of all handguns and assault weapons in this country.

This petition drive is an important step. <u>But without hard lobbying and the passage of true gun control legislation, it will be only an empty gesture</u>.

That's why we also ask that you please return your petitions with as generous a contribution as you can afford, so that the Coalition can continue its hard-fighting program to institute reasonable restrictions on the sale and ownership of handguns and assault weapons in this country.

Please help honor Yoshi and the thousands of other children that have been needlessly killed by signing your petitions and returning them with a generous contribution as soon as possible.

We have to make a stand—for the sake of the thousands more children and the tens of thousands of adults who will die if we don't act today.

My family and I thank you in advance for your help.

                              Sincerely,

                              Richard Haymaker

P.S. Almost 2,000 children are killed in the United States every year by gunfire. We must refuse to accept those deaths as inevitable. <u>Please sign the enclosed petitions, and return them with a generous contribution to the Coalition as soon as possible</u>.

This petition letter is a classic. It won a MAXI Award from the Direct Marketing Association of Washington. It centers its message on the tragic story of a Japanese student who was killed in the United States by handgun violence. The compelling story received widespread press coverage. While this letter went to existing members of the Coalition, it illustrates all you need to know to write a good petition letter to outside lists as well.

Part II

*Letters for Soliciting
Repeat Gifts from
Your Donors*

When a new donor comes on your file, it most likely is without any thought that he or she may be asked for a repeat gift. However, the experience of most fund-raising organizations tells us that the majority of donors on your file will not object to receiving additional requests for gifts. A person's interest in your cause does not end with the making of a new gift. Quite the reverse is true. It signifies the beginning of an interest in your work. Follow-up requests for giving will be welcome and produce significant results if done in a manner that respects what the donor has told you by his or her previous giving history. And, even if the donor does not send a repeat gift, he or she is better informed of your work and is conditioned to respond at some later date, by giving or possibly by volunteering to provide some kind of needed assistance.

Direct mail fund-raisers experience their best returns from mailings that they make to previous donors. These repeat requests for a gift usually return an excellent net income for the program needs of the fund-raising organization. That's why most experienced fund-raisers are willing to lose money on acquiring a first-time donor. They know that the initial loss will be more than made up by subsequent repeat gifts from the donors they acquire. But you need to have an active follow-up mailing program to your current donor file to realize this additional income. It is not unusual for fund-raisers to mail follow-up appeals to their donors 12 times—or more—a year.

If these follow-up mailings contain new and interesting information to the donor—and if the copy is tastefully targeted to the donors' interests—regular follow-up mailings will not offend your donors. The fact is, they will enjoy getting updated information on an organization in which they're already interested. In this part you will learn how to write these letters. You will see many different types of letters that can be used to produce additional gifts from your existing donors. By sending a variety of interesting appeals, you will keep your donors well informed, and you will achieve maximum results from your donor file.

8

Requesting Additional Funds Through the Special Appeal Letter

The most basic kind of a follow-up request to a donor is what is called a special appeal. By its very name it signifies a subject of a special nature that requires funding now. Here are some examples of special appeal subjects from various mailers: a building destroyed by a fire, a sharp increase in applicants at a hospice, or news that a wildlife species faces extinction. But a special appeal does not necessarily have to focus on a new need that has occurred. It's permissible to ask for special gifts for programs that you have already planned in your budget. Unless you have some extraordinary means of funding these programs, it is reasonable to expect that your current donors will underwrite part or all of the costs. Let's see when and how to write a special appeal to your existing donors.

When to Use the Special Appeal Letter

The most obvious answer to the question, "When should we send special appeal letters?" is simple—when you need the money! Because nonprofit organizations depend on the repeat giving of existing donors for their ongoing success, special appeals ought to be made with regular frequency. How many is the right number? Most fund-raisers consider the total number of mailings they send to a typical donor in a year and make a judgment based on this fact. Some feel that one communication (appeal mailing, newsletter, renewal notice, etc.) per month is about right. You want to balance the need you have for funds with the overkill or aggravation factor on the part of your donors. A word of caution is due here. One or two stinging complaint letters from donors about sending too many appeals isn't overkill. There are people on your list who for a variety of reasons will write you complaint letters presumably about receiving too much mail. It's useful to keep a tabulation of the number of complaints received broken down by subject matter. In Chapter 17 you will see a sample letter to send to a donor who complains about receiving too much mail. Over a period of time a seasoned fund-raiser will know the right number of mailings to send to donors to keep complaints to a minimum and to raise the maximum amount of funds.

There is a seasonal factor to be considered in writing to donors. The months from September through April are generally considered to be the fund-raising season, or as one of my colleagues likes to say from Labor Day to the first warm day in spring! In scheduling special appeals to your donors, emphasis should be given to these months, especially the period from November through January. Year-end tax-giving is a powerful motivator. And the month of January is the top direct response month across the board for all mailers. Now let's take a look at how to construct and write a special appeal letter.

How to Write the Special Appeal Letter to Your Existing Donors

You have a distinct advantage in writing to donors on your file. Individuals who have given once to your organization have told you two important things about themselves. They're interested in your cause, and they give by direct mail. Those are two highly important factors. Do not disappoint your donors by letting them lie fallow in your file without a number of additional mailings. These are not dunning requests that are unappreciated. They contain educational information that donors will find interesting if written along the lines suggested in this chapter. Here are 11 important principles to bear in mind as you develop special appeal letters for your donor file.

1. SEGMENT YOUR DONOR LIST AND PERSONALIZE THE COPY.

If your donor records contain information relevant to the current appeal, you're in a good position to segment those donors and make references in the copy to that previous giving history. If a group of your donors has given to a previous appeal of a very similar nature, it's effective to refer to that fact in the copy.

- Because of your previous concern for _____, I knew you would want to hear about what is happening right now in _____. Your support is what has made our efforts so successful. I wonder if you could make a gift of $ ____ to our special campaign today?

If nothing else, make sure to personalize the copy in terms of the money amount "ask." Categorize your donors by giving level, and ask for amounts that are graduated above the previous giving levels. There are two dangers here . . . you can ask for too much, way beyond the donor's capability. Or you can ask for too little, partly offending your donor who knows he or she is capable of giving more and usually does. So, capture your donor's giving history and target gifts beginning at this level and slightly higher levels. Chapter 20 gives you more extensive guidelines on money amount request amounts.

2. TELL THE DONOR HOW YOU USED THEIR PREVIOUS GIFT.

This is just common sense and good manners. People respect and appreciate at least some word on what happened with the previous gift. By showing that you remember, and telling what good was accomplished with the earlier gift, you establish the right kind of mood for considering the current need.

- Last _____ you made an important gift to our work. It provided a great boost to our _____ project. We were greatly encouraged by your support. Now when we face an even greater need, I am writing to good friends like you to see if you can help us again.

3. DESCRIBE HOW NEW GIFT WILL BE USED.

It's important to be as specific as possible with your existing donors regarding how you will use the new gift. Avoid abstract needs and target, instead, some urgent current need. This does not mean that the gifts received all have to be designated for the particular type of project. In writing your gift response form copy, highlight the stated need but include reference to the entire work your organization is doing. And it's important to report to donors in subsequent communications just what kind of progress you have made on the project to which they gave.

- Today we need your renewed support to finance the beginning construction of our new visitors center. Your gift of $25, $50, $100—or more if possible—will be matched by an anonymous donor. Whatever you give will be doubled in our drive to get this exciting new project off the ground.

4. DON'T DISGUISE THE NAME OF YOUR ORGANIZATION.

This may sound obvious, but it's worth stating. Whatever project or organizational name under which you promoted the original gift should be prominently displayed on the outer envelope and letterhead of your appeal mailing. It's important that your donors know that they are receiving a piece of mail from an organization that they have previously supported. This almost guarantees that they will at least open the envelope and glance at the message. There's a world of difference (in terms of interest) in receiving a message from a brand new organization as opposed to one that you've supported in the past.

5. SHOW APPRECIATION FOR YOUR DONOR.

There's no one quite as special as a donor, especially a person who donates to support *your* work. Your organization would not exist without many such persons. That's why it's a top priority to make sure your donors know how much you value them in each and every piece of mail they receive from you. One of the most common complaints about direct mail fund-raising is that " . . . I get too much mail. I only hear from them when they need money!" You can turn this often-heard lament into a plus simply by weaving a theme of genuine appreciation into your letter.

- Without good friends like you we wouldn't be so successful. Your generous support is a source of encouragement to all of us as we work to _____.

6. RESPECT YOUR DONOR'S INTELLIGENCE.

It goes without saying that your average donor knows a lot less about the in's and out's of your work than you do. But by the same token your donor probably knows a lot more about your cause than the average citizen. That's why the slant in your copy to donors should be one of sincere flattery that he or she is well informed about the issue. Your letter is based on the fact that you're writing to a knowledgeable insider. This does not mean you should write in a ponderous style, but you can be more program specific with existing donors than you can be with first-time donors. Regardless of the audience and the content, always write in a manner that is easy to understand.

- For someone like yourself who is familiar with the struggles that these children go through, it comes as no surprise that there are over _____ kids now without a roof over their heads.

7. USE YOUR DONOR'S NAME.

Dale Carnegie said the most beautiful word in any language to a person is his or her own name. It's important to use your donor's name, especially your higher-level donors. They've thought a lot about you. They have probably been flattered to receive a letter from a well-known person affiliated with your organization. It makes them feel good to know that you know them by name. So use their name if at all possible. And be sure to use it *correctly*.

- That's why I am writing to you, Mr. Kuniholm. You have supported our work in the past. And I feel confident that when I tell you what we're up against now, you'll want to do what you can to see this new project through to success.

8. WRITE WITH A SENSE OF URGENCY.

The need you are requesting funds for should have a touch of urgency to it. After all, you are writing about a special need. You took time to write now, so the donor expects there to be some current or pressing need. If it doesn't come through this way, the donor will wonder why you decided to write at this particular time. Look for bona fide reasons why the gift is needed *today*.

- If it were only one or two cases like this, I suppose it wouldn't be necessary to write you. But the fact is there are only 560 black rhinos left in the world. Unless you and I act today, they may become extinct. And extinct means forever.

9. ASK FOR THE GIFT.

Just because you're writing to existing donors, don't assume they know you want them to send a gift. No matter what kind of letter you send, it's important that the donor know why you're sending it and what you want. You can see a number of different ways to ask for the gift in Chapter 20. Make sure to include a number of "asks" throughout the letter.

- I'd like to ask you to do two things. First, complete and return your survey. Then include as large a gift as you can along with your survey so we can make the results known to Congress and the public at large.

10. OFFER SOME TANGIBLE OR RECOGNITION BENEFITS.

Most donors want to feel that the maximum amount of money they contribute goes for the work specified. At the same time they like to be recognized in some small way. Consider what you can offer that's inexpensive but shows you appreciate what the donor is doing. Listing the donor's name on a special roll, or sending a small token gift, or inviting the donor to a special event all show that you care about the donor.

- When you respond we'll start sending you our quarterly newsletter—and you'll also receive the free bookmark. Of course, the greatest benefit of all is the good feeling of knowing you're doing something to help these innocent victims.

11. INFORM YOUR DONOR.

For the long-term health of your organization, you want to have as informed a constituency as possible. That's why every mailing should convey new and interesting information that you want donors to know about. This will help in gaining future gifts and involvement in other functions. It means that the cause you're fighting for has a large well-informed group of citizens who are on your side.

- On the reverse side I've reprinted the 5 most common myths concerning the research conducted on helpless animals. If nothing else this should convince you that the big corporations are just not telling the truth.

Now, review the special appeal model letter and the array of special appeal letters in this section. See how easy they are to read. This is so because the subjects selected "almost write themselves." The need is very clear. The "ask" for money follows very logically. If you're a donor to one of these organizations you would find these letters interesting reading. And above all informative. To the interested recipient they are not "junk mail!"

Each of the following sample letters was mailed to existing donors of the various organizations. It's important to recognize that the donors will read this copy with interest because they have already given to the work of the requesting fund-raiser. Typically there's a pitch for a higher-level gift for a specific purpose.

Also included is an outbound telemarketing script for a world relief organization.

MODEL LETTER—SPECIAL APPEAL
HALF-WAY HOUSE

Dear _____,

SHOW APPRECIATION FOR YOUR DONOR (POINT #5) AND USE YOUR DONOR'S NAME (POINT 7)

Recently you made a very important gift to ABC House. I want you to know we haven't forgotten that gift, Mr.(Mrs.)_____. And I'd like to share with you just how we have used it . . . and also tell you about an urgent new need to make a difference in helping desperate kids in _____.

TELL THE DONOR HOW YOU USED THEIR PREVIOUS GIFT (POINT 2)

I've enclosed a note from one of "our kids." Jimmy was a tough little fighter when he arrived here. Today he's getting along with his new friends. And he's beginning to understand why some of the hard things happened to him.

He's not ready to make it on his own yet. But without your compassionate help he would still be out there somewhere on the streets . . . <u>with no hope</u>.

DESCRIBE HOW NEW GIFT WILL BE USED (POINT 3)

But today we're faced with a new crisis . . . and need your special help more than ever. Because you have helped in the past I wanted to share the need with you. I know you care for the overwhelming needs of the neglected kids in our city.

Recently we went out on a limb. We bought an old neglected tenement house on Main Street. As you may know this is the highest drug-infested area of our city.

We plan to refurbish this old building. And staff it with some of our case workers. Tonight there are many more "Jimmy's" out there wandering around the city streets. Where will they sleep? Will they be able to resist the lures of the drug pushers? How many will be shot and killed this month?

It's a war zone. But we can have a beachhead with your help. And we can succeed with these youngsters no one seems to care about.

WRITE WITH A SENSE OF URGENCY (POINT #8)

We've just established an Emergency Fund for refurbishing the ABC House. Funds are urgently needed to buy the materials and tools . . . and furniture . . . and some kitchen supplies.

Our volunteers are ready to start work. But we need your immediate help to get started.

DESCRIBE HOW NEW GIFT WILL BE USED (POINT 3)

For $25 we can purchase 8 sturdy two by fours for rebuilding some of the dilapidated rooms. $50 will buy siding for one room. And for $100 we can get the necessary tools to get a few workers started. All of this will make possible a safe haven for some scared and lonely kids.

ASK FOR THE GIFT (POINT 9)

I'd like to ask you to contribute to our Emergency Fund with a gift of $ _____ (2 times donor's Highest Previous Contribution), Or, maybe you could send $___ (1.5 times HPC) or even $_____ (HPC). (See Chapter 20 for a discussion of HPC)

It will mean a lot to kids like Jimmy and many others who have nowhere else to turn.

SHOW APPRECIATION FOR YOUR DONOR (POINT 5)

You have responded generously in the past. I know you will do what you can for this current need.

On the reverse side of Jimmy's note I've included a photo of the building we've just purchased . . .

along with a "shopping list" of our current needs to get it in usable shape for service.

OFFER SOME TANGIBLE OR RECOGNITION BENEFITS (POINT 10)

When the project is completed we plan to have a dedication ceremony with the Mayor and other city officials in attendance. I look forward to meeting you then so I can personally thank you for caring for our city's too-long neglected kids.

Thanks for your support.

Appreciatively,

Executive Director

INFORM YOUR DONOR (POINT 11)

P.S. We just received some good news. The city has OK'd our permit application for a service facility for taking care of 82 kids. We have the property. Now we have the official green light. All we need is the funds in our newly established Emergency Fund to get the house ready. Thanks for your gift.

SPECIAL APPEAL LETTER
AIDS ACTION COMMITTEE OF MASSACHUSETTS, INC.

Dear _____,

It's a terrible thing to outlive your child.

When my son Charles died, I felt as if my life were over, too. For three agonizing years I had fed and bathed him, turned him over, cried for him. After that, I was nearly paralyzed with grief.

Then I came to work as a volunteer at AIDS Action. At first, I was too sad to do much. But in this healing environment, I began to work out my pain and see what I could do to help others.

That's when I took over the reception desk, greeting other mothers' children who are struggling with HIV and AIDS. Often they arrive scared and nervous. My job is to welcome and comfort them. When I can make someone laugh, I feel like a million dollars—and I know I've done a good job.

I am proud to be part of this warm and welcoming place where people who are struggling with HIV and AIDS find the information, resources, and lifeline services they need so desperately.

But this is terribly hard work. When I lose another friend from among the many I've made here, the tears of Charles's death come back to me. I feel all over again the heartbreak of HIV. And I fear for those other mothers' children who, without AIDS Action, would have nowhere to turn. That's why I keep working here, even on the bad days.

Each of us, in our own way, must help fight this deadly virus. I know you have done that by lending your financial support in the past.

Now, won't you join me in renewing your support by sending another generous gift to AIDS Action? As

a mother who lost her child, I thank you for showing how much you care about people with HIV disease.

Sincerely,

Bernice Time

    P.S. The enclosed 1993 calendar is a gift of
thanks for your support—both in the past and now,
again. I hope you will give as generously as you
can.

In short order this appeal letter invokes strong emotions and makes a powerful case for giving. It has a provocative opening and is as personal as any fund-raising letter can be. It pulled over 8 percent in response, with an average gift of $45.75—and at a cost per dollar raised of only $0.14. It shows how a special appeal to existing donors can produce outstanding results.

SPECIAL APPEAL LETTER
WORLD WILDLIFE FUND

In the icy cold waters off Antarctica a gentle giant of the oceans, a minke whale gracefully glides on the surface, drawing in krill and plankton. Suddenly a gun roars on the deck of a small ship nearby. A 100-pound harpoon bomb whistles through the air and finds its target . . . the triangular head of our feeding whale. The sleek massive body of this intelligent creature shudders as the explosive charge detonates—<u>killing the minke whale</u>. A blood red slick spreads out over the waves.

Dear World Wildlife Fund Member,

Unless we act today this grim scenario could again be commonplace. What we have worked so hard to gain could easily slip away if we don't act quickly.

<u>Here's the problem . . .</u> (Problem stated)

<u>Here are the facts . . .</u> (Facts outlined)

<u>But there is a solution . . .</u> (Solution described)

You can help WWF stop the slaughter before it gets out of control . . . and provide a safe haven for these intelligent, beautiful creatures that inhabit this globe with us. <u>We urge you to take the following two steps now . . .</u>

1. <u>Sign the enclosed petition</u>. We need a show of members' strength to help build U.S. government support for the French proposal and counter the erosion of will that threatens our efforts to preserve the whales.

2. <u>Send an emergency contribution</u> of $35, $50, or even $100 to help WWF push for a much-needed sanctuary for these graceful mammals. Let them nurture their young in peace . . .

Reprinted with permission, World Wildlife Fund.

Please respond today. Sign the enclosed petition and return it with your tax-deductible contribution.

With your support WWF will . . . <u>mobilize</u> all who care about wildlife to make their voices heard . . . <u>reach</u> Americans through television, radio, newspapers, and magazines urging them to support the sanctuary proposal . . . <u>launch</u> a nationwide education and information campaign to make sure all Americans know that . . .

At last we have within our power to <u>save and protect the remaining whale species in Antarctica once and for all</u>!

                    Sincerely,

                    Kathryn S. Fuller
                    President

P.S. Your petition—and special gift to WWF today—will help ensure that the minke whale and other whale species will finally be safe and secure in their Antarctic feeding grounds. Thanks in advance for helping to make a difference at this critical time!

The opening "Johnson Box" (see Chapter 19 for an explanation of this technique) on this one uses an illustration to evoke strong emotions on the part of a donor who is concerned about wildlife. The problem is followed up by the solution and includes an effective petition involvement device. It produced an unusually high number of gifts.

SPECIAL APPEAL LETTER
THE OLDER WOMEN'S LEAGUE

Dear Member of OWL,

It's no secret that America's health care system is in total disarray.

But <u>there is a deep and foreboding secret</u> about health care which is frightening in its implications for women. Our nation's patchwork system of medical care, pension and health insurance system <u>discriminates against women</u>—especially midlife and older women.

I want to share with you the facts that show what an alarming situation we face.

And, as you think about these ominous statistics I want you to know one thing. OWL is at the forefront of a fast-growing national movement that is going to ensure that major changes take place.

Later in this letter you'll find some exciting news about OWL's plans and how you can help. But first consider this . . .

- A woman over the age of 65 is unlikely to have private insurance benefits other than Medicare.

- Only 33% of her total health care costs are paid by Medicare.

- And her out-of-pocket health care costs will average $1,300 a year.

Consider too that when it comes to health insurance only 60% of employed women have employer-sponsored coverage. Women are disproportionately at risk for loss of long term coverage due to divorce or the death of a spouse—30% of older women are covered by someone else's employer-based insurance while only 7% of men are.

Reprinted with permission, The Older Women's League.

Health insurance in America historically has been biased toward employed males. Many women—because of their family and caregiving roles and the double burden of sex and age discrimination—end up in low-paying jobs in sectors of the economy that provide no health care benefits.

That's the problem. And that's why older women face a health care crisis today.

But all of this must change.

That's why I am writing you this emergency appeal. I need your help today in what promises to be one of the biggest battles in OWL's history. I urge you to join us and carefully consider the two actions I recommend later on in this letter.

Now let me bring you up-to-date on exactly what OWL is going to do to change things. We're about to launch a campaign to fight for a universal health care system that doesn't discriminate against older women.

OWL is fighting for publicly financed universal health care legislation that . . .

- Removes barriers to basic health care service by providing universal access to quality health care for all women regardless of employment status . . . pre-existing health conditions . . . the ability to pay.

(More specifics of OWL's action program are cited.)

OWL's chapters and members have told us that universal health care is their top priority public policy issue. So, we've nailed these goals to the masthead of OWL's "ship of state." And we're going to work with all the energy we've got.

But, we can't do it alone. We need you.

With your help—and the help of other OWL members—we can muster the resources we need to swing into action at a moment's notice.

At this moment we are evaluating a series of health care bills . . . (bills mentioned)

<u>Your generous gift today will help us to respond quickly and effectively</u> to join issues with Congress and the Administration on a moment's notice.

On the local level, in this past year 17 legislatures introduced universal health care bills in their states. OWL chapters were there in California, Washington, Wisconsin, New York, Missouri and Vermont working to assure that the health care needs of older women are addressed.

With all the new bills coming up—in Congress and in the field—we need emergency funds to ensure that we can make our positions clear. To testify . . . to update chapter leadership . . . to send background Gray Papers to key decision-makers and many more urgent activities.

So the first step that you can take as an OWL member is to . . .

. . . <u>send a contribution today</u>. Whatever amount you're comfortable with right now is all I ask. Your continued support allows OWL to play a leading role in issues affecting mid-life and older women.

I'm confident we will succeed. Why? Because OWL's approach works. Consider these three examples . . .

(Three recent victories listed here)

Yes, our intensive efforts at mobilizing women work. We research the facts. We present logical and persuasive arguments to our lawmakers in Washington and in the states as well.

I'm convinced with your help—and that of thousands of other concerned women—<u>we will succeed</u>.

But to ensure that success . . . there's one more simple—yet vitally important step—you can take to help the cause. When you send OWL your contribution would you also . . .

. . . <u>sign and return the enclosed Petition to the Senate Majority Leader Senator George Mitchell</u>.

By doing this you will give meaning to the word clout. The officials and legislators in Washington do take heed to such petitions. Simply sign and date the Petition urging Reform of Our Nation's Health Care Laws . . . to achieve a health care system which is sensitive to the needs of women of all ages, races, income, and personal life styles.

It's about time that our Nations' health policies respond to women!

The stage is set for victory. We've done our homework. The action is about to begin.

I urge you to join with us in what could be our biggest achievement for women in OWL's second decade of work.

I look forward to hearing from you.

Sincerely yours,

Lou Glasse
President

P.S. There are currently 16 bills being considered in the House and Senate that could have a major impact on a woman's right to adequate health care. Make no mistake—women's lives are at stake! Please take a moment to return your contribution and signed petition today!

This special appeal letter for the Older Women's League produced one of the highest returns of any of its mailings to members in its history. It is a classic on how to write a special appeal to your existing file. It combines the petition technique covered in Chapter 7 with a very compelling argument for one of the central issues that this organization deals with. It generates that effective fund-raising emotion—anger—but the anger is based not on inflammatory statements but on a simple recitation of the facts. It is loaded with solid data on the need for reforming the national health care system for older women. And it bases its case on the fact that OWL has had a lot of previous success on related issues. There are a lot of short very direct sentences. The letter is absolutely specific on what it wants the member to do . . . send a gift and a petition. Study this one carefully. It exemplifies all the right things to do when writing a special appeal to existing members.

BOOK SALES LETTER
WORLDWATCH INSTITUTE

**** Special Pre-Publication Offer ****

NEW—from the Worldwatch Institute

<u>Vital Signs: The Trends that are Shaping Our Future</u>

Whether you are a government policymaker, a corporate planner, an environmental activist, a professor, or just plain concerned about the future of the planet—you need this landmark new work, the first in a new annual series. Order now and receive your limited time pre-publication discount!

Dear Friend,

<u>Vital Signs: The Trends that are Shaping Our Future</u> is jam-packed with critical information that is simply not available anywhere else. And you get it all in one easy-to-use volume.

<u>Vital Signs</u> presents the good news. The bad news. And some surprises about the health of our planet and civilization.

In concise text with fully documented charts and graphs you'll get the very latest data on recent trends . . . (listing of provocative subjects from book).

Worldwatch's award-winning researchers have collected this strategic information from around the globe. Now they offer you the latest data in the form of key indicators that best track change in our environmental, economic and social health . . . as well as other important material that's just become available.

Many of the charts and graphs in <u>Vital Signs</u> cover decades of results . . . and much of this longer-term information has never been available before.

Reprinted with permission, Worldwatch Institute.

<u>Vital Signs</u> analyzes each indicator—whether on food or forests, nuclear warheads or infant mortali-ty—in no-nonsense descriptions and easy-to-read graphs.

You'll learn about some ominous trends that may be telling us we have only a decade left to clean up our act . . .

• Are we entering a new era of water scarcity?

• (Additional questions from book are listed.)

At the same time you'll get clear guidance on the best options we have for preventing the dire conse-quences of today's alarming trends. And you may be surprised at what the future holds for us: (Material from book is presented.)

<u>Vital Signs</u> comes out in early September. And I'm writing you today so you can be one of the first to have this extraordinarily useful new volume. We're offering it to you at a <u>special pre-publication price</u> if you <u>order before Sept. 30</u>.

The list price will be $10.95. Order now to receive your copy of <u>Vital Signs</u> for a <u>discount of almost 30%</u> . . . that's <u>only $7.95</u>! But you must order from this mailing in order to get this savings.

And if you include payment with your order <u>you save an additional $3.00</u> in shipping and handling charges!

To track down the data in <u>Vital Signs</u> would take thousands of hours of research by experts in their fields.

I know. Because that's exactly what our award-winning research team does here at the Worldwatch Institute.

No longer do you have to make dozens of calls. Or make a special trip to the library. We've done it for you.

We track trends, evaluate the data, make comparisons and offer sound conclusions for such important
indicators as . . . (list of indicators).

Because Worldwatch Institute is an independent,
non-political research organization we are able to
gather the most objective data through our extensive
information-gathering capabilities.

The Worldwatch Institute . . . (lists its
research activities).

When you use a fact or a statistic from Vital
Signs you know that you are on solid ground. Only the
most reliable, well-researched and documented data
are used. Each chart or graph is sourced to show you
exactly where the data came from.

All the work has been done for you. Clear.
Complete. Authoritative.

And all of this invaluable information is now
available to you at a reduced pre-publication price
of only $7.95 in softback—a $3.00 savings—and $16.95
in hardcover. And you can save even more with your
pre-paid order.

Whether your concern is about the environment,
social trends, economics or health, you'll find
information in Vital Signs that is simply not acces-
sible elsewhere . . .

It will influence the way you look at global
events. How you present your own data. And even the
way you go about your daily life.

The value to you of only a single specific fact
could far exceed the cost of the entire volume.

And this book is overflowing with information and
analysis that can help you recognize trends and react
at the earliest possible date.

As an added incentive we are able to make you a
special pre-publication offer.

If you order before Sept. 30 you are entitled to
discounts on Vital Signs . . . and savings on other
Worldwatch titles.

See the enclosed Order Form for a full listing of savings that could total $10.00 or more . . . just for starters!

And if you choose to send payment with your order we skip all shipping and handling charges . . . and additional $3.00 savings.

But we need to hear from you soon in order to offer you these special discounts.

<u>Vital Signs</u> is organized to be easy to use, with . . . (mention of other Worldwatch publications and repeat of offer along with quotes from press).

No matter what your interest is—from birth control to the ozone layer . . . from cigarette consumption to bicycle production . . . from soybeans to nuclear waste—<u>you'll find the key trends</u> attractively presented right here . . .

If you want to be informed about the trends that will shape your future . . . and the future of this special planet we call home . . . you owe it to yourself to order <u>Vital Signs</u> today.

Sincerely,

Lester Brown,
President

This letter illustrates how to sell a special publication. It went to Worldwatch's own database as well as a number of outside lists. It was a four-page letter that repeated the prepublication offer on each page. You don't have to read too far in this letter before you get a very good feel as to the content of the book. The letter and order form also went for additional sales of other publications of this nonprofit organization. It produced excellent results for the introduction of their new publication.

MODEL TELEMARKETING SCRIPT
WORLD RELIEF ORGANIZATION

(Calls made to existing donors of $25 or more)

HELLO, Mr. Smith, this is Susan Jones calling from ABC World Relief . . . how are you this evening?

Fine, the reason I'm calling has to do with the crisis in Somalia right now.

Our President, Mr. Jenkins, recently wrote you a letter about the need young women have for medical care in this war-torn country . . . do you remember receiving the letter? (Whether yes or no, proceed to next section).

Right now over 200,000 young Somalian women face a desperate need for prenatal counseling and care. It only costs $25 to provide the medical assistance and medications for just one young pregnant woman.

The reason for my call this evening is to share some recent good news with you. We have received a special matching grant for our Somalian Emergency Medical Relief Fund. But I'm calling you tonight because the grant is good only through (date).

That means your gift of $50 at this time will be matched by an equal amount for a total of $100 . . . that will provide help to four needy women.

Can I count on you for a tax-deductible gift in our special drive for Somalia relief? That's just great. Thank you.

Which credit card would you prefer to use? (Take credit card information . . . name of credit card, in whose name, account #, expiration date, confirm address.)

<u>If prefers to pay by check</u>

That's OK, we'll send you a pledge confirmation statement acknowledging your tax-deductible gift.

Make sure to use the return envelope we enclose so your gift will be properly credited to your account.

<u>If person wants to think it over</u>

Why don't we do this . . . let me send you a confirmation of our phone conversation tonight . . . along with a special on-the-scene report by our Somalia Field Director. You make the decision later. If you can, fine. If not, we understand.

<u>If amount too high</u>

I understand, would a gift of $25 be more convenient for you just now? Remember it's matched by our generous donor so ABC World Relief gets twice as much help from it.

<u>If still a "no"</u>

I certainly understand. We have appreciated your wonderful support of ABC World Relief. It means a great deal to all of us. Thanks a lot. And good night.

(Note: See Chapter 11 for another telemarketing script that provides answers to a variety of possible objections.)

9

Getting the Most from Renewal Series Letters

To get repeat gifts you will need the renewal letter—or more properly a series of renewal letters. This is one of the most productive types of letters to send to your member/donors. And the good news is this: Renewal letters are relatively simple to write, and they can be extremely productive year after year.

People on your list who are receiving tangible benefits—such as a subscription to a membership publication—need to be prompted on the anniversary date of their initial contribution with a renewal opportunity so their benefits may continue. Even organizations that have fewer benefits can send renewal letters to their donors. This is done because donors in many cases have such a strong sense of affinity or loyalty to the nonprofit organization they welcome the opportunity to renew their commitment. Most people are conditioned to respond automatically to invoices they receive in the mail. While a membership renewal reminder is not an invoice per se, it is a "near relative" and tends to be acted upon by the recipient almost as if it were an invoice.

Even organizations that send a number of other types of special appeals to donors throughout the year can add a renewal series to their mailing program. While the renewal series is being actively mailed, however, other special fund-raising mailings are usually skipped. This period of time is what is called the "renewal window."

155

When to Use the Renewal Series Letters

Renewal letters can be sent out at either one of the following two different times: on a year-end calendar basis to all active donors on the file or on the anniversary of the member/donor's original gift. If the year-end calendar basis is followed, some cut-off date is needed so as not to "renew" members who have very recently contributed. As a general rule it is desirable not to send renewal letters to donors who have contributed within the last three months. If the annual letter series is adopted the copy should be worded in such a way that the donor understands that this is the practice of the nonprofit organization, that is, that all supporters of the work are being contacted for a renewed commitment as the new year approaches.

Organizations that promote on the anniversary of the first gift, code that date in the donor's record. Then all the donors who have come in during a particular month can be promoted 12 months later. Organizations that have smaller-size files group the months into quarters and promote renewals on this basis.

Whatever timing is selected, it is desirable to follow the same pattern year after year; you make it easier for yourself to keep sending renewal notices on a regular schedule.

How to Write the Renewal Series Letters

There are two ways to look at renewal letters. The first approach is the "annual report" renewal letter. This type of letter is more likely to be followed if there haven't been too many other types of mailings and communications to donors throughout the year. The assumption here is that the nonprofit is making an annual review of all the achievements and victories of the last year. The renewal letter is the basis for a review outlining the new challenges and the need for renewed support. Renewal letters of this type tend to be longer because they present fairly extensive material.

The second type of renewal letter—which is by far the more common—is of the "short and sweet" variety. Here the assumption is as follows: the member/donor has had a full year to enjoy the benefits and to get familiar with the nonprofit organization. No matter how long and extensive the copy, the donor's response will be predicated mainly on the assessment he or she has made of the nonprofit organization during the past year. The guidelines that follow relate to this more prevalent type of renewal letter series.

Most fund-raisers send between five to seven renewal letters spaced one month apart. The first letter is typically sent two to three months in advance of the anniversary date of the original contribution.

Here's a tip to help you determine just how many letters you should send out in the renewal series. Take a look at the percentage return of the current last letter in the series. You can expect to get about one-half of that if you add one more letter. And if that estimated return is higher than what you get on outside list mailings, it makes sense to add one more renewal effort. While there's a limit on how many you can send without appearing to be too intrusive, many fund-raisers find that adding one or two more efforts to their renewal series is a cost-effective way to acquire repeat giving. The guidelines to follow in writing the series are as follows.

1. BE VERY CLEAR ABOUT THE RENEWAL REQUEST AND STATE IT EARLY.

The first sentence or paragraph should clearly state the offer. In the early efforts in the series the assumptive approach is followed: You assume that the loyal core of donors will respond early. In these earlier letters in your series you flavor the copy toward someone like this who is very friendly to your work and will automatically renew as soon as he or she is advised. In the later letters in the renewal series an element of urgency is injected because the member/donor hasn't responded to previous notices. Usually the copy will assume complimentary reasons for lack of response such as busy schedules and so on. All letters in the series should treat the member as a friend who is still interested. Even in the last effort I recommend not asking the donor/member to "rejoin." Even at this late stage you are asking someone who has shown a previous commitment to *renew* that commitment. This copy platform is preferred to one that assumes the donor has made an active decision not to renew so you're imploring him or her to reconsider and renew.

2. DESCRIBE THE BENEFITS THAT WILL CONTINUE WITH RENEWAL—OR WILL BE LOST WITH LACK OF A RENEWAL.

If a publication is included with the membership—or is sent to all the active donors—make sure to state that a renewal is necessary to keep it coming. If there are other benefits that are tied in with the active status of the member/donor, describe these as well. It isn't necessary to do a long promotional piece of copy on these because—as mentioned earlier—the member has probably made a judgment on the benefits' value. But you should point out that renewal is necessary to keep them coming.

3. ASK FOR AN UPGRADED RENEWAL GIFT AMOUNT.

This is especially important in the first two letters of the renewal series. Those who renew at the earliest notice are the better members who will be open to adding something extra to their renewal gift if asked. When the magical moment of writing out the check arrives, a person is probably most responsive to a suggestion to add a few dollars to the amount of the check. If the member/donor isn't asked, he or she probably will not do it unsolicited. Ask for the upgrade renewal amount, and a portion of your members will follow your suggestion.

4. SHARE IMPORTANT VICTORIES DURING THE LAST YEAR.

Your member/donor is probably not aware of all the successes you have had during the year. If there are news clips of special achievements or awards your organization has received, mention them. People like to be identified with winners. This can be important to individuals on your file who aren't totally persuaded by benefits.

Some people may never look at your magazine or take advantage of other benefits, but they do like to be associated with a group that is doing good things—a group that is doing things they value. For this group of donors it's important to build up the image of success and important achievement.

5. OFFER A PREMIUM OR SPECIAL BENEFIT.

There are two schools of thought on this point. The first is to reward your best members who renew early (e.g., on the first notice) with some little extra benefit. The second school holds that you don't offer anything extra to those who are going to renew anyway. This latter theory says offer the extra benefit only to the holdouts at the end of your renewal series. Both approaches have their points. My suggestion is to offer a premium early in the series but to offer it for a specified upgrade dollar amount. Sample renewal letters #1 and #2 for the Center for Science in the Public Interest that appear at the end of this chapter illustrate how to offer a premium for an upgraded renewal amount. By doing it this way, the additional cost of the premium can be offset—or more than offset—by the higher gift amount.

MODEL LETTER RENEWAL #1—
REGIONAL ENVIRONMENTAL ALLIANCE

Dear Member of the Regional Environmental Alliance,

BE VERY CLEAR ABOUT THE RENEWAL REQUEST AND STATE IT EARLY (POINT 1)

As the time approaches to renew your membership in REA, I have enclosed your 1995 window sticker and a statement for your next year's dues.

Please take a moment now to return your statement to me with your check or credit card information to be part of REA's special brand of prudent activism for another year.

DESCRIBE BENEFITS THAT WILL CONTINUE WITH RENEWAL (POINT 2)

When I receive your renewal, I will immediately extend your subscription to REAlert, our newsletter that has gained regionwide recognition for its direct and accurate reporting on environmental problems and praise for its sound and logical solutions to those problems.

OFFER A PREMIUM OR SPECIAL BENEFIT (POINT 5)

And if you renew for an additional $5 or more, I'll also send you our "secret," member's-only booklet, "The 12 Most Beautiful Places in the Region." It is the REA guide to tranquility, solitude, and the wonders of nature, all within 25 miles of the center of the city.

ASK FOR AN UPGRADED RENEWAL GIFT AMOUNT (POINT 3)

There are some strong reasons why we need your support for another year—and why I hope you will renew your membership at a higher level by adding just $5 or $10 to last year's amount.

SHARE IMPORTANT VICTORIES DURING THE LAST YEAR (POINT 4)

The first, and most obvious, is that our regional watershed and ecosystem is not yet safe from unwise development, pollution, and species decimation. Last year, you helped us save the Smith Corners marshlands from developers by creating a regional wetlands; and you helped us bring back the bluebirds when we designed and sold more than 2,000 bluebird bird feeders. And with pressures of development mounting, it is safe to say that your clout and financial support will be needed next year as much, if not more, than this year.

You should also know that the cost of saving the environment is rising. Paper—especially the recycled paper we use for <u>REAlert</u>—costs more and more, and postage (as you know from personal experience) is going up every day—adding more than $7,000 next year to an already small budget.

Paying quality staff, finding expert testimony, writing news releases, all of this takes money—and that comes from our loyal members who share our vision of an economically healthy <u>and</u> green region for the future.

Please take a moment to return your dues statement with your check or credit card information. And display your window sticker proudly.

OFFER A PREMIUM OR SPECIAL BENEFIT (POINT 5)

As soon as I receive your statement by return mail, I'll extend your subscription to <u>REAlert</u>, and if you add just $5 or more to your renewal this year, I'll rush your "12 Most Beautiful Places" brochure to you.

Thanks for renewing for another year,

John Jones

Executive Director

MODEL LETTER RENEWAL #2—
REGIONAL ENVIRONMENTAL ALLIANCE

Dear member of the Regional Environmental Alliance

BE VERY CLEAR ABOUT THE RENEWAL REQUEST AND STATE IT EARLY (POINT 1)

I am sending you this advance notice because your membership in REA is due for renewal in a month.

Please renew today so we can continue to send you <u>REAlert</u> and all the other benefits of membership I've listed on your enclosed renewal statement.

OFFER A PREMIUM OR SPECIAL BENEFIT (POINT 5)
ASK FOR AN UPGRADED RENEWAL GIFT AMOUNT (POINT 3)

<u>And if you renew at just $5 or more over your last year's amount, I will send you our "secret," member's-only booklet, "The 12 Most Beautiful Places in the   Region.</u>" It is the REA guide to tranquility, solitude, and the wonders of nature, all within 25 miles of the center of the city.

SHARE IMPORTANT VICTORIES DURING THE LAST YEAR (POINT 4)

In the past year, we've scored some impressive victories for ourselves and our grandchildren: saving Smith Corners from the developers—doubling the number of bluebirds in the area—working for a regional agreement on lawn pesticides that are causing fish kills in local streams—educating local officials on the need for parkland and open space.

It is my hope that you will continue to support REA in these and future efforts.

DESCRIBE BENEFITS THAT WILL CONTINUE WITH RENEWAL (POINT 2)

When I receive your renewal, I will immediately extend your subscription to <u>REAlert</u> our newsletter that has gained regionwide recognition for its direct and accurate reporting on environmental problems and praise for its sound and logical solutions to those problems.

And you will know that you, as a member of REA, are helping to make a future for our region that is green <u>and</u> prosperous. A region of economic vitality without sacrificing the birdsongs, the sight of beaver and muskrat and deer, the beauty of trees and wild-flowers that make living in our region such a joy.

Sincerely,

John Johns
Executive Director

P.S. Your early renewal will help save future mailing and postage costs of follow-up reminders. Renew today so we can make every penny count here at REA—and let us add your clout to our efforts for another year. Thanks.

RENEWAL LETTER #1
CENTER FOR SCIENCE IN THE PUBLIC INTEREST

Dear Member of CSPI,

It's time to renew your subscription.

To continue receiving the award-winning <u>Nutrition Action Healthletter</u>, simply return your renewal payment with the enclosed statement.

This year, we've had to raise the regular price of <u>Nutrition Action</u> to $24. But because you've been a friend and long-time subscriber, I'm going to give you <u>a chance to renew now for only $20</u>—the price for the last fifteen years!

And, while you're at it, why not extend your subscription for two years? That way, you'll <u>save an extra $7.00</u> off the regular two-year price—and protect yourself from possible future price increases!

It may seem a bit early to remind you your subscription to <u>Nutrition Action Newsletter</u> is coming up for renewal . . . but it's not.

<u>Early renewals are very important to a non-profit consumer group like CSPI</u>. They save us the cost—and save you the nuisance—of follow-up reminders. And since CSPI is a non-profit, every dollar that's saved can go back into waging the battle for good health, nutrition, and a safer food supply.

And I know you won't want to miss one issue of the nutrition newsletter that Jane Brody of <u>The New York Times</u> calls "my personal favorite."

Just look at the areas we will be covering in upcoming issues of <u>Nutrition Action Healthletter</u>. Each one is essential for your own and your family's well-being:

(Listing of interesting article titles follows.)

We've increased our budget for food testing because <u>you rely on us to get the facts to you</u> for wise and healthy eating. And you can't always get honest information from food manufacturers! Our ground-breaking studies of Chinese and Italian restaurant food revealed that many popular dishes contain more fat and salt than you should eat in an entire day!

<u>Nutrition Action's</u> Product Comparison section will tell you which food brands are the worst and best buys!

And, to replace unhealthy processed foods in your diet, the <u>Healthy Cook</u> section of <u>Nutrition Action</u> will give you recipes that are delicious, quick, and healthy. It also provides you with hard-to-find low-fat recipes for Asian, Mexican, and Italian dishes.

As always, you'll be the first to hear about food scams and misleading food labels—like . . . (itemized cases).

And don't forget—<u>Nutrition Action accepts no advertising</u>. We're beholden to no one but you—the consumer. That means you can rely on our dedicated staff of scientists and nutritionists for honest, unbiased information.

So why not pick up your pen and <u>send in your renewal now</u> while it's still fresh in your mind!

I look forward to receiving your prompt renewal so you won't miss a single article designed to help you and your family eat better and stay well.

Yours in good health,

Michael F. Jacobson, Ph.D.

Publisher and Executive Director

P.S. <u>Nutrition Action</u> is much more than a news-letter: Your subscription also supports our <u>vital work as an effective watchdog</u> of the government and food industry. You make possible the activism that has made CSPI synonymous with consumer protection, honesty, and integrity!

This first letter in the series does a lot of the right things. It makes the renewal pitch early in the letter. And it makes a special offer to long-term member/subscribers. It tells why early renewals help a nonprofit organization. It lets members know of interesting material coming in the members' publication, and it includes some "cause-oriented" reasons for renewing.

RENEWAL LETTER #1 FOR MEMBERS COMING UP FOR THEIR FIRST RENEWAL—CENTER FOR SCIENCE IN THE PUBLIC INTEREST

Dear Reader,

Not too long ago you subscribed to <u>Nutrition Action Healthletter</u>, our nationally acclaimed, award-winning newsletter on nutrition and health. I hope you're enjoying and discovering a lot from it!

Because you're a first-time subscriber, I want to give you an early opportunity to renew your subscription. Early renewals are very important to a non-profit organization like ours—they save us the unnecessary cost—and you the nuisance—of follow-up reminders.

<u>And if you renew NOW, I'll pass those savings along to you</u>: You can have another year of <u>Nutrition Action</u> at a <u>special price of only $15</u>!

You'll <u>save $9.00 off</u> the regular renewal price of $24.00! That's a whopping 38 percent!

If you want to be healthier, <u>Nutrition Action</u> can help you. It's a medical fact that by eating right you can reduce your risk of developing debilitating diet-related diseases like cancer, heart disease, and stroke. <u>Nutrition Action</u> translates the latest medical research into specific, practical advice on what you need to eat, what you should buy in the supermarket, and what you should avoid!

If you need to watch your weight, we'll help you . . . the healthy way. <u>Nutrition Action</u> tells you about the tastiest low-fat, low-calorie foods, and gives you some great recipes in every issue.

You can even live longer. You can learn from <u>Nutrition Action</u> how to avoid food poisoning . . . and avoid dangerous food additives and contaminants. The sad fact is, if you live in the United Sates, there are pesticides in your food. But <u>Nutrition</u>

Reprinted with permission, Center for Science in the Public Interest.

<u>Action</u> tells you how to minimize your consumption of them.

   <u>To make your renewal simple</u> . . . all you have to do is return the specially marked renewal statement and your payment in the enclosed postage-paid envelope.

   Take this <u>early-bird opportunity</u> to renew and you can enjoy tomorrow's nutrition news at yesterday's prices. So do it now, before this opportunity passes you by!

                    Sincerely,

                    Michael F. Jacobson, Ph.D.
                    Publisher and Executive
                    Editor

                    <u>Nutrition Action</u>
                    <u>Healthletter</u>

   P.S. Don't forget: As a first-time subscriber, you are eligible to renew for only $15. That's $9.00— 38 percent—off the regular subscription price of $24.00!

This is also a #1 renewal letter, but as you can see from the text, it is directed to subscriber/members who are coming up for their first renewal. Note how the copy refers to that important point in different places. It shows that the nonprofit is aware of the new member's situation. It also makes a special offer: a reduced price renewal rate. Because new members are acquired initially through a reduced-price offer, this organization wisely repeats a special price offer on the first renewal effort.

   Note: The first three letters in CSPI's renewal series are split into two groups: one being long-term members and the other one being first-time renewers.

RENEWAL LETTER #2
CENTER FOR SCIENCE IN THE PUBLIC INTEREST

Dear Friend,

I think you'll want to renew your subscription as soon as possible when I tell you the exciting things we're planning for <u>Nutrition Action Healthletter</u>.

To continue receiving the award-winning Healthletter—and take advantage of the <u>special $20 renewal price</u>—simply return your renewal payment with the enclosed statement.

We've got some important articles coming up in <u>Nutrition Action</u>, so I'm sure you'll want to keep your subscription up-to-date. Right now, our staff of scientists and nutritionists are putting the finishing touches on:

(Listing of upcoming article titles follows.)

Because of your support—and that of 700,000 other subscribers—<u>Nutrition Action</u> remains <u>completely independent of any government or industry funding . . . or advertising</u>.

That means we can provide you with reliable, unbiased, no-holds-barred information. It also means we can name brand names, and tell you which foods and supplements promote your health—and which foods and additives endanger it!

You'll want to keep getting <u>Nutrition Action</u> when you find out how we're making it <u>better than ever</u>.

How? To start with, we're moving ahead to expose more advertising hoaxes like . . . (cases enumerated).

It's critical for you to receive the most up-to-the-minute information on nutrition and food safety. So we're doing research on a whole range of important issues—from food contaminants to fake fats to the links between diet and disease.

Reprinted with permission, Center for Science for Public Interest.

And you can be sure we'll warn you about deceptive ads and rip-offs at the checkout counter! We'll bring you the latest information about exactly which food brands are the best and the worst buys—and why.

With features like <u>Food Porn</u> and <u>Brand-Name Product Comparison</u>, <u>Nutrition Action Healthletter</u> is the liveliest, best-written, most-read nutrition newsletter in the country. <u>You can't afford to miss out on it</u>.

Pick up your pen and send in your renewal <u>now</u>, while it's still fresh in your mind.

I'm looking forward to receiving your renewal by return mail, so you won't miss a single article designed to help you eat better and stay well. <u>It's all yours</u> . . . when you renew!

Sincerely,

Bonnie Liebman
Director of Nutrition

P.S. If you add $5 to your 1-year, 2-year, or 3-year renewal, we'll send you <u>our exclusive</u> and popular canvas grocery bag. This colorful, 16" x 18" x 7" wide bag is environmentally friendly and is perfect for toting home groceries or for recreational use. The bag is made of 14-ounce natural twill, and the handles are double-stitched for extra strength. <u>You can't find a bag of this quality for this price anywhere else</u>!

This renewal letter does something very important: It tells the members how they will be getting a "new and improved" magazine. This gives a nice boost to the copy style. As you saw in renewal letter #1, this letter makes the renewal pitch early in the copy and in very specific terms. There's no guessing as to the letter's purpose. The P.S. goes for an upgrade gift amount by offering an extra premium. This is also an excellent idea for people who are the longer-term members.

RENEWAL LETTER #3
CENTER FOR SCIENCE IN THE PUBLIC INTEREST

Dear Subscriber,

Your subscription to <u>Nutrition Action Healthletter</u> is due for renewal. Simply return your payment in the postage-paid envelope provided.

I know you won't want to miss one issue of the publication Jane Brody of <u>The New York Times</u> calls "<u>my personal favorite</u>."

I don't have to tell you about the usefulness and quality of <u>Nutrition Action</u>. Just look at the areas we'll be <u>covering in upcoming issues</u>: (Listing of article titles follows.)

We're also planning to increase our food testing because we know that you rely on us for the ingredient information you <u>can't get anywhere else</u>.

Of course, each issue will also contain one of our popular product comparisons, which focus on the healthiest fresh, packaged, and prepared foods.

The "Eater's Digest," "Healthy Cook," and "Dr. Tastebud" sections of <u>Nutrition Action</u> will give you practical advice, recipes, and tips on better eating.

And don't forget the <u>lively Food Porn and Right Stuff</u> sections!

Because we accept no advertising and are financially independent of the food industry and government, <u>we can answer to no one but you</u>. We can really tell it like it is!

So now it's up to you.

Reply now by using the enclosed form and postage-paid envelope while it's still fresh in your mind.

Reprinted with permission, Center for Science in the Public Interest.

```
                        Sincerely,


                        Michael Jacobson, Ph.D.
                        Publisher

     P.S. As a way of saying "thank you" in advance
for renewing, I've enclosed a handy card to carry
with you to help you eat healthier.
```

More urgency is injected into this letter—more than the first two efforts preceding it. Note the effective use of an up-front premium. (See Chapter 3 for a full discussion of such premiums.)

RENEWAL LETTER #4
CENTER FOR SCIENCE IN THE PUBLIC INTEREST

IMPORTANT MESSAGE FOLLOWS

DEAR <u>NUTRITION ACTION</u> SUBSCRIBER:

YOUR SUBSCRIPTION TO <u>NUTRITION ACTION HEALTHLETTER</u> EXPIRES, EFFECTIVE WITH THIS NOTICE.

WE NEED YOUR O.K. AT ONCE TO REINSTATE YOUR SUBSCRIPTION.

ACTION IS REQUIRED NOW . . .

RETURN ENCLOSED RENEWAL FORM TODAY, REPEAT, TODAY. WE WILL PROCESS IMMEDIATELY SO YOU WILL CONTINUE RECEIVING THE NATION'S MOST RESPECTED NUTRITION ADVOCACY NEWSLETTER.

THANK YOU FOR YOUR PROMPT RESPONSE.

MICHAEL F. JACOBSON, PH.D.
EXECUTIVE EDITOR

P.S. RESPOND NOW AND RECEIVE A YEAR OF <u>NUTRITION ACTION</u> FOR JUST $15! THAT'S $9 OFF THE REGULAR PRICE! ACT NOW TO SAVE!

This fourth renewal effort was done in the style of a Western Union telegram. Headline copy at the top of the form stated: ACTION ALERT— Urgent You Reply at Once. In Chapter 22 you will see how and when to use an "Emergency Style" format. As you can see from this effort a good place is in the latter efforts in a renewal series. The fuller copy groundwork has been laid in earlier efforts—now it's time to act and a telegram highlights that point.

RENEWAL LETTER #5
CENTER FOR SCIENCE IN THE PUBLIC INTEREST

Dear Friend,

Time has run out on your subscription.

Unless you renew <u>immediately</u>, you will no longer receive <u>Nutrition Action Healthletter</u>, the award-winning newsletter that's been praised by <u>The New York Times</u>, <u>USA Today</u>, and <u>U.S. News & World Report</u>, as well as by physicians, nutritionists, and dieticians.

To show you just how important I personally think it is for you to continue to receive <u>Nutrition Action</u>, I'm going to make you a <u>special reduced-price offer: $9.00 off</u> the regular renewal price of $24.

<u>For only $15</u>, you can now receive a full year (10 issues) of <u>Nutrition Action</u>.

<u>For only $15</u>, you'll get the latest diet and health findings our research uncovers . . . the good taste and good sense of the recipes we give you . . . the questions we answer that translate nutrition theories into practical everyday advice.

<u>For only $15</u>, you'll get a special FREE BONUS gift I'll tell you about in a moment.

What price can you put on sound, reliable information that helps you stay healthy? If eating right keeps you healthy, it can be worth thousands of dollars in doctor-bill savings and uncountable savings in pain and suffering.

That's why <u>Nutrition Action</u> for only $15 is such a valuable investment!

Look at the kinds of subjects we'll be tackling in upcoming issues of <u>Nutrition Action</u> . . . each one is <u>essential to your health and well-being</u>:

(Listing of article titles follows.)

Frankly, there's also a more <u>personal reason</u> why I want you to renew: It's to help keep you and your family from having to experience the sadness that comes from the premature loss of a loved one, or the pain of your own personal illness.

Don't cut yourself off from our life-giving information . . . especially since you can have it now for the special price of only $15!

Here's what you'll get:

- a one-year renewal subscription to Nutrition Action for $15—that's more than one-third off the regular renewal price . . .

- our money-back guarantee on your subscription . . .

- "10 Tips for Safer Eating" enclosed with this letter—a handy guide that can help protect you and your family from many of the additives, toxins, and other contaminants in our food supply.

Simply return your payment in the postage-paid envelope provided. Do it now, while the urgency is fresh in your mind.

Sincerely,

Michael F. Jacobson, Ph.D.
Publisher and Executive
Editor

P.S. As a token of my appreciation for your renewal, I'll also send you a FREE BONUS gift: CSPI's Healthy Cook, our 28-page booklet that is brimming with good-and-easy recipes for all seasons and all tastes. It will be as helpful in your home as it is in mine.

One word characterizes this well-done renewal letter: OFFER. Page 1 features the low-price offer. The letter also includes the up-front premium that was utilized in the previous renewal effort. Page 2 recaps the basic benefits and refers to the money-back guarantee. Then it goes one step further in the offer: a special back-end premium for renewing that is mentioned in the P.S. (See Chapter 4 for a full discussion of the Back-End Premium offer).

RENEWAL LETTER #6
CENTER FOR SCIENCE IN THE PUBLIC INTEREST

Dear Subscriber,

Okay, <u>you're a tough customer</u>. You want a bargain, but you care about value.

You've resisted all my previous notices about renewing your subscription to <u>Nutrition Action Healthletter</u>.

<u>Your subscription has now ended</u>, but I'd like to urge you one more time to renew. So I'm making you a valuable offer that even our toughest customers can't resist:

<u>A full year (10 more issues) of <u>Nutrition Action for only $15—$9.00 off the regular renewal price of $24.00</u></u>! Plus a FREE copy of our handy Eating Smart Fat Guide.

Issue after issue, <u>Nutrition Action</u> helps more than a million people separate nutritional fact from fiction. We'll help you in your personal quest for better health with

- Clearly written, easy-to-follow articles on the <u>links between diet and health</u>.

- <u>Revealing brand-name comparison charts</u> listing the calorie, fat, sugar, and sodium content of all kinds of foods—from spaghetti sauces, fresh fruits and vegetables, and cereals to soups, cookies, and frozen entrees.

- Answers to questions on <u>food safety</u>: from artificial colorings and preservatives to safer food preparation, from packaged food labels to vitamin supplements.

<u>And it's about time you heard the truth about what's in your food</u>. Testing foods in an independent laboratory is expensive—up to $15,000 per test! But

<u>Nutrition Action</u> is doing that in order to give you the reliable and unbiased facts.

And because we accept no advertising and are financially independent of the food industry and the government, <u>we answer to no one but you</u>. We can really tell it like it is! How to stay trim . . . cut your cholesterol . . . control your blood pressure . . . and more.

In fact, from <u>The New York Times</u> to <u>USA Today</u>, <u>Nutrition Action</u> is recognized as the leader in consumer nutrition and health.

<u>So now it's up to you</u>.

Reply now and receive the very next issue of <u>Nutrition Action</u>! Simply use the enclosed form and postage-paid envelope.

                    Sincerely,

                    Michael F. Jacobson, Ph.D.
                    Publisher and Executive
                    Director

    P.S. Renew now and I'll send you CSPI's most popular and handy slide guide, the <u>Eating Smart Fat Guide</u> . . . a pocket-sized listing of the calories, fat, and saturated-fat content of over 250 foods. It's my way of saying THANKS for your renewal!

The copy in this letter addresses the nonrenewing member as a "tough customer." It then goes on to do what it has done so successfully in the earlier letters: highlight the offer. Also please notice that in all these *Nutrition Action Healthletter* renewal letters the P.S. is used very effectively to pitch the offer.

RENEWAL LETTER #7
CENTER FOR SCIENCE IN THE PUBLIC INTEREST

Dear Reader,

It's now or never. That may be a bit of an exaggeration, but nevertheless this is "the end of the line" for you and Nutrition Action Healthletter.

We want you back. I urge you to take me up right now on our best and last renewal offer: one year of Nutrition Action for a rock-bottom low price of only $10.

I'm sure it's not going to be easy for you always to know what's healthy to eat and what isn't. But you can have the leading experts working for you again. You can know the answers. For example . . . (illustrative examples).

Every issue of the award-winning Nutrition Action Healthletter contains complete answers to questions like these. I'm inviting you to again read and enjoy this nationally acclaimed newsletter on food and health.

Nutrition Action names names. We tell you exactly what's wrong (and what's right) with hundreds of brand-name foods. We tell you the truth—straight out—about "fraudulent" foods: (examples cited)

Facts. Life-enhancing, life-preserving facts. Facts unearthed by the scientists and nutritionists who work for Nutrition Action Healthletter. And because Nutrition Action accepts no advertising, the facts are honest and unbiased.

(Specific magazine content cited.)

And now you can have tomorrow's nutrition news at yesterday's prices! For only $10, you can have a full year of Nutrition Action, along with our no-questions-asked, 100% money-back guarantee.

I've made it as inexpensive and risk-free for you as I possibly can. Now you just have to take advan-

---

Reprinted with permission, Center for Science in the Public Interest.

<u>tage of it</u>. Please use the enclosed order form and
postage-paid envelope for fast service.

Sincerely yours,

Stephen B. Schmidt
Editor, <u>Nutrition Action</u>
<u>Healthletter</u>

P.S. Remember our best and last renewal offer—if
you renew your subscription <u>now</u>, we'll give you the
lowest renewal rate we offer: <u>$10 for 10 issues</u>!

We've seen how this nonprofit organization handles the copy on seven
renewal efforts. Throughout, the offer is the key. In the earlier efforts an
attempt is made to go for a higher-dollar response . . . either a longer-term
subscription or an extra gift. As the series progresses the offer gets better.
In this last effort the nonrenewing member gets the lowest price of all the
letters. Above all each and every letter is clearly written and the reason for
writing is set forth very early in the copy.

MODEL TELEMARKETING SCRIPT
MEMBERSHIP RENEWAL

(Occurs after completion of the direct mail
renewal series.)

HELLO, I'd like to speak to Mr. John Doe. Thank
you.

Good evening, Mr. Doe, how are you this evening?

I'm Roland Kay calling from the Reston
Environmental Trust. Our records indicate that your
membership expired two months ago . . . and we
haven't received your renewal yet.

(If he says he's renewed, thank him; if he hasn't,
proceed to next section.)

We'd like to send you a special map that outlines
the rivers and trails in Reston County.

To receive your free map, all I need tonight is
your OK on a two-year renewal for only $36. We'll
also reactivate your subscription to your members'
newsletter, the "Restonian Environmentalist."

How does that sound? (If positive) Fine, we'll
get your subscription started right away, and I'll
send you your free map along with an acknowledgment
invoice. Thanks so much. (Confirm renewal . . . con-
firming name, address, and term for two years at
$36.)

(If hesitating) I understand, maybe a one-year
renewal for only $18 will work better for you right
now. (If positive, confirm as per above.)

(If still hesitating)

May I make a suggestion. Let me do this. I'd like
to send you the current issue of the newsletter
because it has some information on a possible toxic
waste dump in Reston that I think will be a concern
to you. I'll also include an invoice . . . if you
want to keep your membership alive—and the newsletter
coming—simply pay $18 and your copies will continue.

If you're still not convinced, simply write CANCEL on the invoice and you'll be under no obligation.

Fair enough? OK, now let me confirm (as per above).

(<u>If still no</u>)

Thanks for your past support. We'll be in touch with you in the future on issues of importance to Restonians. It was good talking with you tonight.

(Note: See Chapter 11 for another telemarketing script that provides answers to a variety of possible objections.)

10

Reaping Substantial Funds with the Major Donor Letter

Effective fund-raising is based on what is called the 80-20 rule. This rule states that 80 percent of the total dollars contributed will come from 20 percent of your donors. While the exact percentage numbers in this formula may vary from one organization to another, it is generally true that a large percentage of total contributions will come from a small percentage of donors. For example, a direct mail effort that I am familiar with produced the following results: Of the total $841,336 contributed from two successive direct mail letters, $450,361, or 53.5 percent of the total, came from only 13.8 percent of the donors who were the highest-level donors.

Results like this are not unusual. But they do point up a crucial fact: All donors are not equal. A typical donor list will have donors spread out by a number of giving amount ranges. It's important to segment your donor file by these giving levels and in each mailing to your active donors ask for gifts at continually higher levels. For example, donors who have given $15 in the past, might be asked to give $25, $35, and $50. Donors at the $100 level might be asked to give at the $150, $200, and $250 level. There are various formulas for upgrade giving like this. The exact formula varies from fund-raiser to fund-raiser. Some are more aggressive than others. The key point is to keep asking donors to give at higher levels. The goal is to get the highest number of donors possible in your top giving levels.

Donors will eventually end up giving at a level that is consistent with their ability to give and their motivation to support your cause. Or, said another way, they will give at a level consistent with their demographic and psychographic profile. If you, as a fund-raiser, do not consistently work to upgrade giving levels you will have a lot of unrealized giving potential residing with your donors.

In this chapter we're going to look at a critically important letter to get donors to give at the highest levels. This is the major donor letter that invites current donors to consider upgrading to the highest giving levels. Typically, giving clubs are established for these top levels. Each club will have varying membership levels ranging from $100 to $10,000. Let's take a look at the right timing for mailing such a major donor letter and how to write it.

When to Use the Major Donor Letter

The major donor letter should be sent when you have succeeded in developing a number of donors at higher giving levels. For example, let's say your organization has 100,000 active donors who have made a contribution within the last 12 months and that 2,500 of them fall in the $100 and up category, 7,500 in the $50–99 category, and the balance ranging between $15 and $49. Those 10,000 donors in the $50–100-category would make good prospects for a series of mailings offering membership in a special club with membership categories ranging from $250 to $1,000. There is really no hard and set rule when to mail such a major donor letter. It's important to have staff personnel that can administer the program before you send out the invitation letters. You want to be absolutely sure that you can deliver on the special benefits you promise and also be able to cultivate these donors in a personal way. It's obviously counterproductive to go to the extra effort to solicit major donors and then give them no more follow-up cultivation than is given the lower-level donors.

How to Write the Major Donor Letter

There are a number of factors that will make for success in writing the major donor letter. Here are the key factors to consider in writing the major donor letter.

1. ESTABLISH CLUBS WITH INSIDER CONNOTATIONS IN THE NAME.

While donors may politely tell you that they don't want special recognition . . . they just want to help the good cause, don't believe them. All donors—especially those who give extra-large gifts—do like to be recognized. A simple way to do this is to give your special giving club a name that connotes insider connections (President's Club, Founder's Society, The Committee of 1,000 and 1, etc.).

2. GIVE SPECIAL RECOGNITION BENEFITS.

Do the highest-level donors go that extra mile in giving without being promised any special benefits? Consider this story. A fund-raiser had just received a $10,000 gift in the mail from an individual. The fund-raising staff members were elated. They were doing a little victory jig around the office to express their elation. Then a small note popped out of the donor's envelope that they hadn't noticed earlier. In it she asked if she ". . . could have a free copy of the booklet that was being offered to donors!" That came as a huge surprise. I guess they thought that such a big gift was motivated only by an altruistic interest in the cause. My point? Human nature is pretty much the same and doesn't change because the donor adds a few extra zeros to the number on their contribution check. The benefits offered the high-level donor, however, should focus on recognition of the donor. Benefits such as their name listed on a plaque or in the annual report, invitations to attend special functions, presidential update letters, art prints, and books are all effective and appropriate. Another subtle benefit is simply the name of the membership level within the club. Names such as benefactor, founder, sponsor, and so on are typical of the effort to convey status through the name of the membership level.

3. THE LETTER SHOULD BE SIGNED BY A PEER.

Individuals who give at the highest levels are probably best reached by people they consider to be their peers. That's why the letters of this type come from the chairman of the board or president. This high-level office lends a special dignity to the letter and gets attention from the prospect.

4. THE TONE OF THE LETTER SHOULD BE UPSCALE.

While all the good direct mail techniques of Chapter 1 still apply, they are dressed up a bit in terms of language for the major donors. A *maitre d'* at an elegant French restaurant gives similar information that a hostess at a regular restaurant does, but the words and tone are different. The same upscaling of language for the highest-level donors is effective. The major donor letter should be infused with flattering words. These are not insincere. They simply recognize that your donor in this category is a person of the deepest commitment to your work.

5. SPECIFY SOME SPECIAL USE OF THE FUNDS.

It will be more effective if a unique use of the funds is outlined. This would be a special use that an insider can be expected to appreciate. This ties in with the honest flattering style of the letter. You compliment the donor for being in that core group that understands the intricacies of your work.

6. USE A REFERRAL FROM ANOTHER CLUB MEMBER.

A referral from someone the donor knows and respects can work like magic. It's easy to turn down an invitation from someone you may never see personally, but it's much harder if in the normal course of daily living you encounter the person who has flattered you with a nomination. That's why it's not a bad idea to ask members of your high-level giving clubs for names of friends and associates they think would enjoy participation in the club. These names should be followed up using the techniques of this chapter as well as those in Chapter 14 on the referral letter.

MODEL LETTER—MAJOR DONOR SYMPHONY ORCHESTRA

Mrs. Lillian Williams
444 11th Lane
Alexandria, VA 22222

Dear Mrs. Williams,

USE A REFERRAL FROM ANOTHER CLUB MEMBER (POINT 6)

Dottie Johnson suggested that I write to you about a special NoVa Regional Symphony program you may find of interest.

ESTABLISH CLUBS WITH INSIDER CONNOTATIONS IN THE NAME (POINT 1)

Dottie and I, and a select group of friends who support the Symphony, are members of the Conductor's Circle, and we would like to invite you to join us.

GIVE SPECIAL RECOGNITION BENEFITS (POINT 2)

As a member of the Conductors Circle, you will enjoy certain privileges. You may choose a work to be performed during the season by the Symphony; you are invited to join Artistic Director Smith for special Conductor's Circle parties before each performance; and you are welcome at our very popular monthly "Tea with the First Chairs" and to invitation-only lectures by national and regionally acclaimed critics, performers, teachers and conductors. Of course, you will be listed in both the annual report and the programs.

SPECIFY SOME SPECIAL USE OF THE FUNDS (POINT 5)

But most important, this select group provides to musically gifted youth in our area a truly rare opportunity: the chance to compose "real music" and/or conduct real rehearsals of the Symphony. (Here list details of the program.)

I know of no other program like it in the country. We view it—as we hope you do, too—as a vital part of the long-range plan to bring talented youth into the classical music tradition. To infuse them with the excitement, the joy, of—not just listening to—but of actually creating the wonder of Bach, Mozart, and Berlioz for an audience.

And not coincidentally, these young people will be able to actually work with professional classical musicians—the able members of the NoVa Regional Symphony.

THE TONE OF THE LETTER SHOULD BE UPSCALE (POINT 4)

In a day when more and more musically talented youth fall prey to the siren of popular music, we felt a need, indeed, a duty, to start this program, which we began just last spring.

As you may imagine, such innovative programs are costly, and finding foundations or corporations to support such "frills" is very difficult.

That is why I hope you will join Dottie, me, and others by contributing $2,500 or more to join the Conductor's Circle, enjoy unique benefits, and help ensure that Prokofiev, Dvorak, Beethoven, Haydn, Tellemann, and Elgar live on in live performance for generations to come.

Dottie will call you in a few days to get your answer. Thanks so much.

Sincerely,

THE LETTER SHOULD BE SIGNED BY A PEER (POINT 3)

Ralph Wilson

Volunteer Chair
NoVa Symphony
Conductor's Circle

P.S. At a time when budget constraints are taking
music out of our schools, our program is even more
important, and I hope you can join us.

SAMPLE LETTER—
ST. JOSEPH'S INDIAN SCHOOL

Dear Mr. _____ ,

How much of your life-savings would you like to leave in the hands of federal and state governments?

If you don't have a Will the law has already decided how your possessions and savings will be distributed!

A Will seldom seems like an urgent matter. However, every year millions of estate dollars go to the government because many people put off making their Wills.

How sad it is when the surviving spouse or child or relative must ignore the wishes of a loved one and abide by the decisions of a judge—especially when it doesn't have to be that way!

No matter what your age, preparing a Will is one of the wisest things you will ever do. It is actually a simple task.

Drawing up the Will itself takes only a couple of hours and is usually done for a moderate fee. It's the surest way to arrange and distribute your personal affairs so your family and friends will be remembered the way you wish.

Enclosed is a leaflet entitled "You Have A Will . . . No Choice About It!" I think you will find it enlightening as well as useful.

If you feel you would like to learn more about making a Will but find it difficult to get started, I suggest you send for a free copy of our fact filled booklet, "An Attorney Answers Questions About Your Will." Simply check the space on the attached form, we will be happy to send this handy reference at no obligation on your part.

Reprinted with permission, St. Joseph's Indian School.

God bless you and yours—please know you are important to us at St. Joseph's. Without friends like you, these Lakota children would have nothing at all.

Sincerely,

Brother David Nagel
Director

Some of the largest gifts come to nonprofit organizations through bequests. Occasionally these arrive unexpected from donors who have not necessarily been the highest level donors over the years. But a wise fund-raiser will make it easy to help donors prepare their wills. Here is a straight-forward letter that makes the case for having a will and encloses a leaflet on the subject—and offers to send a booklet with additional information. One or two substantial gifts through bequests can add significant amounts to the overall revenues you raise from your donors. It's not a bad idea to offer to send this information by check-off boxes in other communications such as newsletter and acknowledgment mailings.

SAMPLE LETTER—
WETA (PUBLIC TELEVISION STATION)

Dear Mrs. Kuniholm,

When I was asked to chair the 2691 Club member-ship drive, I was quick to accept. For a long time I have wanted to send my thanks and appreciation directly to you. This letter gives me a wonderful opportunity to do so.

You see, you and I share a special relationship.

Your continuing support of WETA made WETA's support of "The Civil War" possible. That makes us part-ners, you and I. Burns and Kuniholm. We're forever linked by our shared regard for what is perhaps the most important and remarkable public broadcasting station that ever was. And "The Civil War" was our contribution to it.

The "Civil War" exists because WETA exists. When I needed help, WETA was there to give it. WETA provided the seed money and later helped obtain the underwriting to make "The Civil War" possible. Without WETA, I would have been the tree falling in the forest without anyone there to hear it.

Now, it's my turn to help ensure that WETA keeps its ability to recognize and develop quality programs for the future. Your membership in WETA's special 2691 Club will help greatly to ensure that future programs continue to reflect your taste. WETA is one of the few stations in the entire PBS system which has no city, state or university sponsor.

(Copy follows on outstanding programming of WETA.)

Make no mistake about it. WETA has an uncanny ability to take the courage of its members and use it to develop great programs that few other stations would risk. WETA bet on "The Civil War"—to the great

Reprinted with permission of WETA, Washington, D.C.

benefit of all. That's what public television was
intended for. And WETA is public television at its
best.

   On November 7, the 2691 Club will hold its annual
Gala to welcome new members. This year's Gala will be
in the ballroom of the historic Willard Hotel. I'll
be there along with Sharon Rockefeller, Ward Cham-
berlin, Sally Wells, and others you'll know from WETA
programs. I hope you can come. And if you do, please
let me know personally that this letter helped you
decide to join.

                              Sincerely,

                              Ken Burns
                              Honorary Chairman
                              The 2691 Club

   P.S. Please try to return the enclosed membership
acceptance by October 7 so that your Gala invitation
will arrive on time.

The highly acclaimed creator of "The Civil War" television series, Ken
Burns, signs this letter inviting the recipient to join in WETA's high-level support group, the 2691 Club. Genuine flattery comes through as Burns identi-
fies himself with the recipient and goes on to say how recipient's support
has made such a wonderful series possible. A major event is planned—a
gala—and the acceptance to the high-level giving club is tied in with this
special function.

MODEL TELEMARKETING SCRIPT—
LOCAL LIBRARY

HELLO, may I speak to Mary Jones. Thank you.

Good evening Ms. Jones . . . I'm calling you tonight on behalf of the Northwest Library. Is this a good time to speak with you?

(If not, schedule another time to talk.)

Fine . . . here's why I'm calling. At Northwest we're planning to add a new children's wing to include books, magazines, and tapes for young people ages 7 to 12. How does that sound to you?

Great. As a Friend of Northwest Library you know that our library serves all the citizens in the three northern counties. And, until now, there has been no library for our youngsters.

We have a matching grant from the A-Z Foundation . . . and in order to receive it we need to receive $50,000 from our local citizens.

Because you have helped in the past—and because you know the value of good books for young people—I'd like to ask you to pledge $500 for the construction of this new wing.

You can pay it in installments over the next year if you prefer. All I need from you tonight is your OK . . . this will help qualify us for that wonderful matching grant.

Your name will be listed as a Northwest Library Sponsor on a plaque to be maintained in our lobby. And when we send you your acknowledgment we will send you a packet of 12 bookplates.

Can we include you as a special donor? If positive, confirm name, address, amount, and fact that a pledge reminder mailing will be sent.

<u>If negative or hesitating</u> . . .

I understand . . . we can still use a lot of gifts in the $250 range to qualify for the grant.

<u>If still no commitment</u> . . .

Why don't we do this . . . I'd at least like to send you a brochure on this new children's wing so you will see what our plans call for. Then at a later date if you change your mind you can easily make a gift. We have a deadline of _____, so I urge you to give it your serious consideration by then.

It was nice talking with you tonight. And, on behalf of the Northwest Library, I want to thank you for your past support.

(Note: See Chapter 11 for another telemarketing script that provides answers to a variety of possible objections.)

11

"Calling In" Funds with the Telemarketing Script and Follow-up Letter

Asking for contributions by telephone has become a staple of most fund-raising organizations today. Some organizations have these calls made by internal staff members. If the nature of your appeal is highly complex or technical, this might be the wiser course. However, many more fund-raisers today engage outside telemarketing firms for this activity. These professional telemarketing firms have highly specialized equipment for making calls and well-trained, polite personnel. In the past there has been a hesitancy to contract with outside telemarketing firms on the fear that their paid callers will not properly answer questions or come through with the right tone. With the proper training of the telephone sales representatives these concerns fall into the background. The reality is that outside telemarketing firms—in most instances—can do a much better job than in-house callers in getting results, and they do it with a minimum of complaints. They can also handle a much larger volume of calls than can be done internally.

The best results from telemarketing come from a coordinated campaign combining the telephone with direct mail. In this chapter we're going to look at a telemarketing script to understand just how this copy should be written. Then we'll see different types of direct mail letters that are used in conjunction with a telemarketing campaign—letters that are sent in advance of a telemarketing call as well as the follow-up letters to confirm the pledge and get the gift.

The telephone can be used to solicit major contributions from the high-dollar portion of your list. Or it can be used to renew members or reactivate lapsed donors. All these approaches are made to individuals who have made a previous contribution to the cause and are familiar with your organization and what it does. Telemarketing works best when the calls are made to people who are already familiar with the calling organization.

There are some instances, however, where a fund-raiser will use the phone to solicit new donors from cold prospect lists. This is usually done if the nonprofit organization has an available source of names with phone numbers for a very specific audience they are trying to reach; for example, a volunteer fire or police department that serves a specific community. People living in the defined geographical area can be presumed to have an interest even though they haven't previously contributed.

The one key point to keep in mind about telemarketing for gifts is that the call is *interactive*. This is not true in direct mail where you decide in advance what to ask for and what size gift you want—and you are limited on the purpose and amount. On the phone you can start out with a certain amount and then negotiate varying levels depending on the responses given. The telemarketing representative can also listen to particular questions and answer these accordingly. This interactive negotiation aspect is what makes telemarketing so effective.

When to Use the Telemarketing Letter

RENEWALS

Most fund-raisers will send a series of renewal letters first. At some point they will switch to the phone to solicit a renewal from the tougher prospects. Direct mail, with its lower cost than telephoning, can be used to gain the early, easy renewals. The phone, with its more intensive personalization, is utilized after the direct mail series has run its course. Some fund-raisers test the calling at different points in the series—in the middle or in some few cases early on. The typical scenario is direct mail series first, followed up by a phone call with confirmation letters and invoices to those who say "yes" on the phone.

REACTIVATIONS

Members who have not responded to any renewal efforts or appeals typically end up on the inactive file. These names should be regularly solicited because in most instances they will respond better than any outside list of names. Former members or donors have given once so they have some familiarity with your work. A phone call updating these former donors on some new benefits or some new campaign being launched can reactivate them at a very acceptable cost. Reactivation calls and follow-up confirmation notices are best done with the most recent lapsed donors. Fund-raisers will work their way back into a file, the earliest lapsed names first and then the older names, to see how far back they can go cost effectively.

SPECIAL APPEALS

It may come as a surprise but the phone can be effective in soliciting large-size gifts—up to $1,000. These gifts will come from donors in your active file who have given above-average contributions (e.g., $50 to $500). A person who has responded to a general direct mail appeal with a gift of $100 can reasonably be assumed to have a much greater giving potential if approached on a more personal basis through a telephone call. Because there are always "sleepers" on the list, it's wise to experiment with different giving-level donors to assess their ability to upgrade their contributions. Calling for high-level contributions should probably be limited to once or twice a year to the same file segments. Each fund-raiser tests to find the right combination of direct mail and telemarketing appeals. A balance needs to be struck between results and promotional overkill.

How to Write a Telemarketing Script

Probably the most important factor to bear in mind with a telemarketing script is that the telephone representative has a live prospect on the phone. And this is usually a person who has knowledge of the cause—both general knowledge through previous giving and, in some instances, more specific knowledge through an advance telemarketing letter. This means the script can focus its attention on two main points: First, there is the gift negotiation aspect. The prospect reacts (either positively or negatively) to the size of a potential gift that the telephone representative is asking for. You'll see how tastefully this is done in the Medic Alert telemarketing script in this chapter. Second, the telemarketing representative can answer objections that are unique to the particular prospect. This type of interaction is one of the reasons telemarketing gets such a high response rate. Again the Medic Alert telemarketing script illustrates how each type of objection they encounter can be answered. Plus, note how it's possible through telemarketing to learn different facts about your donor/member that can be tastefully incorporated in the follow-up letters.

How to Write the Advance Call Telemarketing Letter

Some fund-raisers will make telemarketing calls without any advance notice. If the purpose of the call is straightforward and not requiring much elaboration (e.g., a renewal or a reactivation of support), then an advance letter is probably not necessary. However, if your fund-raising project is more complex, then it is a good idea to send an advance letter (e.g., a major drive to raise funds for a new building). Here are some of the points to consider in writing a letter in advance of a telemarketing call.

1. ADVISE THAT A CALL WILL BE MADE TO DONOR SOON.

Typically the advance letters are for major campaigns. The "ask" for the gift is not made in the letter—that will be done in the subsequent phone call. But it's absolutely essential that the donor know that a call is coming shortly and that a request for a major gift will be made on the phone.

2. GIVE A TIP-OFF ON THE AMOUNT OF THE GIFT.

Sometimes fund-raisers will note the specific amount that's going to be asked for. The preferred practice, however, is to indicate that you're going to ask for a "substantial commitment" and then leave it to the telemarketing representative to negotiate the amount.

3. OUTLINE A MAJOR NEED.

Because telemarketing is an out-of-the-ordinary approach, it should generally be limited to very special campaigns for larger than average gifts or for very targeted efforts such as a renewal or reactivation of a membership. Make sure to outline a major new need in the letter.

4. ADOPT A HIGH-LEVEL FLATTERING TONE.

This should come naturally considering that you're probably going to call the best segments of your list. It helps to genuinely flatter the recipient who has been specially selected to receive this call.

How to Write the Postcall Telemarketing Letter

Letters that are written after the telemarketing call has been made are different in nature and should follow these guidelines:

1. ACKNOWLEDGE GIFT OR PLEDGE IMMEDIATELY.

Once a decision is made on the phone, the follow-up letter should go out within 24 hours. People tend to have short memories, and you want to reach them while they still have an active memory of the decision made on the phone.

2. ACCURATELY CONFIRM THE PHONE COMMITMENT.

Whatever decision the person made on the phone should be clearly confirmed. A decision has already been made, so it's important to keep faith with the donor on his or her pledge made on the phone.

3. INDICATE CLEARLY HOW PAYMENT IS TO BE MADE.

The phone follow-up closely resembles a billing mailing. The donor has agreed to a specific gift amount. Confirm that amount on the enclosed invoice.

4. THANK DONOR.

It never hurts to add one more word of thanks. Make sure donors know how much you value their support.

5. ASK FOR AN UPGRADE.

This should be done with the utmost delicacy. You already have a commitment, and you don't want to lose the sale by being too aggressive. On the other hand, there is a portion of donors who, when the checkbook is open, are also receptive to an invitation to give a little bit more. If you do this, do it gently and in good taste. Some fund-raisers will offer an extra premium for the upgrade-level gift.

6. RESTATE THE CORE NEED OR BENEFIT.

This is done mainly for reinforcement. The sale has been made. So this copy should be written with that slant. You are not trying to get the initial decision. You already have that, but it doesn't hurt to recap what is most significant in your campaign, be it a major new project for which you need support or some special benefits the donor will receive.

MODEL LETTER—ADVANCE TELEMARKETING LETTER— PUBLIC TV

Dear Friend of WXXX,

ADOPT A HIGH-LEVEL FLATTERING TONE (POINT 4)

Because you have been a strong friend of WXXX, I would like to share some exciting news and a major challenge with you. It is a challenge I believe we can and must meet, if public television is to remain in the forefront of quality television—indeed, if you share with me the desire to see quality television overcome the "sitcom blizzard" we see on commercial TV.

OUTLINE A MAJOR NEED (POINT 3)

Here is the news: An anonymous donor has offered $50,000 to WXXX for the creation of a quality mini-series. (Here elaborate on the product.)

The challenge is this: Under the terms of that generous gift, we must <u>match</u> that $50,000 with an <u>additional $50,000 from WXXX members before (deadline)</u>.

Thus, the total of the gift would be $100,000 for WXXX.

ADVISE THAT A CALL WILL BE MADE TO DONOR SOON (POINT 1)

When you think of what this seed money could do for public television, you will understand why I have asked a representative to telephone you in the next week. The stakes are high and the deadline is soon. I do not want to miss this one-time opportunity to "jump-start" what could become one of the more innovative programs in public television today.

If our representative calls at a bad time, by all means tell him or her, so that we can arrange a better time.

GIVE A TIP-OFF ON THE AMOUNT OF THE GIFT (POINT 2)

But I do hope you can take a moment then to hear details about this wonderful matching gift and what we hope to accomplish with it, and, if you can, help us match that $50,000 with a significant gift of your own.

I am excited about this "seed money." We may start another series, which would attract additional funding—or it might be a low-cost but high-impact program on the environment or child care or . . . who knows?

If you have suggestions as to what kinds of special miniseries should be created with your seed money, by all means tell my representative when he or she calls.

But in any case, I do hope you can help us match this $50,000 gift with a major gift of your own.

You will be investing once again in the future of quality.

                              Sincerely,

                              Executive Producer
                              WXXX

MODEL TELEMARKETING SCRIPT—RENEWAL
MEDICALERT

INTRODUCTION TO DONOR

Hello, Mr.(s.) _____, this is _____ and I'm calling on behalf of the MedicAlert Foundation.

Thanks to you and other members, Medic Alert has been able to provide peace of mind for over 4 million members, worldwide who wear the MedicAlert emblem—and now we plan to add an extra safeguard for you or someone you love in case of an emergency. Because of your support, MedicAlert will soon be able to provide immediate transmission of EKGs, lab tests and other image technology right to the scene of an emergency. So, doctors can have your most current documents and records right there on hand.

Mr.(s.) ____, we urgently need your continued support this year to keep our life-saving services operating at peak efficiency. We must keep our technical equipment up-to-date so we can provide immediate information about our members in an emergency . . . and, to train all emergency workers to look for the MedicAlert emblem.

Mr.(s.) _____, can we count on you to renew your support of MedicAlert this year with a tax-deductible gift of 1.5 times $HPC or 2 times $HPC?

(If yes) GO TO CLOSE FOR WILL PLEDGE/SPECIFIC AMOUNT.

(If yes/no specific amount) GO TO CLOSE FOR WILL PLEDGE/NO AMOUNT.

(If unresponsive) GO TO APPROPRIATE RESPONSE.

(If financial objection) GO TO APPROPRIATE RESPONSE.

(If maybe/no) GO TO SECOND REQUEST.

(If special objection) SEE APPROPRIATE RESPONSE.

FINANCIAL OBJECTION

I respect that, Mr.(s.) _____, and we understand not everyone can help at that level. You were so generous to help with $HPC in the past, can we count on you to help with that much again?

(If yes/specific amount) GO TO CLOSE FOR WILL PLEDGE/SPECIFIC AMOUNT.

(If yes/no specific amount) GO TO CLOSE FOR WILL PLEDGE/NO AMOUNT.

(If maybe) GO TO MAY PLEDGE.

(If no) GO TO NOT INTERESTED OR THIRD REQUEST IF APPROPRIATE.

SECOND REQUEST

(Respond) Your continued support is so important because <u>MedicAlert's</u> quality protection depends on keeping our medical response systems running smoothly and effectively. Cuts to any of our programs could have a devastating effect on people, like you, who count on us to be there when they need us.

You were so generous to help with $HPC in the past, can we count on you to help with that much again?

(If yes/specific amount) GO TO CLOSE FOR WILL PLEDGE/SPECIFIC AMOUNT.

(If yes/no specific amount) GO TO CLOSE FOR WILL PLEDGE/NO AMOUNT (If maybe) GO TO MAY PLEDGE.

(If no) GO TO NOT INTERESTED OR THIRD REQUEST IF APPROPRIATE.

THIRD REQUEST

(Respond) Is there any gift you feel you can help with at this time?

(If yes) GO TO WILL PLEDGE/SPECIFIC AMOUNT.

(If yes, but won't commit to an amount) GO TO CLOSE FOR WILL PLEDGE.

(No specific amount) GO TO CLOSE FOR WILL PLEDGE/NO AMOUNT.

(If maybe) GO TO MAY PLEDGE.

(If special question/objection) SEE APPROPRIATE
RESPONSE.

(If no) GO TO CLOSE FOR NOT INTERESTED AT THIS TIME.

CLOSE FOR WILL PLEDGE/SPECIFIC AMOUNT

That's wonderful, Mr.(s.) _____. We'll be writing
you a letter to thank you for your $XX contribution,
so let me just verify your address. (Verify full
address including apartment # and zip code.)

In with our letter will be a special envelope to
mail back your $XX gift. Thank you again for renewing
your support, Mr.(s.) _____. Goodbye.

CLOSE FOR WILL PLEDGE/NO SPECIFIC AMOUNT

That's terrific, Mr.(s.)_____. We'll be sending
you a letter to thank you for your contribution, so
let me just verify your address. (Verify full address
including apartment # and zip code.)

Mr.(s.) _____, so we can effectively plan our
programs for the year, is there a minimum amount you
feel comfortable with for our budget projections?

(If yes) Great! That will help so much! In with
our letter, there will be an envelope to return your
$XX gift. Thank you very much. Goodbye.

(If no) That's fine. Please watch for our letter
in the mail, and thank you so much for speaking with
me today. Goodbye.

CLOSE FOR MAY PLEDGE

Thank you for your consideration, Mr.(s.) _____.
Let me just verify your address, and we'll get a letter off to you right away, along with a return envelope. (Verify address . . . .)

Terrific! Please watch for our letter in the
mail. Thank you for taking the time to speak with me
today, and I hope to hear from you soon. Goodbye.

CLOSE FOR NOT INTERESTED

(If the objection is financial or time related) I
can understand if this isn't a good time. Even if you

waited 30 days or so to send your 19__ contribution, it would help us meet our financial goal for the year, and make a tremendous difference to our programs. Do you feel you could help in the next 30 days?

(If yes) GO TO CLOSE FOR WILL PLEDGE/SPECIFIC AMOUNT.

(If no) I'm sorry to hear you won't be able to help us right now. But we thank you so much for the support you've given us. Thank you for taking the time to speak with me (today/tonight). Goodbye.

(If objection isn't financial or time related) I'm sorry to hear you won't be able to help us right now, but we thank you so much for the support you've given us. Thank you for taking the time to speak with me (today/tonight). Goodbye.

I DON'T RESPOND TO PHONE SOLICITATIONS

I respect that. If you like, I can make a special note that you prefer not to be called. Would you like me to do that for you, Mr.(s.)____? (Flag record.)

If you think you might be interested in helping again this year, we would be happy to send you a letter instead.

(If no) GO TO NOT PLEDGING AT THIS TIME.

(If yes) Great! Let me just verify your address so we can get that letter to you right away. (Verify full address.) Enclosed with the letter will be a special return envelope. Thank you for speaking with me. Goodbye.

"I HAVE TO DISCUSS IT WITH MY SPOUSE"

I appreciate that, Mr.(s.) _____. I'll just go ahead and send you a letter and return envelope. Is your address still . . . (Verify full address . . . .) Great! You and Mr.(s.) _____ have been so generous to help with $HPC. Do you feel you'll be able to help with that much again this year?

(If yes/specific amount) GO TO CLOSE FOR WILL PLEDGE/SPECIFIC AMOUNT.

(If still noncommittal, record as maybe.) That's fine. We'll certainly appreciate whatever you can send at this time. Thank you for speaking with me today. Goodbye.

"I'M RETIRED AND ON A FIXED INCOME"

Thank you for telling me that, Mr.(s.) _____, I didn't know that. Would a gift of $10 or $15 be better for you at this time?
(If no) GO TO NOT INTERESTED AT THIS TIME.

"I GET SO MANY REQUESTS FOR FUNDING, I CAN'T GIVE TO EVERYONE."

We appreciate the fact you must be selective in your giving, and we're so grateful for your loyal support.

Medic Alert is a non-profit organization, and without your support, we can't maintain our life-saving services.
(Close with appropriate financial request.)

"I CAN'T AFFORD TO GIVE RIGHT NOW."
"THIS IS A BAD TIME FOR ME."

I can appreciate that, Mr.(s.) _____. Even if you waited 30 days or so to send your 19__ contribution, it would help us meet our financial goal for the year, and make a tremendous difference to our programs. Do you feel you could help in the next 30 days?
(If yes) GO TO CLOSE FOR WILL PLEDGE/SPECIFIC AMOUNT.

(If no) I'm sorry to hear you won't be able to help us right now. But we thank you so much for the support you've given us. Thank you for taking the time to speak with me (today/tonight). Goodbye.

"WHAT DOES THE ONE-TIME MEMBERSHIP COVER?"

Your one-time membership covers your MedicAlert emblem and annually updated wallet card. MedicAlert deliberately keeps membership fees low so that everyone who needs protection can afford it.
(Return to script.)

```
     (If  unresponsive)  Is  there  a  particular  reason
why  you're  unable  to  help  again?  We're  very  interest-
ed  in  your  comments.
     (Listen  carefully  and  try  to  counter  objection
based  on  scripted  response.)
```

This telemarketing script for MedicAlert illustrates a number of important points. The calls are being made to previous donors who have an interest and familiarity with the calling organization. Note particularly how the script is written to be *interactive*—the donor's reactions are taken into account and respected. The telephone representative adjusts his or her responses according to what the prospect says. Also you can see that a telemarketing approach like this is highly courteous—simple clear answers are given to various responses. Even those who don't contribute as a result of this approach will feel good about the organization and be open to further appeals, either direct mail or telemarketing. Note especially that those who don't want to be called on the phone are flagged and handled in accordance with the prospect's request. All in all a very well done and tasteful outbound telemarketing script.

SAMPLE LETTER—TELEMARKETING
FIRST FOLLOW-UP FULFILLMENT LETTER TO LAPSED
MEMBERS WHO RENEW OVER THE PHONE—STATION KQED

Dear _____,

Thank you for speaking with (name fill in) on the telephone and for renewing your membership in KQED with a $XX contribution. <u>By renewing today, you will receive all the benefits of membership at $5 off the 19XX rate</u>!

(Variable Paragraph)

<u>If person gives favorite programming</u>

Your contribution directly supports the programs you told us you enjoy most like XXXXXXXX, XXXXXXXX, and XXXXXXXX.

<u>If person doesn't give favorite programming (Default)</u>

Your contribution directly supports the programs you enjoy most like Masterpiece Theatre, The MacNeil/Lehrer News Hour, and Great Performances.

Our number one priority at KQED is to bring you the programs you enjoy with as little interruption as possible. That's why we went out on a limb in June and cut our on-air pledge drive in half!

<u>Putting our viewers ahead of profits makes KQED unique</u>. But it doesn't keep us from feeling the financial pinch. And right now, we urgently need your renewed support to make up for the funding we sacrificed when we reduced our on-air campaign.

In fact, we must renew <u>38,000 active members</u> and <u>reinstate 5,878 prior members</u> like you to meet our operating costs and keep all of your favorite KQED programs on the air—plus bring you provocative new programming like KQED's production, <u>The San Francisco History Project</u>, Ken Burns's <u>Baseball</u> and <u>The Three Tenors in Concert 19XX</u>.

Reprinted with permission, Station KQED, Inc. and TransAmerica Marketing Services, Inc.

Thank you so much for stepping forward once again to show you care about the future of public broadcasting here in the Bay Area.

With your ongoing support, our hope is to continue reducing our pledge weeks to keep bringing you your favorite programming without interruptions! Thank you again.

                    Sincerely,

                    Patricia H. Wilson
                    Director of
                    Membership

P.S. Please return your $XX membership today, and I will send you your new KQED membership card which entitles you to special discounts at Bay Area restaurants, museums, theaters and other attractions. Thank you and best wishes!

The following variable P.S.s are incorporated only if donor <u>volunteers</u> the required information over the phone. The operator does not prompt responses in any way. If the following information is captured, the appropriate P.S. will replace the P.S. which currently appears as part of the fulfillment letter.

HAPPY BIRTHDAY

P.S. I understand from (first name fill-in) you recently celebrated a birthday! Please accept my best wishes for a happy and healthy year!

NEW JOB

P.S. I understand from (first name fill-in) that you recently started a new job. Congratulations! Please accept my best wishes and the best of luck to you!

```
JUST PURCHASED A NEW HOME

     P.S. I understand from (first name fill-in) that
you recently purchased a new home! Congratulations! I
wish you the best of luck and much happiness.
```

(Note: A number of similar variable P.S.s may be used for a variety of experiences, including celebrating retirement, person is expecting, birth of a child, marriage, engagement, etc.).

Here's an excellent example of a well-written follow-up letter. It clearly acknowledges the gift amount. It is nicely personalized, utilizing viewing preferences that the member shared on the phone. It states a specific objective of the campaign. And it repeats the reduced price membership offer and the special benefits of membership. Don't overlook the importance of the highly personalized P.S.s based on information that the donor volunteered over the phone. Direct mail is most effective when it is tastefully personalized. In this follow-up letter you are seeing personalization at its best.

SAMPLE LETTER—
TELEMARKETING, SECOND FOLLOW-UP FULFILLMENT LETTER TO LAPSED MEMBERS WHO RENEW OVER THE PHONE—STATION KQED

(DONE IN TELEGRAM STYLE)

(xxxxxxDATExxxxxx)
(Name and Address)

A COUPLE OF WEEKS AGO, YOU SPOKE WITH (NAME FILL-IN) BY PHONE AND SAID YOU WOULD LIKE TO TAKE ADVANTAGE OF KQED'S DISCOUNTED RENEWAL OFFER BY RENEWING YOUR MEMBERSHIP RIGHT AWAY. THANK YOU SO MUCH.

PLEASE DISREGARD THIS REMINDER AND ACCEPT MY DEEPEST APPRECIATION IF YOU HAVE RECENTLY RETURNED YOUR $XX MEMBERSHIP, AND MY LETTER IS CROSSING WITH YOUR RESPONSE IN THE MAIL. <u>HOWEVER, IF YOU HAVEN'T HAD A CHANCE TO SEND YOUR CONTRIBUTION YET, I URGE YOU TO TAKE A MOMENT AND DO SO TODAY</u>.

I THOUGHT IT WAS IMPORTANT TO WRITE YOU AGAIN TO REMIND YOU THAT I MUST HEAR FROM YOU SOON TO ENSURE YOU RECEIVE A FULL YEAR OF EXCEPTIONAL PROGRAMMING AT THE 1993 RATE.

EFFECTIVE JANUARY 1ST, KQED'S BASIC MEMBERSHIP RATE INCREASED TO $40 A YEAR, AND OUR LIMITED INCOME AND FAMILY MEMBERSHIPS INCREASED BY $5, AS WELL.

<u>HOWEVER, BY RENEWING YOUR MEMBERSHIP TODAY, YOU WILL RECEIVE ALL OF THE BENEFITS OF MEMBERSHIP AT $5 OFF THE CURRENT RATE. BUT I MUST HEAR FROM YOU RIGHT AWAY</u>!

I URGE YOU TO USE THE RETURN ENVELOPE I'VE ENCLOSED TO SEND YOUR $XX MEMBERSHIP CONTRIBUTION TODAY. WE NEED YOUR ONGOING SUPPORT TO CONTINUE BRINGING YOU THE PROGRAMS YOU ENJOY MOST.

THANK YOU AGAIN FOR YOUR SUPPORT OF KQED.

```
                              SINCERELY,


                              PATRICIA  H.  WILSON
                              DIRECTOR  OF  MEMBERSHIP
```

<u>FOR TEST SEGMENT (PREMIUM)</u>

```
    P.S.  AS  SOON  AS  I  RECEIVE  YOUR  $XX  MEMBERSHIP
CONTRIBUTION,  I  WILL  SEND  YOU  A  XXXXXXXXXXXXXX  AS
OUR  SPECIAL  THANK  YOU  FOR  RENEWING  YOUR  SUPPORT.  I
LOOK  FORWARD  TO  HEARING  FROM  YOU.
```

<u>FOR NONTEST SEGMENT (NO PREMIUM)</u>

```
    P.S.  I  MUST  HEAR  FROM  YOU  RIGHT  AWAY  TO  RECEIVE
THE  SPECIAL  DISCOUNTED  RATE  AVAILABLE  ONLY  TO  PAST
KQED  MEMBERS.  PLEASE  RETURN  YOUR  MEMBERSHIP  CONTRIBU-
TION  TODAY.
```

This follow-up letter repeats much of the argument for renewing what was in the first letter, yet in a much more urgent tone. It effectively uses underlines to highlight the offer and the "need to renew copy." Also note that an offer test was done on the phone and the letter contains a variable P.S. reflecting this test. See Chapter 24 for a review of the important items that should be tested in direct mail efforts.

SAMPLE TELEMARKETING, FOLLOW-UP GIFT RESPONSE FORM—STATION KQED

From: XXXX Name Fill-in XXXX
XXXX Address XXXX
XXXX City, State, Zip XXXX
To: Patricia Wilson, Director of Membership

___ YES! I spoke with XXXX (name fill-in) on the phone and I want to take advantage of the discounted renewal rate for former KQED members only.

Enclosed is my $XX membership contribution, which is $5 off the 19XX rate.

___ I would like to receive more benefits by joining at a higher membership level. Please renew my membership at the following level:

___ $60 Family Membership (Helps parents and children get more from KQED's innovative children's programs and Bay Area learning resources.)

___ $100 (Entitles you to the "KQED Passport" full of valuable coupons redeemable at local restaurants and retailers.)

___ $250 Leadership Circle (Allows you to participate more fully in KQED with a variety of special events, benefits and activities.)

___ Please charge my membership to my credit card:

___ AMEX ___ MASTERCARD ___ VISA ___ DISCOVER
ACCOUNT NUMBER _____
NAME ON CARD: _____
EXPIRATION DATE: _____
___ I've made my check payable to KQED.

This gift response form does something very important. It confirms the agreed-upon membership amount for payment, and it provides for upgrade giving opportunities. When a person has the checkbook "at the ready," so to speak, it is an easy matter to consider a higher amount in writing out the check—or making the credit card charge. The higher amounts suggested on this gift response form are tied in with additional benefits. Raising the average gift amount this way is a critical factor in determining the success of fund-raising.

12

Acquiring Regular Monthly Donors with the Sustainer Letter

There are a variety of ways that donors give to nonprofit organizations. Donors who need a strong current reason for giving are most likely to respond to the type of special appeal mailing outlined in Chapter 8. These donors need the increased emotional stimulation that a special appeal makes. On the other hand another portion of your donors are more likely to give in a regular "bill-paying mode." They like to give each month at the same time as they make out their checks to pay for household and other expenses. These are the systematic givers. They are conditioned to give on an automatic basis to a charity that they have predetermined is a good one and that needs their regular support. It's similar to people who have pledged to their church or synagogue and then make weekly or monthly contributions on a predetermined schedule.

These monthly donors are called sustainers and typically give a small to average monthly amount, ranging from $10 to $25 per month. However, consistent giving like this, even when the individual successive gifts are relatively small, can add up. Sustainer donors also like the idea that a greater portion of their gift will go to the cause as opposed to fund-raising expenses. Once a person has signed on as a sustainer he or she should be excluded from most of the other mailings to regular donors. They have made a commitment to the particular nonprofit's work and will give on a regular planned basis. Yet they do need monthly reminders or statements to let them know the current amount due. It's a good idea to assign the responsibility for the sustainer donors to an individual in your organization who becomes familiar with these donors as much as possible. Little birthday notes or comments on things happening in the sustainer donor's life can be very effective in cementing a warm personal relationship with the fund-raising organization. Donors will give faithfully when they know that there is a real person at the other end of the line who is looking for the monthly gift. This personal link almost becomes a benefit in and of itself.

When to Use the Sustainer Letter

The normal time to recruit sustainer donors is early on in the donor's relationship with your organization. Basically you want to canvass all your new donors as they are being added to the file to give them an opportunity to give on a regular monthly basis. This invitation would go to donors who give at the average money amount levels, for example, in the $10 to $25 range. The higher-level donors are best left out of the sustainer appeal in the hopes that you can upgrade them to substantially higher individual gift amounts. Many fund-raisers make the sustainer appeal in conjunction with the acknowledgment of the donor's first gift.

How to Write the Sustainer Letter

1. BEGIN WITH APPRECIATION FOR THE DONOR'S INITIAL GIFT.

Here's an important point to remember. A donor's first gift to your organization probably took more time and consideration than the donor will ever expend over making any subsequent gift. You can reasonably presume that your first-time donor's interest level in your work is at its all-time peak right after mailing you that first check. During the first few weeks or what we might call the "honeymoon" period—complimenting the donor for giving or joining is very much in order. It furthers the bonding process.

2. INVITE THE DONOR TO JOIN A SMALL CADRE OF EXCEPTIONAL DONORS WHO GIVE ON A MONTHLY BASIS.

Early in your letter tell about a special group of donors in your organization who go the extra mile and allow you to accomplish some very special things. These are the monthly donors or sustainers. The more "insider-ish" and special you can make this group sound the better. And this is not insincere. They really are special through their commitment to monthly support. It is flattering to be asked to join an inner circle. That's the way the sustainer letter copy should sound.

3. GIVE A GOOD OVERVIEW OF YOUR ORGANIZATION'S PROGRAM.

Sustainer giving "sustains" your organization. That's why it's important to indicate that there are many programs that will need support throughout the year and in subsequent years. The donor needs to have that good feeling that each month's gift is really making a difference, that is, going to something of major importance.

4. ALLOW THE DONOR TO MAKE SUBSEQUENT CHANGES IN THE COMMITMENT.

One concern that monthly donors have is the necessity to change or stop their giving if their individual circumstances change. You don't want to make the sustainer commitment sound so iron-clad that it scares off donors. Include some terminology that indicates monthly sustainer donors can change their giving amount or drop off altogether at a later date if necessary.

5. SEND MONTHLY REMINDERS TO THE DONOR.

These updates are necessary to keep the giving active. Each month a mailing should go to the donor reminding that the monthly payment is due. A brief word on current activities and use of funds is effective. Some organizations include a statement that recaps all the giving to date. If the donor has missed two or more payments, a special letter to see if a change is necessary is desirable. If someone gets too many months in arrears it is difficult to get caught up to date. It's preferable to adjust the current amount and go on from there.

MODEL LETTER—SUSTAINER— NATIVE AMERICAN CHARITY

Dear Friend of the Native American Fund,

BEGIN WITH APPRECIATION FOR THE DONOR'S INITIAL GIFT (POINT 1)

I was deeply gratified to receive your recent gift of $_____.

I included it with others I received this week and was able to send a check directly to our New Mexico mission 200 miles north of Santa Fe. There, it will be received just in time to buy warm winter clothing for students and fuel oil for the three-room school we have established in the little town of

_____.

We chose this location three years ago because the need is great. Regular schools are a long bus ride away. The Native American children there work with their parents on small farms, and schooling is seen as a luxury—not a necessity.

And yet it is a necessity, if we are to break the cycle of poverty and ignorance, and bring the love of God to these children and their parents.

GIVE A GOOD OVERVIEW OF YOUR ORGANIZATION'S PROGRAM (POINT 3)

In just three years, we have made wonderful strides. We have built three schools and staffed them with Native American teachers. We have brought arithmetic, reading, music, and art to young lives. And we have started to make a difference. Already, families are seeing their children "graduate" from our little schools, and are allowing them to take the trek on busses to the faraway high school. They have seen the value of learning!

INVITE THE DONOR TO JOIN A SMALL CADRE OF EXCEPTIONAL DONORS WHO GIVE ON A MONTHLY BASIS (POINT 2)

And that is why I am asking you to become a member of the NAF Children's Circle.

You see, I can't support this little mission and dozens of others like it with "just in time" checks. We desperately need a steady source of income. And that is why I am turning to you.

We started the Children's Circle just last year, and the response has been wonderful. We ask people like you—perhaps of modest means, but who see clearly the need—to give $10, $15, or $25 each month to sustain the work of our missions to Native American children in the Southwest.

In return for your caring and regular gifts, I will send you a monthly reminder, along with an update on the children you are helping so directly.

Often, Sisters at the mission will write to me about one of their successes, or a child will write about his or her hopes and dreams, and I will share those letters with you.

ALLOW THE DONOR TO MAKE SUBSEQUENT CHANGES IN THE COMMITMENT (POINT 4)

Please take a moment now to fill in the enclosed Acceptance Form. You can decrease, increase or stop your pledge at any time, just by letting us know.

The important thing is to begin, so we can continue helping the Native American children who lead such desperately poor lives.

Once more, thanks for your recent gift. And I do hope you can join us in the Children's Circle.

Yours in God,

Fr. John Francis
Senior Advisor
Native American Fund

SUSTAINER INVITATION LETTER— CENTER FOR MARINE CONSERVATION

Dear Member,

I'm writing to invite you to join a small, select group of Center members who have undertaken a very special effort to help marine wildlife and their habitats.

I'll tell you more about this special group, but first let me tell you why it was created.

Each day there are growing abuses to precious marine animals and the oceans in which they live. Driftnets are laid across miles of open sea to catch squid, tuna, and salmon. But every day these curtains of death also entangle and drown marine mammals, seabirds, and sea turtles. The Japanese alone set more than 7,000 miles of deadly driftnet every day.

If that isn't enough, dolphins are being killed at an alarming rate . . .

(Subsequent paragraphs talk more about the threat and what the Center is doing to promote its program.)

What we have learned from our fights to protect marine wildlife and their habitats is that the ingredients for victory include foresight, commitment, continuity and sustained effort.

And that's why we have formed this special group of members—a group I hope you will join. We call it the <u>Marine Wildlife Preservation Fund</u>.

During the *Exxon Valdez* disaster, I asked a few individuals to join me in creating this special Fund. The response exceeded all expectations . . . . <u>These special individuals made a commitment to provide steady income to the Center—month after month—for emergency response work and funding for unforeseen demands in our many program areas</u>.

Because of the exceptional dedication and enthusiasm shown by the founding members of this program, we are extending our invitation to other committed Center members. I hope you will accept my invitation to join the Marine Wildlife Preservation Fund, by pledging to make a contribution each month of $15, $20, or $25.

In a year's time a monthly contribution of just $15 (that breaks down to just 50 cents per day) can make a real difference by helping us to . . .

(Project descriptions follow.)

While the general operation of the Center's programs is made possible by annual membership contributions and extra donations, it is the regular monthly contributions of this special group that will sustain our <u>special efforts</u> on behalf of the world's marine wildlife . . .

I realize in asking for a monthly commitment I am asking a lot. It may even mean a personal sacrifice on your part. But I wouldn't be asking if the challenges and opportunities were not so great. In return, I can promise you that your donations will be put to immediate and effective use.

Every month, as a Fund member you will receive a special "insider's" report on our activities, a pledge reminder, and a record of your giving history.

I hope you will take the time right now to take an extra step to help marine wildlife and their habitats by making a monthly pledge today. I have enclosed an enrollment form where you may indicate your monthly gift preference and a reply envelope for your convenience.

With your help we can strengthen the fight and together make important gains to protect marine wildlife and their habitats. Only with your support can we ensure that the decade we are about to enter becomes the one when we helped save our marine heritage.

Sincerely,

William Y. Brown
Chairman of the Board

This sustainer invitation letter gives a very clear explanation of how the monthly sustainer funds will be used. It also tells how the organization started the sustainer program. And there is a lot of excellent copy that flatters the donor for being invited to join this insider group. The donor is clearly asked with specific money amounts and is told what to expect each month. The letter also makes an excellent case for the overall needs of the organization.

SUSTAINER INVITATION LETTER— WORLD WILDLIFE FUND

Dear World Wildlife Fund Member,

I am writing you today to extend my heartfelt "Thank You."

<u>I am personally encouraged by your recent commitment to join WWF</u> and help us protect rapidly disappearing wildlife habitat and critically endangered species.

As I said in a previous letter to you, if we are to succeed, we need a core of committed members like you who are dedicated to moving beyond "just talk."

<u>You see, your membership participation is the path to action</u>. By contributing to World Wildlife Fund, you are part of a vast citizens' conservation force that can literally reach across the world to many remote areas most in need of our attention.

That's why I'd like to ask you the question, "<u>Are you willing to take the next step</u> to help ensure the survival of the world's remaining wildlife and their habitat?"

If you are, I invite you today to join a select group of members that we call the Guardians' Circle.

This special group of members has agreed to band together to make regular monthly contributions to support World Wildlife Fund's international wildlife-saving projects.

<u>This is an especially critical time right now and we desperately need to accelerate our work</u>. With regular monthly support we can invest more of our resources where they can bring the highest and most enduring returns for future generations.

And I think you, more than anyone, know exactly what is at stake.

<u>Right now, WWF's main priority and greatest conservation challenge is saving tropical forests</u>. I

Reprinted with permission, World Wildlife Fund.

can't emphasize that enough. I can't say it as forcefully as I know it must be said.

(Copy follows on the issue of rain forest decimation and what WWF is doing to prevent the tragedy.)

We must not let this tragedy happen!

Please take just a minute right now to consider
how critical your second step will be to the future
of the rain forests.

I've enclosed a WWF Guardians' Circle pledge form
for your convenience. Simply indicate the monthly
amount you can send and mail your completed form in
the postage-paid return envelope. As a member of our
Guardians' Circle, you will continue to receive your
bimonthly WWF newsletter, FOCUS, as well as regular
statements to provide you with a record of your
monthly support. I hope we can count on you to join
us in this worldwide campaign.

If each of us gets involved, we will have the
resources we need to protect the world's tropical
forests.

You have my heartfelt thanks for your continued
commitment.

                                        Sincerely,

                                        Kathryn S. Fuller
                                        President

P.S. I've set a goal of adding 2,800 new members
to our Guardians' Circle this year. And if each of
these new members give only $15 a month, we'd have
an additional half-million dollars this year alone
for our critically important wildlife, habitat and
resource protection projects.

P.P.S. I've enclosed some special information
about WWF's Convenient Giving Plan—please read it.

Here's a sustainer invitation that is sent to new donors. It appeals to the new donor to go the "second step." A very specific major problem is cited for the need, saving the world's threatened rain forests. In the P.S. a targeted goal is set and shows how substantial additional income can be achieved through a small number of donors giving on a monthly basis. World Wildlife Fund also allows donors to pledge through electronic funds transfer. These donors can elect not to receive any follow-up mailings at all. The donation is simply deducted from their bank account each month—a very nice tie-in with sustainer giving (See Chapter 21 for guidance on how to word the response form for the electronic funds transfer offer.).

13

Reactivating Donors with the Lapsed Donor Letter

In regard to former donors or members we're faced with a terminology problem. The words "lapsed" and "expired" tend to convey that people on a list with such a label are hardly breathing and probably not worth the effort of any further contact. Many alert fund-raisers, however, find these names to be much more responsive than any outside list so they mail them on a regular basis. In this chapter you'll learn just how to write a letter to reactivate lapsed donors. The truth is that people who have given to you previously but for various reasons haven't given in the last few years are generally a more productive list than any outside list you can rent. They're like a gold mine that's waiting to be worked a little bit more. Some gold nuggets still reside there if you will only take the time and trouble to dig for them. And the obvious advantage is that these are "your" names on which there are no list rental costs. Reactivating donors from the lapsed file will cost less than soliciting new donors from outside lists. That's why it's important to institute a regular series of reactivation efforts: direct mail and telemarketing.

The definition of what constitutes a lapsed donor varies from organization to organization. Many groups will consider that anyone who has given within the past 24 months is an active donor and the 25 + month donors are "lapsed." Here's how to determine what age donors should fall in the lapsed file. Analyze the results from your appeal mailings by recency (e.g., donors who gave 0–12 months, 13–24 months, 25–36 months). When the returns from the older names on your file become marginally productive, transfer them to the inactive file to receive the special lapsed donor efforts.

Before you send letters to your lapsed file, consider this important point. For these reactivation efforts to be successful, it's critical that the names on the lapsed list be kept up to date. (See Chapter 23 for information on how to correct addresses on an inactive list.) Periodically list-cleaning efforts should be made to make the latest address changes or deletions as appropriate. Some mass-mail fund-raisers will simply delete the names on which they receive an address change to save on list maintenance expenses. They've found it's cheaper just to delete the name from the file as opposed to keying in the new address. This decision should be based on the relative productiveness of the lapsed file. If your lapsed file is a highly responsive list, compared to outside lists, then the changes probably should be made. If this is not the case, then deletions are probably in order.

Why do lapsed letters work so well? For one reason you know you're writing to people who have an identified interest in your organization. And you also know they respond by direct mail. Those are two very important marketing pieces of information. The reason the lapsed donors haven't given recently may have nothing to do with their ongoing interest in your cause. It could have been simply that other needs and concerns temporarily crowded out the ability to give again to your work. But people's circumstances are always in a state of flux. That's why repeated follow-up efforts to former donors will be successful if done right.

You also have the "guilt factor" working for you. People don't like to turn down repeated requests to renew. But the people on the lapsed file have turned down a number of your previous renewal and special appeal solicitations. With the passage of a little time, their circumstances may be different, and they just may feel a little guilty about saying "no" so many times earlier. I experienced that feeling when, just after turning down a winsome telemarketer from my alma mater, I received a piece of fund-raising mail for the annual fund. I had some residual twangs of guilt from that telephone turn-down that worked to the advantage of the direct mail letter. And I sent in a gift. The point is: Don't ever give up on former donors until the results simply tell you it isn't worth mailing them any more.

When to Use the Lapsed Donor Letter

The lapsed donor letter is sent usually two to three months after the last regular renewal effort has been mailed. In one sense the lapsed letter series represents an extension of the renewal series with a time lapse period in between the two types of letters. Do not let the expired names stay on your file for too long a period before any reactivation activity begins. The longer you wait, the colder the names become. Some time needs to pass before you start promoting expired names, but a two to three-month period is about right.

How to Write the Lapsed Donor Letter

1. FEATURE THE COPY THEME THAT ATTRACTED THE DONOR IN THE FIRST PLACE.

You have in your possession one strategic bit of information. If you have coded your file by the original package or theme that sold your donor you can utilize a similar theme to reactivate that individual. Your donor's basic desires and interests are probably pretty much the same. Use that theme but couched in a copy framework that indicates you know you are dealing with an old friend.

2. TELL THE LAPSED DONOR YOU MISS HIM OR HER.

All of us value friendships. We don't enjoy terminating a relationship with someone we like. This same feeling pervades a lapsed member of a charitable organization. At one time they valued what you did—and supported their concern with a gift. You valued that involvement and you miss the person not only because of the drop-off in giving but because you've lost a valued partner in your work. It is appropriate and effective to tell the former donor how you feel about having one less supporter.

3. RESELL THE BENEFITS.

If you have benefits of value such as a colorful magazine and visiting privileges at a museum, resell them. And one of the important benefits is the positive emotions attached to your cause. See how these feelings are rekindled in the two sample letters at the end of this chapter—The National Parks and Conservation Association and The Navy League.

In earlier chapters of this book we've seen that featuring member benefits is a good way to acquire the new donor. There's no need to abandon this approach when writing to former member/donors. As the old saying goes, "If you've got it (benefits), flaunt it (benefits)!"

4. UPDATE MEMBER/DONOR ON THE CURRENT STATE OF YOUR CAUSE.

You can't assume former donors are up to date on the latest happenings in your field. As a matter of fact, an update of this sort is a good copy platform or reason for writing. It's an easy way to demonstrate your concern for the former donor—that you want to keep a valued friend apprised of what's going on in your field. This is an age of information. Your lapsed donor letter can key in on this need very effectively.

5. MAKE A "WELCOME-BACK" OFFER.

It never hurts to sweeten the offer a little bit, especially for a former member. For some unknown reason they have not given recently. Mainly you want to get them back in the habit of writing out checks to your organization. A special offer, such as a half-price membership discount or a special premium, is a good idea. Once the person is back in the fold, so to speak, he or she will start getting special appeals and other mailings. These efforts will be the ones to solicit the larger gifts. The primary goal of the reactivation letter is to restore the former donor to an active status. A special welcome-back offer is a good way to accomplish this objective.

6. ASK FOR A "YES" OR "NO" DECISION.

A simple survey response is effective with reactivation letters. Basically you're trying to get the former donor thinking about your work again, and it is hoped, a gift will come along too. However, you may learn some strategic bits of information from former donors. They could very well have some answers that will help you do a better job of writing your appeal letters to your donors. There may be some objection that you haven't adequately covered in your copy. Former donors can supply you with some good field intelligence. It is always flattering to be asked to help. It conveys that you still believe the former donor is a valued member of the team, even if a recent gift hasn't been made. Respect that knowledge of your former donor, and gifts will follow.

MODEL LETTER—LAPSED DONOR—
LOCAL PRESERVATION SOCIETY

Dear former member of the Middletown Preservation Society,

FEATURE THE COPY THEME THAT ATTRACTED THE DONOR IN THE FIRST PLACE (POINT 1)

What do you see when you drive through Middletown today?

Do you see things that bother you? Uncollected trash here and there? Zoning violations?

RESELL THE BENEFITS (POINT 3)

It's my guess that you joined MPS in the first place to fix what was wrong in our town—and to make things more beautiful.

TELL THE LAPSED DONOR YOU MISS HIM OR HER (POINT 2)

Well, that's why we want you back! We miss you!

Because your clout and financial support are what keeps our streets clean and our parks beautiful, and our city a great place in which to live.

UPDATE MEMBER/DONOR ON THE CURRENT STATE OF YOUR CAUSE (POINT 4)

Have you driven past the empty lot on Main Street? Now it's a new park—thanks to MPS. And the big house on Pleasant Street is preserved as an MPS project. You've probably noticed that the garish signs on Park Avenue are gone—thanks to MPS pressure on the zoning committee.

And the big recycling effort that is the right thing to do and saves the city money—that's an MPS initiative, too.

But we could do more—and we need to. Because we must stay vigilant to pressures to diminish our city's beauty.

Won't you join us again? We miss you and need you—and your city needs you.

MAKE A "WELCOME-BACK" OFFER (POINT 5)

Please join us again, now, with the enclosed card, which features a special "welcome-back" dues discount of $10. So when you drive through the city again, you can take pride in being part of creating the beauty that makes Middletown so special.

Sincerely,

Mildred Jones
President

ASK FOR A "YES" OR "NO" DECISION (POINT 6)

P.S. We would welcome you back, but even if you can't rejoin now, please return the card to me with your answer, so we can avoid bothering you with more requests. Thanks.

FORMER MEMBER LETTER—
NATIONAL PARKS AND CONSERVATION ASSOCIATION

Dear Former Member,

Do I have reason to worry?

We've written several times now, asking you to renew your NPCA membership and . . .

. . . now your membership has expired.

Please take a moment while you have this reminder in hand to renew your membership. We need you!

Maybe I haven't said it strongly enough—as strongly as it must be said—but your dues are NPCA's lifeblood.

Your dues enable NPCA to buy critical lands adjacent to, and sometimes inside of, National Parks to keep them out of the hands of developers.

Your dues allow NPCA to protect threatened and endangered species like the Florida panther, grizzly, bald eagle, mountain lion, wolf, sea otters, and more.

Your dues permit NPCA to develop school programs and educate Americans of all ages about how to use, enjoy, and care for their parks.

Your dues enable NPCA to fight in the halls of power here in Washington to protect our National Park System's living mask of green for ourselves and future generations to enjoy.

All this is to say that your renewed support really is critical.

So please, convince me that I have no need to worry.

Take a moment right now to renew your membership in NPCA.

Renewing is easy.

Just complete the enclosed Annual Renewal Statement and return it along with your tax-deductible dues check. Today if at all possible.

```
            Sincerely,


            Paul C. Pritchard
            President
```

This organization sends out a series of renewal letters. This "former member" letter is a blend between a very late renewal effort and a lapsed member reactivation letter. It illustrates how important it is to begin promoting lapsed names fairly soon after the renewal series stops. There's a nice, but brief, recap of what dues accomplish and a strong pitch to renew, which, as the letter states, "is easy."

LAPSED DONOR LETTER—
THE NAVY LEAGUE

From the Office of Theodore Roosevelt

Dear Navy Leaguer:

When I first endorsed the idea of the Navy League—I had but one thought in mind: The building and maintaining in proper shape of the sea services.

And the Navy League can't do that without your support.

You see, it seems to me that all good Americans interested in the growth of their country and sensitive to its honor, should give hearty support to the policies for which the Navy League is founded.

Your membership . . . your support of this broad and farsighted ideal, is perhaps the best calling an individual can answer.

Only with your continued participation can the sea services of your great nation thrive and survive to adequately defend American interests.

It is with heartfelt pride that I ask for your help in this most important endeavor. I am most proud of our sea services and the place of honor they have in our nation's history. I am proud of the job that they perform today—and will unswervingly do in the future.

Share with me this symbol of our collective patriotism, and begin anew your dedication to the Navy League.

Sincerely,

Theodore Roosevelt

This award-winning letter to lapsed donors illustrates a very important point in writing effective copy. When you get the copy platform right,

Reprinted with permission, The Navy League.

the rest is easy. It was an extremely clever idea to have the letter signed by a long-since-dead president who was the founder of The Navy League. This fascinating approach got the attention of the former donor and made the copy fairly easy to write. A little whimsy was used on the outside envelope with the teaser line: Delayed Mail! Learn from this one. Do some hard creative thinking first, then write. You'll be amazed at the results you can get.

Part III

Letters That Accomplish
Special Purposes

There are a number of other letters you will need to write to balance out your fund-raising program. So far in this book we have looked at letters that make a direct ask for a contribution—either a first time gift or a repeat contribution. These are your "front-line" letters that get the job done, so to speak. They raise the money to support your work. At the same time you need to have some other letters backing up these front-line letters. And, as in every good military campaign, victory can turn on the effectiveness of your "behind-the-lines" support.

In this part you're going to see what other types of support letters you will need to write and how to write them, and as in Parts One and Two, you'll get actual samples of these letters that you can adapt for your own needs. For example, you may want to ask your donor/members for special help in terms of suggesting names of referrals. Or you may want to ask them to become activists or volunteers in your work. For very special needs you will want to make a funding request to a foundation or a corporation. You'll see just how these letters should be drafted. And then there are the "housekeeping" type of letters: how to acknowledge new gifts and how to answer complaints and other correspondence from your donors. You'll see all these types of letters and more in this part. Each chapter gives you information on when to write these letters and how to write them. Just one effective letter from this part could pay big dividends in all your efforts to raise the maximum amount of funds for your cause. Be sure to study these carefully.

14

Adding to Your Donor/Member List with the Referral Letter

Donors to your organization can help you in a number of ways. They can make additional gifts as we saw in Part Two. Now, in Part Three we'll review special additional nonmoney ways that donors can come to the aid of your cause. It should be clear by now that the cultivation of your existing donors is one of the most productive activities you can engage in as a fund-raiser, whether it's to ask for financial support or some other sort of help. In this chapter we're going to look at a very strategic way that your donors can provide immeasurable assistance to your program, that is, by sending you a list of referrals that you, in turn, can invite to join or support your work. Each of your donors has a circle of friends about whom they have intimate knowledge—knowledge, for example, about which of these friends would be likely prospects for giving to your work. That's why it makes a lot of sense to ask your active donors from time to time for names of friends whom you might contact for membership.

Here's why referral name promotion is so significant. For many organizations, acquiring the names of prospects is expensive. And the reality for many organizations is that the supply of outside rental names is very limited. This is especially true for organizations that have a fairly specialized area of interest. One such organization is The National Association of Railroad Passengers. This group with a highly targeted market has found that the referral name letter is an excellent way to acquire new members with an interest in promoting better intercity rail passenger service. Look at it this way. Assume for the moment that you are a specialized nonprofit organization with a list of only 12,000 donors, and that a good outside list rental market just doesn't exist for you. But it's a fair assumption that each of your existing 12,000 donors knows a number of people who might be logical prospects. The trick is to first solicit those referral names from your existing donors, and then to follow-up with well-written referral letters. That's what you're going to learn in this chapter.

When to Use the Referral Name Letter

We first have to ask the question, "When is the best time to solicit names of prospects from your existing donors?" That will determine when we should send the referral name solicitation letter to your donors. There are a number of times when your current donors should be asked to send you names of referrals. One of the best times is shortly after the donor has sent you an initial contribution. From my experience, that is when the donor's interest in your organization is at a peak level. Then too it makes sense to regularly poll your members throughout the year. Your donors will have conversations with friends and attend various functions throughout the year when they come in contact with good prospects. So my suggestion as to when to ask your current donors for referrals is as follows: *First*, shortly after they have sent the first gift. This can be done as a separate letter request or incorporated in your new donor acknowledgment mailing. *Second*, include inserts asking for referrals in your regular newsletter and other informational mailings. It's not a good idea to ask for referrals in your special appeal mailings that ask for a gift. By doing this you give your donor too many options and a possible "out" not to send a gift. It's better to include the referral name request when it doesn't compete with your direct appeal for a financial gift.

How to Write the Referral Name Letter

Here are the essentials to include in the referral name letter sent to prospects that an existing donor sends in.

1. MENTION THE NAME OF THE DONOR WHO REFERRED YOUR PROSPECT.

This is the most critical element of the referral letter. There exists a personal relationship between your donor and the prospect he or she referred. Using the nominator's name adds a high degree of personal interest to the referral letter and is one of the main reasons why its response is so high. I have tested referral name letters with and without the name of the donor-nominator and have found that mentioning the name of the donor-nominator doubles the response. In the name solicitation model letter at the end of this chapter (that is, the letter you send to your donors asking for referral names) you'll see how to write the letter to get the donor's approval of using his or her name. There will be a handful of donors who will tell you not to use their name, and, of course, it's important to honor this request. However, for the great majority of your donors, they will allow you to use their name if you phrase the request as you see it in the model letter.

2. EMPHASIZE THE EXCLUSIVE NATURE OF THE NOMINATION.

It's important to bear in mind you are writing to a very special person. After all, this person has been nominated by a personal friend. In your letter you should convey the privilege it is just to have been selected for the receipt of the letter. It really is the case and it adds a lot of interest to the copy.

3. INCORPORATE CONTROL COPY ELEMENTS IN THE LETTER.

The sales points that attracted the donor nominator will probably appeal to the referral prospect. You are writing to people with similar interests as your existing donors. That's why using elements from the control letter that attracted your current donors makes a lot of sense.

4. FEATURE THE BENEFITS OF MEMBERSHIP.

If your organization has tangible benefits, they should be stressed in this type of a letter. The conferring of benefits is a natural tie-in with nomination. It tends to give validity to the nomination.

5. SEND THE LETTER RIGHT AFTER RECEIVING THE REFERRAL.

While this isn't a writing suggestion, it is an important point. For whatever reason, referral names have a short "shelf life." Once a donor has sent you a referral he or she is apt to mention it to the nominee. So, if your letter comes on the heels of this personal discussion, you stand a much better chance of getting a response.

6. FOLLOW-UP THE REFERRAL WITH AT LEAST TWO LETTERS.

In the model letters that follow you will see how to write two follow-up letters. A second follow-up letter works well because of the high response that you typically get from two efforts. Experience shows that two mailings produce anywhere from a 5 to 12 percent response. This is many times better than normal outside list mailings, and it generates members/donors from a quality source. These are members who are likely to renew and keep on giving for years. But don't throw away the names of the people who don't respond to the two-effort series. They should be added to your prospect file and be regularly promoted for membership and/or contributions in your regular mailing program. You have already paid for keying them into your file so subsequent promotions to them will be done at a very low cost.

MODEL LETTER—
SOLICITING REFERRAL NAMES FROM EXISTING DONORS

Dear Member,

There's a simple but important way you can help us grow the membership of _____—that is, by suggesting names of your friends who would have an interest in our work.

As a donor/member you are familiar with the mission of _____. (Provide a sentence on what your organization does.) And I'm sure you have acquaintances who, like you, identify with these goals—and who would appreciate receiving some membership materials and an invitation to join.

We have found from experience that members acquired through the recommendation of existing members—like yourself—are really the best source of long-term support. (Note: This paragraph is the way to tell your donor that you plan to use his or her name in the referral letter.) When we send our membership invitations to carefully selected nominations, we can limit our "mass mailings," which, as you know, are expensive. By contrast the nominations mailing is the most cost effective way we have of increasing our membership. And our support.

To nominate your friends, simply list their names and addresses on the reverse side and return this letter in the enclosed postage-paid envelope. That's all there is to it. We do the rest. We'll simply send out membership information to your friends along with an invitation to join.

And if you send us five or more names, we'll send you a little "thank-you" gift I think you will enjoy. (Describe gift.)

I want you to know how much we value your involvement with _____. I hope you can help us now in this special membership drive. If we were to acquire only one new member for each existing member we could double our support overnight.

I look forward to receiving your list of nominees. Please accept my thanks for this special help.

Sincerely,

(Side two of letter requesting referral names from existing donors)

I am pleased to nominate the following individuals for membership in _____. I understand I am under no obligation by forwarding these names. Please send each of the listed friends information on _____ and an invitation to join.

(Leave spaces for listing names and addresses.)

(Note: Put an asterisk at name #5 with note: For sending five or more names you will receive a free gift of _____.)

(Note: A simple one-page letter with spaces on the reverse side for your current donors to list the referral names and addresses is all that is needed to collect these names. And it is helpful—but not essential—to offer a small premium for sending in five or more names. Your goal is to acquire logical prospects, so don't suggest that your member give as many names as possible. You want only the ones who are good prospects and ones that the donor's name has some meaning to.)

MODEL LETTER—
FIRST FOLLOW-UP TO REFERRAL NAMES

Dear Member-Elect,

MENTION THE NAME OF THE DONOR WHO REFERRED YOUR PROSPECT (POINT 1)

I am pleased to inform you that one of our members, _____, has nominated you for membership in _____.

We recently asked a few of our special friends to nominate individuals who, they felt, were concerned about (state goals of your work.)

EMPHASIZE THE EXCLUSIVE NATURE OF THE NOMINATION (POINT 2)

You can feel proud that your friend considered you for such an honor. Members of _____ form a very special group of insiders who are interested in _____. While your support at this time is especially needed, you should know that your membership will provide you with a number of new benefits.

FEATURE THE BENEFITS OF MEMBERSHIP (POINT 4)

As a new member of _____, you will be entitled to:

(List all major benefits and privileges.)

Your new membership nomination comes at a particularly important time for us. Right now we're in the process of adding to our support base in order to accomplish some important new goals. For example, . . . (State current goals).

Please take a moment now to return your membership acceptance form. It's not necessary to include payment with your response. But we do need to hear from you soon.

And, as a special way of welcoming you to our membership, we will mail you a copy of _____ as soon as we receive your membership acceptance.

On behalf of the Board of Trustees—and on behalf of your nominating friend—I look forward to welcoming you to membership.

Sincerely,

MODEL LETTER—
SECOND FOLLOW-UP TO REFERRAL NAMES

(Three weeks after sending out the first follow-up, it's important to mail a "simulated" carbon copy follow-up. This means a carbon of the original printed on light yellow stock with a written-out statement at the head of the letter. The normal letterhead can be dropped to the bottom of the letter to make room for this written-out statement. When you mail the follow-up only three weeks after the original, it's not necessary to remove the responses from the first mailing. Recipients will understand that the letters crossed in the mail. And by using the statement below you will avoid complaint letters. Here's how to word the written-out statement on the carbon.)

    There's still time to join _____ and receive
a free copy of _____. But I must hear from you
soon. That's why I'm sending you this copy of my
recent letter. If our letters crossed in the mail,
please accept my thanks. But if you haven't responded
yet, I urge you to do so soon. There has never been a
time when support for (name of organization) is more
needed.

REFERRAL NAME ACQUISITION LETTER—
NATIONAL ASSOCIATION OF RAILROAD PASSENGERS

Dear NARP Member,

It's a pleasure to report to you that NARP has almost doubled its membership in the last two years. Our current total is 7,000.

With this larger constituency, NARP is gaining greater recognition for its basic thrust . . . to see that our country gets an improved rail passenger service. A dramatic example of this was the May 8 appearance of our Executive Director, Ross Capon, on Walter Cronkite's CBS-TV Evening News, responding to Secretary Adams' proposal to eliminate 25% of Amtrak's route miles.

Even with our nice membership increase, however, one of my goals is to increase the NARP membership even more. With your help I think this is an attainable goal.

Here's what I am asking you—and your fellow members—to do:

Send NARP the names of your friends and acquaintances who share your concern about improving our nation's rail passenger service. We would like to invite them—as your nominees—to join NARP.

There are a growing number of citizens who are beginning to see why an expanded rail service is a vital key to solving our nation's energy and transportation problems. The challenge is to locate these logical membership prospects without excessive cost.

If you—along with all our other members—were to send us just five names, NARP would have 35,000 excellent prospects. Many of these people will join NARP after learning of our successful action-oriented programs.

It will take just a few moments to come up with these names. Consider that fellow associate at work,

Reprinted with permission, National Association of Railroad Passengers.

a friend who rides the commuter train with you, a
neighbor, some friends from your Christmas card list,
or a fellow club member.

   Simply list these names on the reverse side of
this letter. There's no obligation to you or your
nominees. You send us the names. We do the inviting.
Please accept my thanks for your help.

       Sincerely,

       Orren Beaty, President
       NARP

    This nonprofit, with a specialized type of membership, successfully uses the referral name approach. A case is made as to why more members would help. It clearly tells the goals, how to send the names, and the benefits that will result from more members. The reverse side of the letter provided spaces for listing up to ten names of referrals. See the next sample letter on how these names were followed up.

REFERRAL NAME FOLLOW-UP LETTER—
NATIONAL ASSOCIATION OF RAILROAD PASSENGERS

Dear _____ ,

It is a pleasure to inform you that you have been nominated for membership in the National Association of Railroad Passengers by (name of member-nominator).

By accepting this nomination you will be lending your support to the rail passenger's only full-time representative in Washington. NARP's eleven years' work are marked by solid accomplishment. We have played major roles, among other things in: (achievements cited . . . .)

As a member you will receive some tangible benefits as well. Each month you will be mailed the members-only newsletter . . . to keep you up-to-date on legislation and actions affecting good rail service. You'll be issued a NARP member's card showing your support of our goals. (See enclosed brochure.) NARP's Washington office can take up, directly with the Amtrak officials responsible, any problem which you have using their service.

And you'll be invited to attend our regional meetings.

Citizens of all economic levels should be able to travel from one part of the nation to another—in reasonable comfort—at rates they can afford. And I'm sure you're aware of the important part good passenger trains must play in any overall program to cut energy consumption and improve the quality of life.

To make your acceptance of this invitation as attractive as possible at this time we're offering you one full year of membership in the National Association of Railroad Passengers at the reduced rate of $10 (one-third off the regular rate).

Reprinted with permission, National Association of Railroad Passengers.

To accept your membership nomination submitted by our member, simply complete the enclosed acceptance form and return it in the postpaid envelope. There's no need to enclose your payment unless you prefer. We'll be happy to bill you later.

Make sure to clearly print your name and address exactly as you want them to appear on the membership card you will receive from the National Association of Railroad Passengers.

Sincerely,

Orren Beaty, President
NARP

This excellent letter and just one follow-up letter produced a 12 percent response from the nominees. It does all the right things. It mentions the name of the member-nominator. It tells how the cause will be advanced and what individual benefits the member will receive. Finally, it sweetens the offer with a reduced price membership rate and a bill-me option.

15

Obtaining Financial Support with the Foundation and Corporate Request Letter

Almost all nonprofit organizations hope to receive some degree of support from foundations and corporations. This is understandable, because in the United States, there are over 30,000 active private and community foundations. There are also more than 2,500 corporations that actively support philanthropic endeavors. Wise nonprofit agencies try to develop a broad base of support, including foundation and corporate grants. For newer nonprofit agencies, foundation and corporate support may be quite substantial during their start-up years. The immediate net income from these grants can be much more substantial than that from any other source and help get the nonprofit off the ground. Of course, it's wise to plumb all sources of contribution income. Foundations and corporations like to see this diversity of support realizing that they won't be saddled with a nonprofit for years and years. Foundations and corporations want their grant investment to help strengthen a nonprofit's effectiveness. They do not want to foster dependency.

Remember, foundations, trusts, and corporations that want to give financial help are targeted by dozens of nonprofits. Each wants support. Therefore, the requests become competitive. In fact, some trusts and foundations will say that grant requests will be reviewed on a competitive basis. Even when they don't say that, it is part of the selection and evaluating process. And, most often, you are not privy to the competition or the alternative opportunities for a grantmaker to become involved. All the more reason to use the letters and follow the suggestions for writing the foundation and corporation request letters outlined in this chapter.

We're going to look at the type of letter to write to get a positive relationship started with the institutional giving entity. It's clear, however, that the first letter of inquiry is just the beginning with these institutional givers. Very rarely do grants come in as a direct response to one letter request, especially if your nonprofit agency is not widely known. Once the door is opened with an effective letter, however, you stand a good chance of cultivating a relationship that will add thousands of dollars to your income. If you're fortunate enough to get a positive response to your first letter, be prepared to devote time and effort to cultivating the relationship. The aim is to develop a strong relationship. There also needs to be a marriage of interests between the institutional donor and your nonprofit's goals. If you are prepared to be in it for the long haul, you will find that this can be one of your most cost-effective sources of new revenue.

Finally, be aware that the ultimate goal of letters to institutional givers and all the attendant follow-up that takes place is to develop trust. This trust must be based on integrity—the integrity of the program, the integrity of the agency requesting help, and the integrity of the person writing the letter or making a personal face-to-face presentation.

When to Use the Foundation/Corporate Request Letter

Let's make a point by indicating the worst time to send such a letter. If your organization is faced with a current financial emergency and you need a quick infusion of cash, forget about writing to a foundation or corporation. If nothing else, this timing tells the recipient that your group is not well managed.

The short answer to the question on "When to write the first letter of inquiry?" is, "When you have done your homework!" It helps to read all you can about a foundation, its history, stated objectives, interests, limitations, deadlines for queries, and application for grants. And whenever possible, you should scrutinize the kinds of grants a foundation has given to over the last two years.

Some foundations will only consider grants at a certain time of the year. Others consider requests continuously. And still others have two, three, or four periods of the year when grants are received and reviewed. For corporate inquiries it is important to know when their fiscal year ends. Again, many corporations have someone who handles the grant inquiries.

There is now a *Who Gets Grants/Who Gives Grants Guide,* 2nd edition. This publication lists 17,000 nonprofit organizations and more than 50,000 grants. It is also helpful to subscribe to publications such as *The Chronicle of Philanthropy* that gives the latest news on grants that have been made. Possibly the best source for directories and handbooks about grant makers is the New York–based agency, The Foundation Center (79 Fifth Avenue, New York, NY 10003-3076, Telephone 1-800-424-9836; in N.Y. State 212-620-4230). The Center provides free walk-in service to the public and has a large range of resources and files about foundations and corporations pertinent to philanthropy. For those wanting a resource for grants to aid religious causes, there is *The National Guide to Funding in Religion*. It gives more than 4,000 foundations and details about 3,600 grants. For those working with senior citizens, there is *The National Guide to Funding in Aging, 3rd Edition* that gives a customized list of grants made. Another directory is called *The National Guide to Funding for Women and Girls, 2nd Edition*. In this resource, 1,000 foundations and corporations are listed and all of these have a specific interest in women and girls. Then there are guides for funding for children, youth, families, the economically disadvantaged, AIDS, alcohol or drug abuse, environmental protection, and many others.

On the corporate side there is *The National Directory of Corporate Giving* that gives information on 2,300 corporate philanthropic programs. One outstanding fund-raiser that I heard of also made it a point to study a particular corporation's financial statements prior to making an appeal. When your letter comes on the heels of an excellent financial year for the corporation, your letter is bound to get a better reception.

There are a large number of corporations that help projects in their communities or sphere of influence. Therefore, appealing to that interest of a corporation cannot be overstated. This is often true where grants are needed for a particular program that is of concern to the citizenry of a certain community or for buildings, such as a communications center, a music library, or some other facility that a nonprofit wants support for within the immediate vicinity of the corporation. Sharing the dream for a building by way of an artist's impression of the proposed facility can ignite the imagination of even the most harried corporate CEO.

Sometimes, the interests of a foundation will be expressed with important variations depending upon the directory where listed. In a regional directory you may find some of the interests expressed by a certain foundation varying from the entry in the national directory. That difference can be crucial. That's why it's important to dig a little deeper by looking at the state directories as well. For example, *The Alabama Directory* lists about 200 foundations, while *The Guide to California Foundations* has over 600 foundations listed. Your local library with its interlibrary abilities is an excellent resource for information.

When you've done sufficient homework to know that a project or program you want financed matches the concern or interest of the institutional giver, then a letter of inquiry is in order.

How to Write the Letter of Inquiry to a Foundation or Corporation

In Chapter 10 we considered the techniques of writing to major individual donors. These writing tips also apply to writing to foundations and corporations. But here are some special points to keep in mind:

1. LIMIT THE LENGTH OF THE LETTER.

Generally speaking in fund-raising, the longer letters do best (see Chapter 22). This is not the case, however, in writing your first letter of inquiry to foundations or corporations. A letter of one to three pages is advised. The goal of this first letter is to let the giving entity know that you have a project that fits in with its stated goals. Primarily you're looking for a response that says, "Tell us more, there may be some interest on our part." Avoid the temptation to tell a complete history of your organization and its accomplishments. You simply are trying to get over the first hurdle in what will be a longer race to the finish line. A short, interesting first letter is what is called for.

2. DO YOUR HOMEWORK.

Show that you have done your due diligence and that you know something about the foundation or corporation and the kinds of projects/programs they have assisted. Make sure the program you want funded falls within the framework of projects the foundation has supported in the past. Some foundations have very specific guidelines. Doing your homework will indicate whether you need to ask for these guidelines. It is important to find out the name of the person to whom the grant inquiry is to be sent. Some foundations have a number of divisions that handle particular categories of grant requests. Before writing you need to know the right division and the person responsible for receiving your grant inquiry. Then too you will want to read the foundation's program statements and giving policies. Learn its preferences and limitations. For example, some foundations do not give for buildings or scholarships while others do. These are the kinds of vital application facts you need to research before writing.

3. AVOID THE FORMULA APPROACH.

It's easy for a seasoned institutional executive to detect letters that reveal the writer has taken a "how to approach foundations" course or workshop. Your letter, on the other hand, should be sincere, specific, and spontaneous. Your conviction and enthusiasm should shine through. Remember, even though you are writing to an institutional giver, the letter is going to one individual who has feelings and emotions that can and should be touched. Inquiry letters should be businesslike but have heart and soul to them. Avoid tired phrases and cliches. As Robert Reekie, Executive Director of Media Associates International, was told by one foundation executive, "Don't expect the foundation to get enthusiastic or to catch your vision if you don't get that across in how and what you say." This foundation executive went on to say that the most frequent disappointment for him was the lack of vision and vitality in many proposals he had received! Even the toughest executive can be reached when the heart is touched and the mind is given the sup-porting data. Eliciting giving by corporate and foundation people—as it is in almost all types of fund-raising letters you have seen in this book—requires a combination of the emotional and rational.

4. FOLLOW UP WITH THE KEY EXECUTIVE TO LEARN THE AREAS OF GREATEST INTEREST.

A face-to-face meeting with the key executive is important. Here you will learn what really interests that person in terms of making grants. The CEO of a corporation is frequently 100 percent involved in what organi-zations get money and who he or she will listen to. Corporations tend to give to community-building projects and ventures that have a relation-ship to their employees and their product sales. With the corporation you should look for ways that your project meets these criteria. Also, CEOs are often more guided by the heart than the head when it comes to giv-ing money. In other words money is given to what he or she has a per-sonal interest in or a program/project that touches a deep responsive chord.

5. DON'T BE DISCOURAGED BY TURN-DOWNS.

Learn as much as you can from turn-downs. Next year or another time a door may open at that very foundation. Respond in a positive manner to a refusal and say what you can to keep the channels of communication open. You'll see a letter at the end of this chapter (Media Associates to the XYZ Foundation) that turned out to provide a lot of good counsel and eventual financial help to the requesting charity. But it didn't result in an immediate gift. Excellent follow-up correspondence from Media Associates International finally was productive. No response at all on your part to an initial turn-down may be misinterpreted as a lack of interest in pursuing the project another day. While a good letter to a foundation may not bring a grant, it can produce some tangible benefits or provide you with invaluable suggestions for other sources of possible funding. Follow up on all these suggestions.

MODEL LETTER—CORPORATE REQUEST—
HEALTH GROUP

Dear Mr. Jones:

AVOID THE FORMULA APPROACH (POINT 3)

In the battle to cut rising health care expenses, the two biggest potential areas of cost-cutting are prevention and early detection of disease.

HealthWagon is dedicated to early detection of disease through regionwide health screening for diabetes, many kinds of cancer, tuberculosis, childhood diseases, and the "silent killer," hypertension.

The benefit to you as an employer could be enormous in cutting health care costs. The benefit to the entire region and your customers would be equally as great.

But comprehensive health screening depends on funding. It can't be done just by volunteers. And equipment and getting test results is labor intensive and costly.

Yet none of these is nearly so costly as the diseases they detect early.

DO YOUR HOMEWORK (POINT 2)

In view of your past support of the Heart Foundation and the Cancer Society, and the fact that each of your stores has a high blood pressure self-test station, I felt that I should speak to you about the possibility of funding one of our HealthWagons.

The wagon—actually a 2 1/2 ton truck—would have your corporate name and logo on it and would travel throughout our area to schools and places of work and worship, offering screening for many diseases.

**FOLLOW UP WITH THE KEY EXECUTIVE TO LEARN THE AREAS OF GREATEST INTEREST
(POINT 4)**

May I contact you early next week to discuss this
further?

Thank you for your consideration.

Sincerely,

Wilson Smith
Executive Director
HealthWagon

MODEL LETTER—FOUNDATION REQUEST—
LITERACY GROUP

Dear Mr. Randolph:

AVOID THE FORMULA APPROACH (POINT 3)
DO YOUR HOMEWORK (POINT 2)

Our research shows us that illiteracy in the tri-county area is concentrated in the inner city among older youth, and in the outer suburbs among middle-aged and older adults. Sublevel reading skills are prevalent in our affluent suburbs.

Yet here is a startling fact: Most people with low literacy skills believe society is thwarting them in their desire for a good job or a good college!

The bottom line is this: literacy skills are at an all-time low in our area, likely to get worse without concentrated action, and those without the needed skills are not aware of their problem.

We have learned that the Smith Family Foundation has a strong history of supporting education and literacy projects, as well as projects that assume a high literacy level, such as your Science-In-Schools project. Your recent grant to the English as a Second Language organization carried on in that vein.

We would like to approach your foundation with an idea for an innovative advertising campaign that will dramatize literacy deficiencies to those who need added skills, but who are not fully aware of their need, so they will seek out help. Our initial idea would be to put current job applications filled out by typical students in an ad and show that these don't make the grade. We are also planning a radio advertising campaign on country music and soft rock stations.

These are only two ideas. The concept is to reach those who will be a drag on the economy all their lives unless they improve their skills in language and reading.

FOLLOW UP WITH THE KEY EXECUTIVE TO LEARN THE AREAS OF GREAT INTEREST (POINT 4)

I would like to discuss this idea with you further to see if it is in line with the projects you fund. I will call you on the 25th to set a time we can meet.

Thanks for your consideration.

Sincerely,

Roger Danforth
Executive Director

FOUNDATION GRANT REQUEST—
MEDIA ASSOCIATES INTERNATIONAL

Dear _____,

Because of the ___ Foundation's interest in evangelical activities in missions and in evangelism, we are inquiring about making a grant application.

Media Associates International (MAI) is an evangelical 501(c)3 publicly supported Christian agency. We are assisting mission agencies in their literature ministries through editorial training, mission newsletter and magazine guidance, and help with strategic planning for increased effectiveness, through books and printed materials. One of the missions with whom we've had a long association of training assistance is the ___ Ministries.

We want to submit a request for a pilot literature evangelism project that an ___ missionary wants to test in a huge shopping mall in Bangkok. Although ___ does not have the money to put into this shopping mall outreach, they are supportive of the concept's possibilities and are encouraged by MAI's willingness to assist them in developing this innovative project. Ninety percent of Bangkok's 12 million population are Buddhist. They are virtually unreached by the traditional Christian bookstores (8 of them) in the city. The pilot project will place a book stall into a mall where a recent Burger King study showed that 80,000 shoppers come on any given day.

The cost of the project, including space rental, book stock, and staff for one year will be $12,000. We would like to submit a grant request for $4,000.

We look forward to receiving grant application forms and procedures. MAI is a member of IFMA and ECFA.

```
With  warm  Christian  greetings,


                                Sincerely,


                                Robert  B.  Reekie
                                President
```

This letter, while only one page, in its original form, gives clear evidence that the writer has done his homework. He has asked for support for a project that is in line with what the foundation is interested in. The fact that he is asking for only a third of the total needed communicates to the foundation that other funding sources will have a stake in the success of this project. He gives some relevant financial validation information by referring to known auditing agencies. And he asks for an application knowing that this letter of inquiry is only the first step in the process.

FOUNDATION GRANT REQUEST—
MEDIA ASSOCIATES INTERNATIONAL

Dear _____,

We are submitting this proposal to the XYZ Foundation because of their concern for agencies that are making known God's love within the harsh realities of the modern world.

Media Associates International (MAI) is a 501(c)3 publicly supported Christian agency. It was formed in 1985 with a mandate to foster and encourage relevant printed materials written by creative Christian men and women in Africa, Asia, and Latin America. MAI's commitment to training creative people to express God's love and concern for justice, is driven by the stark reality that very, very little writing by local Christians has been done.

In Africa, Asia, and Latin America (not to mention the former East European countries) less than 10% of all available Christian books are written by national authors. As a result, Christian leadership in places such as Africa is hurting because they do not have books and printed material that are derived from the soul and soil of Africa. Dr. _____ is one world Christian leader who is concerned deeply about the dearth of excellent Christian books written by national writers. For that reason he has encouraged the aims of MAI. Enclosed is a copy of his last letter to us.

Not only is there a dearth of nationally authored fact based Christian writing, but very little is being done to encourage story writing and novels authored by Africa Christians. To try to do something about this, MAI held the first Christian story writing training program in Ghana, West Africa last October. About 25 talented Christian men and women came for hands-on guidance. The group was led by an award winning Christian novelist, _____ and his

wife, _____, who is also a published author. From
that training program will come an anthology of short
stories by African writers.

Tied to fostering national authorship is another
top priority: the urgency for training African
Christian writers to become trainers of others. One
person who is willing to work with MAI in this training trainer program is Ghanian novelist _____.
Last November in Toronto, Canada, he received the
coveted British Commonwealth Prize for excellence for
his first novel. He is also managing editor of the
largest Ghanaian Christian magazine and is also a
newspaper columnist for a major newspaper in Kenya.
This author's creative writing talents were encouraged by MAI.

We need financial help to move forward with these
training programs for African writers and for training trainers. The need for this year is $15,000, and
we are asking for support of the XYZ Foundation.

The money will be used for the training programs
outlined in this letter. Our initial concentration
will be in West Africa with targeting in Ghana, Ivory
Coast, and Nigeria.

We will be pleased to submit a full proposal. We
hope our inquiry falls within the priorities of the
XYX Foundation, and if so we look forward to receiving the grant application package.

Thank you for considering our inquiry.

                              Sincerely,

                              Robert B. Reekie
                              President

P.S. Enclosed is our brochure and two recent
issues of our newsletter, <u>Profile</u>. MAI is a member of
IFMA and of ECFA.

This letter brought a favorable response, not an immediate grant but some very useful information. First, the foundation director was very positive on the programs of MAI on which funding was requested. But he went on to say that this foundation, located in the United States, was setting up an African foundation to handle such grants. So the first step was positive. MAI is hopeful that the strong link this letter forged will eventually result in a grant for its African work. The foundation also referred MAI to some other foundations that target gifts for such purposes. It illustrates that success with foundations comes over the long haul with well-targeted requests and with attention to follow-up.

16

Soliciting Nonmonetary Assistance with the Volunteer/ Activist Letter

Americans love to give. Individual charitable giving has been well in excess of $100 billion in recent years. It's important to realize that this strong underlying drive to give to nonprofit organizations is not restricted to money alone. There are some people who have such a deep interest in your work that they will also want to give of their time to aid your efforts by volunteering. Cause-oriented organizations call these individuals "activists." Activists volunteer their time to write letters to Congress, to make telephone calls, to participate in rallies and other special events, and in general to be available to do what you ask them to do when needed. Because these supporters will aid your efforts without any remuneration, their words speak loud and clear. They are individual citizens, exercising a very basic right, to speak up on behalf of a cause they hold dear.

Other charities need volunteers to serve as ushers in a theater group, docents at a museum, or clerks in a gift shop, for example. Local PTAs, scouting troops, and church groups—all need volunteers to make their efforts successful. And the time these volunteers contribute to your work is worth a significant amount of money. If you didn't have the volunteers, you'd have to raise funds to pay for staff. Let's take a look at some of the principles involved in writing letters to gain activists and volunteers for your work.

When to Use the Volunteer/Activist Letter

People are most likely to volunteer their time and services to your organization when their interest level is at a high point. That's logical, but the question remains, just when is that interest level at a high point? As we have seen in earlier chapters, for causes that solicit new members by direct mail, excitement about the work (not necessarily knowledge about the organization) is probably at a peak just after the prospect has made that key decision to send you an initial gift. People who have just joined a new group tend to be a lot more excited and enthusiastic than members who have been on the rolls for years. That's why a follow-up mailing to new donors a week or two after the first gift is an excellent time to solicit activist participation. However, some groups provide a check-off box on the initial new donor gift response form for activist volunteering. This is something that should be tested. From my experience I've found it's better to first get the new contributor safely in the fold and then shortly thereafter to write and ask for activist participation. The reason? It may be off-putting to some prospects on the initial effort to think that they may have to give time in addition to a gift. Most cause-oriented organizations find that no more than 10 percent of their total file will also volunteer to perform activist duties. So don't put what may seem like a negative in the minds of 90 percent of your prospects when they're considering making the initial gift.

Even though I recommend making the activist/volunteer pitch shortly after the first contribution, it's also important to keep the need for volunteers before your donors/members on an ongoing basis. Regular articles in a newsletter are effective in this regard. It's desirable to print testimonials of volunteers in different walks of life and just how they feel about helping out. People's circumstances are constantly changing, and you want to be in their minds at these critical junctures. For example, one of your donors may have just retired and is looking for some meaningful activity to occupy his or her time. Whether you write a special letter to your active donors asking for volunteers or you incorporate the request in a newsletter or some other type of mailing, there are certain points to be covered. Let's take a look at the best way to write these letters and announcements.

How to Write the Volunteer/Activist Letter

Most of the techniques that you learned earlier in writing letters to ask for gifts apply to letters that make a request for volunteers. Yet there are five major points that should be emphasized. Here they are:

1. DESCRIBE THE BENEFITS OF BEING A VOLUNTEER.

Think first in terms of what the donor will get out of volunteering time and effort. People do volunteer for the good feeling of helping a cause they believe in. They know inherently that some of the charities they support wouldn't function without volunteers. That's fundamental. But—as is true in the case of making a gift of money—donors like to know something of the personal benefits they will receive by volunteering. In fund-raising you never get too far from the "What's in it for me?" question. Talk with your current volunteers and find out just how they feel about what they do for you. Why do they do it? What's the best thing about it? When you ask for new volunteers put some of these emotions into your appeal. It will work.

2. OUTLINE THE DUTIES OF A VOLUNTEER.

People don't like to be surprised. And most people are a little suspicious anyway. So it's important to tell them in very specific terms what you want them to do. Also consider some easy ways of orientation to see if the volunteer prospect would really like it. Conduct special meetings so volunteer candidates can hear from those who are currently volunteers. There may be some nagging little questions that can easily be answered in such face-to-face sessions. Also, allow for flexibility to the extent that the volunteer can back out if he or she has a change of mind. You don't want to scare the volunteer-prospect away, making it sound like an irrevocable lifetime decision. At the same time you want to convey as much as possible the satisfaction and fun of being a volunteer.

3. PORTRAY THE VALUES TO THE ORGANIZATION THROUGH VOLUNTEERS.

What would happen if your organization had no volunteers? What indispensable services do volunteers perform so effectively? Give the donors who are interested in volunteering answers to these questions so they know just how vital a service they provide. It may be—as in the case of a girl scout troop or a local church or synagogue—that the work wouldn't be possible without volunteers.

4. ISSUE A SPECIFIC INVITATION.

In fund-raising we know it's important to make a specific request for the gift and to tell the prospect exactly how much you want. The very same principle applies to making a pitch for volunteers. Give a definite invitation and indicate specifically what kind of duties are requested. People may feel that volunteering is something that can be done at their option when they're up to it. You can overcome this built-in lethargy by outlining a very specific need. It is also helpful to include a deadline for getting their response.

5. SHOW APPRECIATION FOR THE VOLUNTEER.

Don't assume the volunteers know just how much you appreciate their efforts. Tell them. And tell them frequently. And it's not a bad idea to hold special functions just for volunteers to show you value them. Probably one of the biggest benefits of volunteering is the good feeling of being an integral part of an important group in the community. It's not a bad idea to give volunteers pins or some other recognition items that they can use to make known their affiliation with your cause. They probably are the best spokespersons for your work. Give them a little help in reaching out to others in the community who would be influenced by the volunteers' testimonials.

MODEL LETTER—VOLUNTEER APPEAL—
SCHOOL SUPPORT ASSOCIATION

Dear Parent,

How would you like to earn $100 for an hour's work on Saturday May 8th at the Elm Street School Fun Fair?

<u>Of course</u> there's a catch!

You do the work . . . the money goes to Elm Street School Association.

PORTRAY THE VALUES TO THE ORGANIZATION THROUGH VOLUNTEERS (POINT 3)

But here's the good part. The work is easy, and the money from the Fair goes to buy important things for Elm Street School that aren't in the budget.

OUTLINE THE DUTIES OF A VOLUNTEER (POINT 2)
PORTRAY THE VALUES TO THE ORGANIZATION THROUGH VOLUNTEERS (POINT 3)

So, for an hour running the ring toss or Moon Bounce or fish-for-pennies games at the Fun Fair, you can play a real part in making sure that all our children have the books—videos—field trips—posters—they need for a rich, productive school experience.

The fact is, if it weren't for last year's Fun Fair, there would have been <u>NO</u> computer classes this school year. So you can see that it's more than a Fun Fair. It's the best (and most fun) way to make Elm Street School all we want it to be for our kids.

ISSUE A SPECIFIC INVITATION (POINT 4)

And that is why we need <u>you</u> for one hour on Saturday the 8th, any time from 9:00 A.M. to 4:00 P.M. And the earlier you sign up, the better the chances you get to have the assignment and time you want.

We're making it even easier for our "money-makers" this year. When you come to the Fun Fair, you'll see a <u>Volunteer Center</u> near the entrance. Just come there, and we'll make sure you have everything you need to make your job easier.

ISSUE A SPECIFIC INVITATION (POINT 4)

Please look at the form on the back of this letter. Fill in your first, second, and third choices for times and jobs and have your child return it to school tomorrow.

We'll contact you by phone to verify your choice before the 4th of May.

SHOW APPRECIATION FOR THE VOLUNTEER (POINT 5)

Thanks for helping. Without special people like yourself Elm Street wouldn't be the outstanding school it is in our county. I look forward to thanking you personally when you come.

See you on the 8th.

Sincerely,

Signed
PTA President
Elm Street School Assoc.

MODEL LETTER—VOLUNTEER APPEAL— COMMUNITY CHURCH

Dear Member,

ISSUE A SPECIFIC INVITATION (POINT 4)

I want to invite you to join a group of people who are having a whole lot of fun in the _____ Church's Sunday School. And it's not costing them a cent.

You're invited to watch these people have fun, to see the smiles on their faces, the perspiration on their brows, the concentration in their faces, the exhilaration in their voices when each session is over.

And yet, for all the fun they have, these people serve _____ Church and the Lord in a wonderful way by teaching the next generation.

It doesn't take long to discover how to have this kind of fun. <u>And we have room to include you</u>!

But there's a catch. You have to be a special kind of person.

Maybe you are. Read on.

DESCRIBE THE BENEFITS OF BEING A VOLUNTEER (POINT 1)

<u>First</u>, are you capable of having fun? Or of learning to have fun? Do you actually like to smile? You'd be surprised how many people don't.

<u>Second</u>, do you believe that children need to be around joyous adults who can demonstrate (even more than teach) to them about love. And giving. And the Bible . . . and Jesus . . . and God.

<u>Third</u>, do you mind being foolish every once in a while? (It's OK. Only the kids will know!)

And, <u>fourth</u>, would you do something important for your Church and for the Lord?

If you answered "yes" to these four questions you qualify . . . as a Sunday School teacher.

OUTLINE THE DUTIES OF A VOLUNTEER (POINT 2)

That's right. Our teachers have fun, whether they are substitutes, volunteering their time every Sunday, working individually or in a team. And teaching Sunday School is one of the most important jobs anyone can do for the Church and its children of all ages.

It won't take more than two hours of your time each week. One hour of preparation and one hour of teaching.

But in the process you're going to learn a lot more about the Bible yourself and its teaching for daily living.

ISSUE A SPECIFIC INVITATION (POINT 4)

I invite you to come see what it's all about. This Sunday the 4th of April come to the Sunday School office at 9:15 A.M. (15 minutes before Sunday School starts).

We'll let you audit an experienced teacher to see what goes on. You'll probably be asked to help a little. And you can decide for yourself later if it's something you'd like to do regularly.

But please call the church office at 000-0000 before the weekend to reserve a space. We need 12 volunteers this week.

SHOW APPRECIATION FOR THE VOLUNTEER (POINT 5)

I want you to know how much I appreciate your support of _____ Church. It's members like yourself who have allowed us to have such a significant impact on our community.

I look forward to hearing from you.

                        Sincerely,

                        Signed
                        Pastor

    P.S. If you can't come this Sunday, please call
the Church office and we'll arrange another time.
Thanks.

MODEL LETTER—VOLUNTEER APPEAL—
SCOUTING ORGANIZATION

Dear Expert,

Perhaps you aren't used to being addressed that way. But to a young scout who wants to learn about the real world, that's exactly what you are!

OUTLINE THE DUTIES OF A VOLUNTEER (POINT 2)

I hope you will consider sharing your expertise and yourself, on a part-time basis as a Merit Badge Counselor for Scout Troop 111.

The hours and commitment will be of your choosing, and the value will be long-lasting.

Merit Badge Counselors are adults in the community who are willing to help young men learn, understand, and pass the test for Merit Badges—special achievement awards in more than 100 areas from camping to computers to a variety of career skills.

ISSUE A SPECIFIC INVITATION (POINT 4)

I have enclosed a listing of Merit Badges, and I would urge you to look at the list to see if there is one (or more) areas you could help in.

If you can, then call me at work at 123-4567 or at home at 345-1234. I can brief you on the knowledge required to pass each badge. Then you can judge if you can evaluate a boy's knowledge and help him learn the more difficult requirements.

DESCRIBE THE BENEFITS OF BEING A VOLUNTEER (POINT 1)

If you could only help one youngster gain more self-confidence on the sometimes difficult road to adulthood, think what a personal joy that would be. Not many today have that deep down satisfaction . . . of really knowing they have helped someone else in a meaningful way.

A boy's simply meeting an adult other than his parents in a real-life situation is one of the big benefits of this program. And while you are not required to become friends with the boys you help, your "adultness" is bound to rub off on each young man and show him what it is like to be a real grown-up. Young people today are turning to the wrong role models. That's why I hope you can help out and be a positive force in a young man's life.

In my opinion, this is the real benefit of the Merit Badge Counselor program.

Are you interested in finding out if you qualify as an "expert" in a boy's eyes?

SHOW APPRECIATION FOR THE VOLUNTEER (POINT 5)

I know you have helped our community in many ways. That's why I am writing today. You are someone who really makes our town such a wonderful place in which to raise a family.

ISSUE A SPECIFIC INVITATION (POINT 4)

Give me a call at one of the above numbers.

I can assure you that working with these boys and young men is rewarding.

Sincerely,

Signed
Scoutmaster
Troop 111

DESCRIBE THE BENEFITS OF BEING A VOLUNTEER (POINT 1)

P.S. If you would like to talk to other men who have served as merit badge counselors, please plan to join in an orientation meeting on June 7th at the Community Center. I think you'll be inspired to hear what our current volunteers feel about the program. It's exciting.

SAMPLE LETTER—EPISCOPAL CHURCH OF THE WORD— LETTER TO INVITE ATTENDANCE AT CHURCH SERVICES

Come Home to God . . .

at Episcopal Church of the Word.

Dear New Neighbor,

Great News! You and your family can come as you are to God and to church. Imagine a church that values you and your needs.

- Caring people where you will find friends
- Contemporary, relevant, and up-beat music
- A safe and fun Sunday School for children to learn about Jesus Christ
- Nursery care where infants through three years old receive tender loving care
- Junior and senior high youth groups where teens find Christian support in growing up with peer pressure
- Small groups where parents and singles can find a place of support and hope while living in fast-paced, stressful Northern Virginia

We invite you to come as you are and to come home to God.

The first worship service of Episcopal Church of the Word in Gainesville is coming soon on a Sunday in December. The church is located 1/2 mile south of I-66 on Rte. 29 in Gainesville, next to McDonald's.

Alison L. Barfoot
Pastor

Reprinted with permission, Episcopal Church of the Word.

A Word About Our Pastor

The Reverend Alison L. Barfoot is the pastor of Episcopal Church of the Word, a new church celebrating a new home in Gainesville with its grand opening coming in December. Episcopal Church of the Word exists to call families home to God, to strengthen and support family life, to invite the heartfelt presence of the Holy Spirit in contemporary worship, and to know the life-changing power of a personal relationship with God.

Alison grew up in Fairfax County and has lived in Manassas for almost three years. Prior to going into the ministry, she taught elementary and secondary school in Alexandria and is sensitive to the needs of families living in the fast-paced, stressful lifestyle of Northern Virginia.

Come as you are . . . come home to God . . . come home to church.

This was the lead letter in a four-effort series of mailings inviting residents in ZIP codes near the church to attend the opening services. It's not a fund-raising letter per se, but it follows a number of good techniques in such letters. It emphasizes the benefits through attendance. It personalizes the effort so a recipient would be comfortable in coming. It answers potential objections that a nonchurch member might envision. This series was very successful in developing excellent attendance at its services.

17

Sending Out a Potpourri of Other Important Letters

The letters we have reviewed so far in this book include all the major types of letters needed to raise funds. However, a well-rounded fund-raising program also includes a number of other more specialized types of letters to gain maximum results. In this chapter we're going to look at five of these more specialized letters so you will have at your fingertips every conceivable type of letter needed for an effective fund-raising program.

The Contribution Acknowledgment Letter

Thanking the donor for the gift is important for two reasons. The first and most obvious reason is that it is the right thing to do. Donors like to be thanked. They gave thought to the decision to send a gift. They appreciate it when they are remembered even with a printed thank-you letter and a receipt. While it is recommended that you send acknowledgment letters to all your contributors, some organizations send these thank-you letters only to donors above a certain minimum level (e.g., $5 and above). The reason? At the lower end of the giving range ($1–4) it costs as much as the donor gave—or even more—to prepare and send an acknowledgment. So it is a waste of the organization's money to acknowledge the very lowest gifts. Other than this possible exception, make certain that you have a system in place to send timely acknowledgment letters to donors for each and every contribution they make.

But there's a second reason to send gift acknowledgment letters to donors. They are likely to respond with a second follow-up gift. A person who has just given your organization a gift has a very high current interest level in what you're doing. That's why some organizations include with the thank-you acknowledgment letter a second remittance form to be used for sending the next gift. Or you may simply enclose a business reply envelope with the receipt to encourage further giving. This is done simply as a convenience to those donors who are motivated to make fairly regular gifts. The main point of the acknowledgment letter is to let the donor know that you received the gift—that you appreciate it—and to give some indication of how you are using the gift.

MODEL LETTER—GIFT ACKNOWLEDGMENT—
CHILD WELFARE GROUP

Dear _____,

On behalf of the staff and Board of Directors here at the Child Welfare Foundation, I want to thank you for your recent generous gift.

I've enclosed your receipt along with a "Children Are a Natural Resource" sticker as a token of our appreciation.

You probably know that __% of our funding comes from gifts from concerned people like you, and without your generosity, we simply could not (state mission of organization).

Your gift will go directly to help our core programs:

1. The Scolitis Screening Program, to test every elementary school student for often overlooked spinal problems

2. The Home Tutors Group, which helps children in high school and junior high school who are in danger of leaving school because of reading and academic difficulties

3. The Family Discussion Groups, in which parents and children can work out their problems on neutral territory, with our trained staff as mediators and helpers

For the last 20 years we have been helping families in our region to <u>stay together</u> and <u>be healthy together</u>. And we have been able to do this because of people like you who see that strong healthy families are the key to creating healthy adults.

Again, thank you. At a time when we are nearly overwhelmed with requests for our services, your gift is making a difference.

If you have any questions about our work, please don't hesitate to call. Or you can use the enclosed envelope to write to us, or to send an additional donation.

Thanks once again for your wonderful vote of confidence in our work and for your ongoing support.

Thank you again, and God bless you.

                              Sincerely,

                              Executive Director

SAMPLE LETTER—GIFT ACKNOWLEDGMENT LETTER—
AMERICAN BIBLE ASSOCIATION

Dear Mr. _____,

It is a special person who gives from the heart so that others can find new life and hope in the Savior, Jesus Christ. And you are such a person!

Thank you for your recent Christmas gift of $_____ to the American Bible Society. Because of your generosity, many now will have a Bible of their own.

For some people, like this man from Nepal India, your gift of God's Word will be their first opportunity to learn about the Lord and His plan of salvation for their lives.

"When I read the Bible, I knew I was on the wrong road," he wrote. "I now know the right one is here in this book. Before I had no idea what the Christian Gospel was all about. But my heart filled with joy as I read those beautiful words!"

And our hearts are also filled with joy knowing that we have a friend like you working with us to take the Gospel to all the world.

Again, thank you for your generosity and concern. You are truly making a real difference in the lives of people everywhere.

                              In Jesus' name,

                              Eugene B. Habecker
                              President

This acknowledgment letter does two important things. First, it makes the donor feel real special for making a gift. Second, it gives a nice example of how the gift has been used. A receipt for the gift was part of this letter form, and there was a second form attached for the donor's use to send an extra gift. This form was worded this way: "American Bible Society Extra Gift Reply Form . . . Yes, I want to send an extra gift so more people can have a Bible at Christmas and throughout the year. Please use my enclosed gift wherever the need is greatest."

The Fund-Raising Letter to a Board Member

Individuals serve on nonprofit boards for the expertise and counsel they can provide and also for the financial gifts they can make. A letter to a board member, asking for a gift, is quite different from a letter to a cold prospect or even a regular donor to your organization. You know that board members have a deep interest in your organization. And you can assume, for the most part, they have a good giving potential. Even so, it is probably best not to be too aggressive with these individuals. A board member letter should be thoughtful, yet not shy away from asking for a substantial gift. There's another very important reason for getting contributions from your board members. When you approach foundations and corporations for a gift (Chapter 15) it will be important to indicate that you have maximum participation from your board. If you cannot show this to these special funding sources, they may question the dedication of the key people behind your work.

Finally, make sure that you prepare a list of your board members and eliminate their names from all your general mailings. A board member who receives a piece of general solicitation mail without any indication that you know who you are writing to is an unhappy board member. And an unhappy board member is less likely to make a substantial gift. Treat board members with much tender, loving care.

MODEL LETTER—BOARD MEMBER SOLICITATION— SCHOOL

Dear (Board Member)

As a Hopkins School Board member, you are part of the arduous but fulfilling task of creating a dream. And I believe strongly that the dream will become a reality.

The architectural plan for the Hopkins School theater is finished. A scale model is on display in the lobby of the old theater, showing the new rehearsal hall, the innovative stage, and the new reception area for alumni, benefactors, and friends.

We are now ready to begin the Theater Fund Drive to bring our dreams into reality, and to give the highly talented students and faculty of Hopkins a real stage to showcase their talents.

But as with any venture of bringing dreams to life, those outside the immediate circle cannot see the dream as clearly as you and I, who helped give it birth. So before we begin to ask alumni, parents, and friends to make real our dream, before we can make our dream theirs, we must show our leadership and commitment first.

After reviewing competitive bids, we know it will cost $3,400,000 to build our new theater, over three years (a little more than $1,000,000 a year).

Before we go public with that number, I want to show that we are already 20% on our way to that goal, and that means getting pledges of $680,000 in the next 30 days.

To that end, I have personally pledged $25,000 over the next three years. I invite you to join me at that level, or at whatever level you are comfortable with.

Those who pledge $20,000 or more within the next 30 days will be honored as members of the "Master Builder's Circle."

The name was chosen because it is the title of one of Henrik Ibsen's most famous plays, and members will have their names engraved on a plaque in the reception area. In addition, you will be invited to join a private reception in honor of our graduate Mark MovieStar, who has agreed to give a private performance and meet benefactors on _____ at the old theater.

You have shared in the vision. I invite you to share in the leadership. I will call you shortly to find out your decision.

Sincerely,

Chairman, Hopkins School Board

The Employee Solicitation Letter

Employees generally fall into two categories when it comes to giving to the organization they work for. Some feel that they are giving enough through their work efforts, sometimes at a sacrifice in terms of income. Obviously these employees will not be too open to making direct financial contributions. However, other employees are agreeable to giving to an organization they like and know a lot about. Here again the key is to be tasteful, to mainly provide an easy opportunity for an employee to give if he or she feels so inclined.

MODEL LETTER—EMPLOYEE SOLICITATION— ENVIRONMENTAL GROUP

Dear John,

As an employee of the Environmental Safeguard Fund, you know better than most what <u>really</u> needs to be done to protect the environment.

We've all discussed over coffee or lunch at great length which of our programs are underfunded—programs that, with just a little more money, could really make a difference.

In approaching you and all our other employees in our annual giving campaign, I want to emphasize three points:

1. This program is entirely voluntary.

2. You can designate which of our programs you want your gift to go to, including the Employee Training program.

3. You can give at any level you wish—but for payroll deduction, you can't deduct less than $1 per paycheck, for efficiency's sake.

I must tell you that I expect such "program-driven" giving by staff to carry weight when we go to foundations for funding. I expect that they will be impressed that the real pro's—you and your fellow employees here at Environmental Safeguard Fund—felt certain programs and efforts were worth personal giving, and that they will look more kindly on funding these "orphan" programs at a higher level.

In any case, your show of support of our organization at whatever level will be greatly appreciated.

And, of course, your contributions are tax-deductible.

I've enclosed a form for you to use. Our deadline to kick in payroll deductions is January 15th. Thanks for your support.

Sincerely,

Executive Director

SAMPLE LETTER—PROVIDENCE HEALTH FOUNDATION— EMPLOYEE SOLICITATION LETTER

Dear Providence Hospital Employee,

Recently, you and I received a letter asking us to consider making a pledge to the Providence Hospital Annual Fund.

I hope you have already sent in your pledge card, but if not, <u>please let me take a minute of your time to ask you to reconsider</u>.

As a Providence employee, you know better than anyone else how committed Providence is to its patients, and to its staff. But even a great hospital like Providence needs help to do all that it wants to do.

<u>The Annual Fund gives you two ways to help</u>. First, you can designate your gift to the Charity Medical Fund, which helps patients who need basic medical care, but simply cannot pay for it.

Or, you can choose to send your gift to the Employee Enrichment Fund, which helps improve the work environment here at Providence, and thereby supports patient care.

Your past support has been a tremendous help. For example, last year's gifts to the charity fund provided desperately needed cribs, clothing and toys for our boarder babies while they waited for foster homes. And your employee enrichment gifts are helping to furnish the new employee lounge, giving the staff a place to rest from the hard work of patient care.

Most of us can spare at least $1 per pay period to help the less fortunate. <u>I appeal to you as a fellow employee to join me in pledging $1 per pay, or more if you can</u>. You have my promise that your dollars will be stretched as far as they can go.

Reprinted with permission, Providence Health Foundation.

On behalf of everyone whom your gift will touch,
thank you, and may God bless you and your loved ones
during this holiday season.

Sincerely,

Robert A. Hutson
Executive Vice-President

Employees of this health care facility are given two different types of
funds to give to: one helps patients who can't pay, the other is to refurbish
a lounge for employees. The letter also suggests a giving amount (i.e.,
pledge $1 or more per pay period). This is a very effective approach for an
organization that has a fairly large number of employees who are intimate-
ly connected with its services.

Gift-in-Kind Request Letter to a Corporation

Many corporations have goods that they are only too happy to contribute to a nonprofit organization. In order for a nonprofit organization to receive these, a gift-in-kind letter needs to be written to the corporation to make it aware of the need. Before writing such a letter research needs to be done as to which companies have assets they might like to contribute. A screening phone call to the corporate offices will reveal whether the company does, in fact, make such contributions and what types of goods they have available for contributing. Armed with this information your letter will more likely receive the type of response you're looking for.

MODEL LETTER—GIFT IN KIND REQUEST LETTER— SOCIAL SERVICES VOLUNTEER AGENCY

Dear Mr. Smith,

Here at the Sequoia Valley Social Services Volunteer Agency, we don't worry about "state-of-the-art" computer systems.

We worry that we don't have enough office equipment to be able to respond to needs throughout the Valley.

Because of that worry, I am writing to you today to suggest a true "win-win" trade.

As you upgrade your computers, please give the old ones to the Sequoia Agency. Our organization will be able to serve troubled families in the Valley far more efficiently, and you can take a tax write-off for the value of the equipment you give us.

Our needs are simple, but critical:

- A 48MB hard disk to maintain data on donors and volunteers (At present, we use a card file!)

- Three computer stations for data entry and management, to keep our files up to date. (We have one computer right now, everyone else uses typewriters that are getting old and difficult to repair.)

- A "new" FAX machine. We have none now.

- A "new" photocopy machine. Our repairman is like a member of the staff!

- A "new" laser printer. We have an old dot-matrix printer now.

These are all pretty basic things for running an efficient operation, but because the lion's share of our small budget goes to people, not things, we are always short of "things."

I hope you can help. I can arrange for a volunteer to pick up equipment, and we have a volunteer computer expert who can set everything up for us.

The work we do for families and children in trouble in Sequoia Valley is vital. No one else does it. And because we are a non-governmental agency, we help keep your taxes down.

I will give you a call next week to see if we can "make a deal." Thanks for your time.

Sincerely,

Executive Director

The Complaint Answer Letter

A complaint letter from a donor—or from someone on an outside list—should be viewed not as a problem but as an opportunity. Look at it this way. Someone took the time and trouble to write you about a particular concern. Now I realize there are some complaints that come from people who hate what your nonprofit is doing or stands for. There's nothing you can do to satisfy the writers of these letters. On the other hand, the great majority of so-called complaint letters come from people who like what you do and have a concern for your work. The fact that they wrote a letter to express an opinion shows they have a genuine interest in your work.

A complaint letter may also give you some critical information that you need to know. Maybe someone has received a mailing from an unauthorized user of your list. Or it could be that there was some mix-up in the inserts or message of your mailing. These bits of information can be very helpful in adjusting your mailing program. Look on these types of complaint letters as useful bits of "marketing field intelligence." Make sure to thank the writers for their help.

Then again there are complaint letters where you have failed to correctly capture the person's name and address or failed to make a change of address. The essential point here is that the necessary adjustment be made quickly and that a response be given to the donor on the adjustment or correction.

For most organizations their complaint letters fall into definite categories. We'll review these and see the kind of a reply that needs to be given to each of these. The bottom-line on all these types of responses is simply to make the facts known to the complaint letter writer and to respond—as much as possible—according to their wishes. Direct mail fund-raising is too important a function for its image to be tarnished by failing to listen and heed the small percentage of complaints that are received.

Here's a listing of the more common complaints and the suggested responses:

"You're sending me too much mail . . . "

We appreciate your concern about receiving too much mail. Our special mailings to members (donors) raise significant support for the impor-

tant programs of _____. Of course, you're under
no obligation to give, but many of our donors
find that these mailings are one of the best ways
to keep up to date on our needs and achievements.
However, if you would like us to cut back on the
number of appeal mailings you receive, we can do
so. Simply indicate on the copy of my letter
(attached) your preference and we will be happy
to comply.

"I received 2 (or more) copies of your mailing . . . "

We make every effort to eliminate duplications
prior to our mailings. Occasionally some names do
slip through. We'd appreciate it if you would
advise us of the various ways your name and
address appear. We'll make sure to check for all
these variations so that you won't receive any
further duplications. If you do receive an extra
effort in the future, you might want to consider
giving it to a friend who shares your interest in
_____.

"How can I stop getting so much junk mail?"

We make every effort to mail only to identified
interested lists of people who have similar concerns as those of (name of organization). If you
prefer not to receive any further mailings from
(name of organization), please advise us and
we'll make sure not to mail you any further
solicitations. In addition, if you prefer to
receive less direct mail in general, I suggest
you write to the Mail Preference Service, c/o
DMA, P.O. Box 9008, Farmingdale, N.Y., 11735-9008
and request that you receive information on their
Mail Preference Service. This will allow you to
have your name eliminated from various types of
national mailings that you don't want to receive.

"You're destroying the environment by all your
mailings."

We share your concern that our mailings do as
little damage to the environment as possible. We
are always searching for ways to make our
requests for needed funds as economical as possible, as well as easy on the environment.

What we want to avoid at all costs, though, is
having to choose between saving trees and (fill
in your organizations' mission). So, here are
some points to consider:

- (Name of your organization) uses recycled paper
  for all its fund-raising mailings, for
  envelopes, and letters. (Note: If you don't do
  this now, specify how you plan to use recycled
  paper in the future. It is competitively priced
  today.)

- There are only a limited number of ways to raise
  the vitally needed funds for (goal of organization). More than __% of our budget comes from the
  gifts of individuals like you, individuals who we
  can reach most effectively through letters in the
  mail. Again, thanks for your concern. We're working hard to be efficient and environmentally conscious, while we concentrate on our primary mission—_____.

Add this additional paragraph if it applies.

We do all we can to cut down on our mailings, and
one thing I would like to suggest to you is
becoming an "electronic giver" to our cause. I've
enclosed a form for you to use, if this is an
option you like. It saves paper and postage
expense, makes it easy for you, and provides us
with the funds we need to _____.

(Note: See Chapter 21 on how to word the automatic funds transfer offer).

"How did you get my name? I didn't ask to get your mailing."

We carefully review lists that include names of people who have interests that match the goals of (name of organization). These are one-time mailings and we only follow-up to those who respond favorably. However, if you prefer not to receive any future mailings from (name of organization), please let us know and we'll be happy to follow your wishes.

"Please don't rent or exchange my name."

Thank you for writing. We make names on our list available on a very limited and controlled basis. We approve every mailing piece that is sent to our list on a one-time list rental agreement. Most of our donors appreciate receiving information that is relevant to their interests. However, if you prefer that we don't rent or exchange your name, please let us know and we'll be happy to comply with your wishes.

Part IV

Easy-to-Use Tips to Make Your Letters Work

There's a lot more to writing a successful fund-raising letter than just the letter itself. The letter is like an engine in an automobile—the essential part of the car to be sure. But there are other parts. If you can't open the door and get in the car, the engine won't do you much good. Or, if the design of the car is repelling you'll probably never consider buying it. It's that way with direct mail fund-raising letters. They aren't delivered in isolation. They come in a carrying envelope. And the mailings usually have other inserts than just the letter. The letter is the engine, but you need to master the other parts of the "direct mail car" to have a successful mailing.

In Part Four you're going to see all the other critical items that you need to know to make your letters work. You will learn what kind of "teaser" copy to use on the carrying envelope to get your mailing opened in the first place. You'll see what kind of copy to use on that all-important gift response form. And you'll learn what types of enclosures work in fund-raising mailings. Don't overlook Chapter 22. In it you get a good understanding of the way to design your fund-raising mailing so you have the greatest chance of getting your message read *and acted upon*.

In Chapter 23 you'll review critical information in printing and mailing your direct mail effort. So many times in direct mail this is really where the rubber meets the road. Know the right way to go about producing your package so you'll save money and ensure that the U.S. Postal Service delivers it. The greatest letter in the world—undelivered to a prospect—will do you no good. And in Chapter 24 pick some vital information on how to keep on learning from a well-thought-out testing program. This book is a great resource for your direct mail campaigns. But to keep the motor running and to keep receiving those additional contributions, see how to learn from your own successes and failures.

18

Getting Your Envelope Opened

Readership of direct mail letters takes place only if the prospect opens the envelope, takes out the contents, and reads some or all of your message. That's why the creative thinking for your package should start with the outer envelope. That's the initial point of contact your prospect has with your message. The copy you put on the outside envelope should accomplish two very important things: *First,* you want to prevent your prospect from throwing out the envelope unopened. This is the negative you need to overcome if you are to have any success at all. *Second,* not only do you want your prospect to open the envelope but you also want that person to open it with a sense of curiosity about the message to be received. That's why cute, clever, and whimsical sayings may get a chuckle but are seldom used in direct mail fundraising. Occasionally a humorous approach works as in one environmental group's outer envelope that shows a bug-eyed whooping crane, with the copy

RELAX. Both of you. (A $10 nest egg will do it.)

This light-hearted approach happens to be on target with the fund-raising message of the enclosed letter on saving the whooping crane's habitat. That's why it works.

Six Tips on Writing Good Outer Envelope Teaser Copy

Teaser copy is the message that you have printed on the outside of the carrying envelope. Some writers recommend that you write these lines first before you write the letter copy. Experienced professionals have long known that the selling starts the moment your prospect's eyes look for the first time at your envelope in the shuffle of the daily mail. These writers make the point that you have to win the envelope-opening battle for your letter to be read at all. How do you come up with this thought-provoking teaser copy? In my experience I have found it effective to read over a first draft of the letter and to single out the one most important promotional point within. Then I write the teaser copy for the outer envelope so it coordinates with this single most important feature. And as you scan your letter for teaser line material, keep in mind these six tips on writing good teaser copy:

1. BE PROVOCATIVE.

It's important to provoke someone's natural curiosity to find out what's inside. Try to find some way to state the main point in an intriguing way.

2. BE ON TARGET WITH THE MESSAGE OF THE ENCLOSED LETTER.

The "bait-and-switch" technique is just as bad in direct mail as it is in real estate or appliance sales. It's counterproductive to tease interest with one subject and then switch to a totally different message in the enclosed letter.

3. PROMISE A BENEFIT FOR OPENING THE ENVELOPE.

The "what's in it for me factor" is always in the prospect's mind. If you can reward the prospect with the thought they will gain some new information or tangible item, they most likely will open the envelope.

4. USE ACTION-ORIENTED VERBS.

The whole point of direct mail fund-raising is to get a response. The sooner this theme appears in your message, the better. Here are some examples of action-oriented phrases that work on the outer envelope as teaser copy:

- `Open this envelope to receive your FREE gift`
- `Join _____ and you'll receive the 10 big benefits described inside...`
- `Complete the enclosed survey and return within 14 days`

- Discover the joy of _____ in the enclosed special limited time offer

5. BE PERSONAL.

Even though it's a printed envelope the teaser copy should have that one-on-one personal tone to it. Never address the prospect as a member of a larger group or "audience."

6. COVER ONE KEY PROVOCATIVE THOUGHT ON THE OUTER ENVELOPE.

The whole point of "teaser" copy is to say just enough to get the prospect to open and start finding out more about an important message enclosed. Serial stories that end each installment on a "cliff hanger" suspense point are effective. Good teaser copy generally has a suspense flavor to it.

The Three Most Universal Direct Mail Appeals

When you write outer envelope teaser copy following these guidelines, you will be helped if you also recognize that there are three types of mail that are at the top of everybody's list of desired mail. Keep these universal appeals in mind as you write your copy and you'll experience great results.

1. MONEY.

I think we can take it for granted that money is at the top of the list of items people like to receive in the mail. Many different types of payments come through the mail: tax refunds, insurance payments, social security checks, pension payments. We're not apt to throw away a piece of mail that brings us a check. There is a sure-fire "teaser-line" that is bound to get your envelope opened—the following phrase showing through the window just to the left of the name and address: "Pay to the order of." Publishers that offer a discount on new subscriptions, nonprofit organizations that offer a reduced introductory membership rate, and fund-raisers who have received a matching grant can utilize a check enclosure with "Pay to the Order of" showing through the outer envelope address window on a safety check format or some copy that indicates that an enclosure with intrinsic value is enclosed.

2. THREE-DIMENSIONAL ITEMS.

Most people will probably open a three-dimensional package on the logical assumption that there is something of value within. Gifts, mail order merchandise, books, and other items of value come in packages. These, we can fairly well assume, are also near the top of the list of items people like to receive.

To simulate the three-dimensional package feel, you can enclose a booklet or some other item that has bulk to it to get attention. A package of name and address stickers, a key ring in a bubble pack, or a multipage brochure can give your mailing that three-dimensional package feel. And outer envelope teaser lines can play on this theme:

- `The material you requested is enclosed`

- `Handle with care`

- `Special gift enclosed for:`

3. PERSONAL MESSAGES.

There's no doubt that we like to receive personal letters from friends. As the mail shuffle takes place, these personal letters are singled out to be opened and read first. That's because there's a message in the personal letter that is for "me only." It's important to know what that personal message is.

This third category—personal messages—is the one that offers the most opportunity for fund-raisers to emulate. The more the outer envelope can be made to look like a personal message, the greater the chance of its being opened. One very simple but effective way to accomplish this is to put the letter-signer's name in typewriter type just above the return address on the outer envelope. By doing this, you convey the following message: "There's a personal letter for me inside." Most people will not throw away a personal letter even if it's from someone they don't know.

Another simple way to convey "personal message enclosed" is to print the outer envelope teaser line in a hand script. The subliminal thought is that the writer of the enclosed letter took a moment to write out a personal last-minute message. This isn't a matter of tricking the recipient; rather, it's more that you are "dressing" your envelope in personal clothes so the subliminal message is this: There is, in fact, a personal message enclosed.

Of course, there's the ultimate in generating curiosity. That's putting nothing whatever on the outer envelope except the name and address of the recipient. Most people will at least open a totally blind outer envelope just in case they may miss something of real importance inside. Or they may want to satisfy their curiosity as to what's inside. While this can generate curiosity, the prospect opens the envelope with many different ideas as to enclosures. What they find inside the envelope may let the prospect down. That's why it's generally better to tip off the prospect with some indication of the contents within with teaser copy.

When you think of the copy and look of the outer envelope that contains your direct mail letter, think about these three universal types of mail that people like to receive: money, packages, personal letters. And in whatever tasteful and appropriate ways you can emulate interest along these lines, you will be on the right track.

Fifty Teaser Copy Lines for Your Outer Envelope

To get you off to a great start in writing outer envelope teaser copy for your mailing, here's a listing of 50 teasers. Many of them come from my own personal file of mailings from other organizations. Some of these may work for you as is. Or they may just stimulate an idea for a slight revision to achieve that all-important goal of getting the envelope opened in the first place. Whatever teaser line you choose, make certain that it coordinates with the subject of your mailing.

1. Your interim membership card is enclosed. Join now at money-saving rates.

2. To be opened by recipient only

3. Please respond in 14 days

4. At 10 he was considered uncontrollable. At 13 he was . . .

5. Even at Christmas this child's nightmare is real!

6. You are invited to try a FREE issue of _____. (No commitment. No obligation.)

7. Emergency . . . Immediate Reply Requested

8. Postmaster: Do not fold or bend . . .

9. She was tough and street hardened . . . yet she was only 14. But the most remarkable thing about Julie was . . .

10. Important Member Correspondence Enclosed For:

11. You have been nominated for membership in ___

12. $15 may not go far anymore, but at _____ it can _____ . . .

13. RSVP

14. Free (*up-front premium item*) enclosed

15. Photos enclosed...do not bend

16. Postmaster: Official Document Enclosed. Not to be forwarded except in the case where the addressee has filed an authorized change of address.

17. Discover the privileges awaiting you as a member of _____

18. We have reserved a FREE Copy of (*back-end premium*) for you

19. Open immediately! You have only a few days left to reply.

20. Enclosed: A personal message from (celebrity) . . .

21. ANNOUNCING: A new campaign to _____.

22. Limited Edition Offer Enclosed

23. (Name and address only with no return address and a precanceled third-class stamp) Principle: Provoke interest by not disclosing what's in envelope. Has to be opened to find out.

24. (Name of letter signer in typewriter type above logo) Principle: Typed name, slightly irregular, conveys fact that there is a personal letter enclosed.

25. (Adapt from a current major new story that relates to your letter theme . . . Hurricane Andrew's Path of Destruction, Mississippi Floods Out of Control, Gulf War's Aftermath, Tax Increase Coming, News About the Administration's Latest Medical Plan Proposals) Principle: Tie your appeal in with what people are thinking about.

26. Verification of Receipt Enclosed For: _____

27. May we list you as a grass roots supporter of _____?

28. Revealed! The identity of a group that has _____. See inside.

29. Discover America's best kept _____ secret

30. This registered membership number is your invitation to . . . "Come an extra mile"

31. (Issue, e.g. Handgun control) is on the auction block . . . unless we take action today!

32. Inside: Your passport to _____

33. New

34. I'm asking you to make an important decision today

35. Please return today

36. Final notice enclosed

37. It's time to put a stop to ____'s lies!

38. Please sign the enclosed petition immediately

39. Immediate action required!

40. Please sign the enclosed ballot and return it to me immediately

41. The future of _____ is in your hands

42. Have we got a fight on our hands!

43. The favor of a reply is requested

44. Please honor _____ by using the enclosed FREE address labels

45. You are invited to try a FREE issue of _____

46. Here's your chance to help stop _____

47. Here's one heartbreaking problem that has a solution

48. Limited-time offer

49. Dated material. Please open immediately!

50. We want you back!

19
Writing Strong Opening Copy

After you have successfully overcome the first hurdle—getting your envelope opened with good teaser copy—as we saw in the preceding chapter—it is important to start the letter with a compelling first line and opening paragraphs. Direct mail prospects first glance at a few places in a mailing to find out what the mailing is all about, and if they find anything of interest in these "first-glance" spots they will read on. I suspect that the order form is one place the reader's eyes go first to learn the "deal." The first few sentences of the letter are also at the top of the list for first glance readership. That's why maximum effort must be put into creating initial sentences that "hook" the prospect into reading further. In this chapter you'll learn just how to develop the strongest possible opening.

How to Write the First Sentence of Your Letter

The first sentence of your letter should be brief and provocative. The principles of envelope teaser copy apply to the first sentence. You are trying to grab the reader's attention to read the first few sentences and, it is hoped, the first page and entire message. Even though first lines to fund-raising letters are short it takes a lot of effort to get them right.

The first sentence of a fund-raising letter should convey one central thought. And it should be a direct link to the main message of the letter. Do not try to combine a number of ideas in the first sentence. You may have been trying to synthesize all the thoughts as you researched the subject, but unloading on the reader like this is bound to confuse. Open your

313

letter with one quick, punchy provocative thought that will link very quickly with the fund-raising message of the letter. To see how it's done, I've listed 25 good examples of opening lines to fund-raising letters that I have received.

Twenty-five Effective Opening Lines to Fund-Raising Letters

1. A little girl, just eight years old, lies on her bed.

2. This is a difficult letter for me to write.

3. This is an emergency.

4. We are embarking on a rescue mission to save the future.

5. I'll get right to the point.

6. I'm really uneasy. I'm not used to writing letters like this.

7. This letter contains an urgent request. I am asking for your help to . . .

8. I'm asking you to act now to_____or say goodbye to . . .

9. Your help is needed immediately.

10. Imagine you're with me on _____

11. We miss you!

12. The problem simply stated is this.

13. Your gift is urgently needed today to _____

14. I am sure you know that _____. What you may not know is _____.

15. Will you join me in this urgent request to _____.

16. I'd like to tell you why an (actor) has joined the fight to _____.

17. I need your help right now to _____.

18. Please don't put this letter aside.

19. I admit it. I'm going to ask you for money.

20. Children shouldn't have to face the devastation of cancer and death. But they do.

    (Statement of facts)
    But you can do something about it.

21. What can you get for $ _____?

22. As I reread my letter to you, I realize some of it may be disturbing—but so much hangs in the balance—please read it.

23. Accept this invitation as a new member of _____ and we will send you a <u>free</u> _____

24. We are embarking on a mission to_____.

    Will you join us?

25. "Please help (my baby live)" This was her urgent plea.

What do these opening lines have in common? They are all serious in nature and very direct in terms of the fund-raising message. Occasionally a clever twist can work in an opening line, but the great majority of effective openers for fund-raising letters are straightforward in terms of the need that the letter will describe. As a general rule the complete case statement for sending a gift ought to be covered in the beginning paragraphs to a letter. Your prospect is looking at this copy with one question in mind: "What's this all about?" Don't presume that they will continue reading your letter if you haven't clearly told them why you're writing early on in the copy.

The Fourth Paragraph Rule—A Special Tip to Help You Find the Best Possible Opening Line

I have found over the years that after I have written a first draft of a letter the best beginning point for the letter is usually buried around the fourth or fifth paragraph of the first draft. That's why I suggest you look down at the fourth or fifth paragraphs of the first page of your first draft and ask yourself if the core idea for your letter isn't found there. More often than not, you will find the best beginning somewhere down the first page. The reason is this. Most of us engage in what is called writer's "warm-up." Because we're writing to an unknown person we want to explain why we decided to write the letter. Or we want to get into the message in a polite way. The truth of the matter is this. Your prospect really doesn't care or want to know the emotions you experienced in deciding to write the letter. Your prospect is looking for a quick answer to one key self-centered question: "What's the main point of this letter?"

Finding this best starting point by looking down to the paragraphs around the fourth paragraph is what I call the "fourth paragraph rule." It's surprising how often this helps locate just the right beginning for a good fund-raising letter.

How to Develop a Winning "Copy Platform" for Your Letter

After you have that compelling opening to your letter you will need a strong copy track to run on. This is what is called the copy platform. It helps to have this platform clearly in mind so your thoughts are logically and interestingly connected. After you have grabbed your prospect's attention with a strong opening line, you will want the message to flow in a logical sequence. Here are some themes—or copy platforms—that you can follow in writing the balance of the letter:

1. WEAVE THE MESSAGE AROUND AN INTERESTING CASE EXAMPLE.

An individual case story with lots of emotion is an effective opening as well as a useful structure for the entire letter. It helps the reader to visualize a single person or case incident that dramatizes your message. To start a letter with this style you need to have one very strong story that epitomizes your appeal. You can intersperse facts about your organization and the overall need throughout the letter. Take a look at the Covenant House letter in Chapter 1 to see a good example of this approach.

2. REPEAT THE CENTRAL COPY PLATFORM.

Each fund-raising letter you send out should be based on a one-paragraph case statement that outlines the need, what will be done to correct it, and what a gift will accomplish. Once you have this copy platform clearly in mind—and committed to writing—you can keep restating it, but always with a different twist. In other words no matter where the reader begins to look at your message, in short order he or she will receive the main point. And if the prospect stays with your message for more than just a few minutes, he or she will get a strong reinforcement as to the central reason why a gift is needed.

3. WHY A LONG COPY MESSAGE WORKS.

It is generally agreed that the longer copy approach works best in direct mail. The reason this is so—in my experience—is that the serious prospect who is interested in responding is already attracted to the subject matter and will read a full exposition to justify the pleasurable act of giving. Those people who are not predisposed to consider your appeal will not be converted with long *or short* copy. So when you hear someone say "long copy works in direct mail," you will understand that "long copy with a good offer *to the right prospect* works in direct mail" is really the key. The *right prospect* loves to read a message on a subject to which he or she is already partial. The exceptions to this longer copy approach are the highly visible organizations that are well known for what they do. The Salvation Army is a case in point. For this organization a long letter is not necessary to acquaint someone with its work. For a group like the Salvation Army or the American Red Cross, the letter can be used primarily as the asking device.

4. THE PERSONALLY REFLEXIVE LETTER.

When you use a well-known person as your letter-signer it's important that the "voice" be appropriate to the personality. While all the principles of fund-raising apply they must be adapted to the style of the famous person. The secret is to get a famous letter-signer who is closely identified with your message. Even if the letter-signer isn't all that well known, he or she can share a number of personal involvement items that relate to the cause. Prospects are interested to read these relevant but personal insider views. There's another popular technique in writing introductory letter copy—it's called the "Johnson Box." This is a block of copy or paragraph that appears just above the salutation. It is named after the first writer who used this technique extensively in his letters. Today it is a very commonplace approach and is used by a wide variety of mailers. Essentially the "Johnson Box" is like an ad for the letter—it sells the content that is to follow in the body of the letter. If done right, it can add to the readership and response to your effort. Let's see how to write one of these so-called "Johnson Boxes."

How to Write a "Johnson Box"

You can either make the main point of your letter in the "Johnson Box," or you can tantalize the prospect to read on by some provocative teaser-type

copy. Here are a few examples of good "Johnson Box" copy. The first example tells the main purpose of the letter:

- This letter deals with today's most critical
  environmental problem . . . your support will
  entitle you to your new wildlife calendar . . .
  with full-color photos of the wildlife you are
  helping to save.

  Dear Friend,

The next example of a "Johnson Box" intrigues with a case illustration:

- Tommy probably doesn't look too unusual to you.
  Could be one of your neighbor's kids. Or a grand-
  child maybe. But there's <u>one big difference</u>—Tommy
  is homeless. His mother lives in our shelter. Her
  husband lost his job. Got violent. Didn't pay the
  rent. She and Tommy were literally shoved out on
  the street.

  Dear Friend,

The following example of a "Johnson Box" features the main issue of the
letter:

- You have been selected to participate in a program designed to correct one of America's most
  critical national problems . . . affecting our
  food supply, our environment, and the heritage we
  leave to our children. It's a crisis affecting
  our farmland. And it's alarming! Please read this
  letter. Then return the enclosed survey along
  with your completed new membership application
  form.

  Dear Friend,

The "Johnson Box" technique works—in my estimation—because the
great majority of prospects have been conditioned by the newspaper article
structure in which the summary of most articles is stated in the early para-

graphs. Readers want to get a grasp of the main message first to determine if they have enough interest to read on. If you're going to take a journey, you want to know your destination before embarking.

Many effective "Johnson Box" messages refer to the action the letter will ask the recipient to take. As the letter is read, there is in the reader's mind a clearly stated response that is being requested. The person is not reading to gain more knowledge (even though that will happen) but to be solicited to send a gift to solve a critical issue. The "Johnson Box" is to the direct mail fund-raising letter what the "Subject:" line is to the interoffice memo.

For additional ideas on opening lines for fund-raising letters, don't forget to review the material in Chapter 1 on the straight contribution letter, especially the section on "Catch attention with a provocative opening."

20

Asking for the Right Gift Amount

The main point of a direct mail fund-raising letter is to ask for and receive a gift from your prospect. It follows then that the size gift you ask for is absolutely critical to the success of your letter. First, we'll see how to determine how much to ask for from a first-time donor and then turn our attention to how much to ask for in repeat gifts from existing donors. We'll also look at the many different ways you can ask for the gift. In the next chapter we'll review the various types of offers that you can make in connection with asking for the gift, that is, all the trappings of what you ask the prospect to do, and what you promise in response.

What's the Right Gift Amount to Ask from First-Time Donors?

The amount of the requested first-time gift—or what you might call an entry-level gift—is one of the essential keys to your success. Ask someone for too much and they'll not respond because the amount is beyond their means. Ask someone for too little and you may either offend the donor, or you may find yourself spending more to get the gift than it's worth. So it's important to know how to peg the right gift amount for first-time donors.

One important point to remember is this. The level at which donors begin their giving to your organization will have a direct bearing on how much they will upgrade their giving level in the future. The higher you can start someone out in giving, the faster they will progress to those all-important higher giving levels. Remember the 80-20 rule outlined in Chapter 10:

80 percent of the contributions will come from 20 percent of the donors. The ultimate pay-off in direct mail fund-raising comes from the core group of givers who give at the highest levels. Motivating someone to give a $500 or $1,000 gift is the ultimate direct mail pay-off. That's why getting a donor to start at the highest possible level is important. You'll reach pay dirt much sooner.

Five Important Tips in Developing the Gift Amount "Ask"

1. HOW MUCH DO YOUR COMPETITORS ASK FOR?

This is a good place to begin. If most first-time gift requests in your field are $15, you should start out asking this amount; if you ask for a higher amount, you ought to have some reason for it—either your program is a better one or you're offering some special gift inducement for giving.

2. WHAT IS THE AVERAGE GIFT SIZE OF THE DONORS ON THE LIST YOU'RE MAILING?

This is an important bit of information to find out before you develop your copy on the gift ask. If you're mailing to a list of donors who have given, on the average, $10 to another cause, you would do well to start at this level. A $50 gift ask would be a stretch for a list with an average giving history of $10. Learn all you can about the list being mailed and take this information into account in coming up with your gift ask.

3. GIVE A RANGE OF DESIRED FIRST-TIME GIVING LEVELS.

Many fund-raisers will suggest a range of possible gift levels. This is done because sometimes the fund-raiser doesn't have that much information on the giving record of the donors on a particular list. It is also done to provide for donors of different giving-level capacities to receive the same form. Typically a range of four to five gift amounts will be used on the gift form. Here's an example of a typical money amount range on the response form:

- __$15 __$20 __$25 __$50 __$100 __Other $__

You provide some flexibility when you use an "Other" option. It signals to donors that they may choose a larger—or smaller—gift.

4. MOTIVATE TO A HIGHER GIVING LEVEL BY OFFERING A PREMIUM.

A good way to get larger gifts is to offer a premium for giving at the higher level. Here's an example of how one fund-raiser utilizes this technique:

- ___YES, I would like to help save (_____).
  Enclosed is my gift of:

- __$50 __$25* __$20 __$15 __$10 __Other $__

- Send $25 or more and receive your FREE _____!

A word of warning is in order, however. If you give a premium for a first-time gift, you are setting yourself up to give premiums for subsequent giving from that donor. There's an important principle at work here: Donors will best repeat their giving by getting an offer similar to the initial offer. Another illustrative example would be the cut-rate offer. If you offer memberships at 50 percent off, donors who accept this offer will look for a similar type of money-saving offer at renewal time. That's why the crafting of the first offer is so important to all your subsequent efforts.

5. TEST TO FIND THE RIGHT INITIAL ENTRY-LEVEL GIFT AMOUNT.

The money amount gift ask is probably one of the most important test items in a direct mail fund-raising program. (See Chapter 24 on testing.) The "ask" refers to the amount of money you request as a gift or the amount of options you suggest for a gift. This should be the subject of regular ongoing testing. And it's important to look at results on a list-by-list basis. Successful initial amounts of giving will vary by list. If your program is large enough, you can group lists into categories and vary the gift amount asks by your test results.

Four Rules for Writing the Gift Response Form Copy

After you have decided on the best possible gift amount ask, you will want to complete the gift response form (order form) following specific guidelines.

All copy in a direct mail effort is important. But with the gift response form it is essential that certain rules be followed; otherwise, the entire effort is jeopardized. Here are the rules to follow in writing this copy:

1. NO AMBIGUITIES ALLOWED.

You have a major problem if the response form copy is unclear or not consistent with the offer made in the letter. If a person is confused as to what the offer really is, the form will be laid aside without action. Here's a suggestion: Have a totally disinterested person or persons read your gift response form copy to make sure it is clear and understandable as to what is offered and what is requested. Do they know exactly how to respond? If they are confused, rewrite the copy until it's crystal clear.

2. REPEAT THE BENEFITS OF THE OFFER.

In addition to being absolutely clear on the gift amounts, the other benefits should be incorporated in the response form. That's where people look to see what they "really get." There's also another important reason to list the thrust of the appeal on the gift response form—namely, some donors look first to this form to see what they're being requested to do and what they get in response for a gift. If you recap the benefits on the response form you are, in effect, making a second pitch for the gift. This is a good rule to follow on all the inserts in your mailing. Does the fund-raising pitch in one form or another show up on every piece and/or page of the mailing? It's important that this happens: Direct mail readership doesn't follow any set pattern, and the more your "ask" for a gift appears, the stronger your response will be.

3. MAKE YOUR GIFT FORM VISUALLY APPEALING.

If the form itself looks crammed and confusing, don't expect your prospect to search and find out some critical ordering information. Make it look easy to use. Also don't try to accomplish other objectives (such as brochure-type information) on your order form. A gift response form should look like a form to be completed and returned. There should only be one obvious thing to do with this form—and that is to return it with a gift!

4. AVOID GIVING OTHER ALTERNATIVES ON THE GIFT RESPONSE FORM.

Prospects who are considering a first-time gift to an organization should not be confronted with additional decisions such as sending in referral names or signing up as a volunteer. While these are valid requests, they are better done on acknowledgment and other follow-up mailings to donors already on your list. From a promotional point of view, you don't want to give prospects an "out," so to speak, from sending in a gift. There is one major decision you want your first-time donor prospects to make—and that is to send you a gift. Do everything to keep their eye on that ball and not confuse them with other decisions.

What's the Right Gift Amount to Ask from Existing Donors?

Once a person has a giving history with your organization, you are in a much better position to target your follow-up copy, including what amounts you ask them to give. That's why it's essential to capture the giving history of your donors as well as other pertinent information about their interests in your program. The whole objective is to send copy to these known donors that is personal and relevant to their interests. Two bits of information included in your donors' records will be helpful in future mailings.

1. HIGHEST PREVIOUS CONTRIBUTION (HPC).

To assess the giving capacity of your donor, it is essential to know their highest previous contribution. The highest previous contribution (HPC) measures the single gift-giving capacity of your donor. If, for example, you have a major project in which you want to ask for maximum size gifts the HPC will help you in targeting the optimum gift amount request.

2. THE MOST RECENT CONTRIBUTION (MRC).

The level of the latest gift from your donor measures their current level of interest. It may also be a measure of their level of interest in the type of appeal made. That's why some fund-raisers also capture the appeal theme data as well. It is most effective in writing to donors to remind them that you remember a particular gift to a particular campaign—and then report the latest results on the project given to. This is fund-raising at its best. You base a current request on genuine thanks for a remembered gift for another important project.

Asking for the Gift in Pieces Other than the Gift Response Form

Fund-raising letters should have either a direct or an indirect gift request on every page of the letter, brochure, or other insert. To some, this may sound crass and overdone. But it really isn't. If every prospect read your mailing in a predictable and similar manner every time, you might get by with one request. But this is not the case. Remember that direct mail readership takes as many routes as there are readers. That's why effective direct mail fund-raisers repeat the gift request as often as they can. Even if you enclose a news clip, for example, it is a good idea to add a little script note that points out the value of the insert and how a gift will be used. Some recipients may look only at the news clip piece. Because asking for the gift is so important, we list here 51 different ways this can be done. This list should serve as a creative idea stimulator to remind you to make different and varied requests throughout your appeal. Here's a special tip to help you improve your fund-raising mailings even more: Keep a special notebook of money amount asks that you see in other mailings and that seem relevant to your cause. This way you'll not come up short when you need to inject these critical phrases in your direct mail fund-raising letters. Now let's take a look at the different types of phrases you can use to specifically ask for a gift in the letter.

Fifty-one Different Ways to Ask for the Gift

1. Any size gift you make will be appreciated. But, if you possibly can, won't you please write a check for $____. Whatever you give, please accept my deepest thanks.

2. Look into your heart. Then make as generous a contribution as you can.

3. Please send your gift today—it will make a difference. Even more important, your gift will _____

4. Thank you for your compassionate response. I look forward to hearing from you as soon as possible.

5. That's the kind of miracle you can create when you give only $_____.

6. There's so much more to be done . . . and we need your help to continue.

7. Support us. You'll be glad you did. We get things done.

8. Your gift will help us reach that ambitious goal.

9. By responding today you will _____.

10. As you sow your financial seed this month, do it as an act of faith.

11. Your special gift of $ _____ will allow us to _____.

12. I hope we can count on you. Your gift will mean so much to _____.

13. I'm asking you to help us help _____ at this critical time.

14. So, give us $ ____, and we'll see that _____.

15. Will you help us reach this goal? Your gift of only $____ will allow us to _____.

16. Your emergency gift is needed today.

17. Please do the best you can. ____ is depending on you.

18. If you cannot make a gift of $____, I hope you will make a gift of $ ___ or whatever you can afford today.

19. Whatever you decide, know that your help is vital and timely.

20. That's why I am writing you today. For I assume that you not only want to talk about it, but that you are concerned with what's been happening and want to do something about it.

21. Together, we can, make a difference.

22. Lend the _____ your personal support.

23. Here's how you can help.

24. Right now we need you, your concern, your compassion, and your financial support.

25. That's a huge sum. That's why we need many more committed members, many more dollars, and _____.

26. Please let me know I can count on you.

27. Our project is ready to go. All we need is a special tax-deductible gift from you to get it started.

28. I am counting on your support.

29. I hope you will send a check, just as large as you can make it, today.

30. Yes, we need you, your voice and your gift of $____. Please help us today.

31. We need money to save the lives of these children and to find better ways to cure _____.

32. Before I ask for your help I want you to know exactly what will be accomplished with a gift today.

33. And while these valiant people can do a lot, there is one thing they can't do. They can't operate without our support. Please help.

34. So—Please say yes! And to show our special thanks you'll be entitled to _____.

35. I urge you to be as generous as you can. Not for me, but for _____.

36. _____ can't solve the _____ problem alone. We need your help.

37. I'm not asking for myself. Your gift will _____.

38. Only you can make that happen . . . through your support of _____. So please take a moment now to send your tax-deductible contribution.

39. Please turn your concern into practical, effective action . . . your gift of $ ____ will allow us to _____.

40. When you give, you'll have the satisfaction of knowing you've done the right thing.

41. Remember, we have no source of supply to help _____ other than what caring citizens send. Thanks for doing your best to _____.

42. When you join you'll receive _____. But the best benefit of all is the satisfaction of knowing that you have helped _____.

43. Only with your support—and that from many other caring citizens—can we _____.

44. Because your past support has made such a difference, I'm asking you today if you could find it in your heart to send a gift of $_____.

45. Don't delay. In the short time it takes you to write a check _____ will take place.

46. Right now you can make a direct impact. Your gift of $ ____ will _____.

47. Remember, we receive no government grants and must rely entirly on private support from people like yourself.

48. Your financial support is greatly appreciated and needed to _____.

49. Our need for your support is terribly urgent right now because _____.

50. Help us. Send your gift today to _____.

51. Please do what you can. We'll all be glad you did.

21

Structuring the Fund-Raising Offer

In the last chapter, we looked at all the different ways to make a specific ask for the gift. Now, in this chapter, we'll look at the ways to wrap an offer around the gift ask. When we say "offer" in fund-raising mailings, we mean all the trappings connected with how much you are asking your prospect to give as well as the terms, conditions and special benefits. There will be a central theme to the letter request . . . a particular project that needs funding. But around this theme or appeal there are a number of items that make up the entire pitch or offer. These include the amount of money being asked for, any premiums offered, terms, discounts, and so on. All these items taken together are what we call the offer. It is one of the most important factors bearing on your success.

Here are 14 different types of fund-raising offers that you can utilize to get maximum response.

Fourteen Different Types of Fund-Raising Offers

1. ASK FOR A SINGLE MONEY AMOUNT.

Here you ask for just one single amount. The advantage is simplicity. It's clear and uncomplicated as to what you want from the donor. Here's an example of this type of request:

```
___ I accept your invitation to membership in the
_____. I will receive all member benefits.
```

```
__ $25 check enclosed, payable to _____.
```

2. ASK FOR A RANGE OF GIVING LEVELS.

This is probably the most widely used approach for a money amount ask in fund-raising letters. The advantage in using a range is that you can provide for donors with different giving level capacities on the same list. In a sense you get the best of both worlds: You can offer a minimum entry-level gift and yet at the same time allow for higher-level giving from donors who have that ability. Here's an example of a giving amount range:

```
I want to invest in students like _____ and see
my gift multiplied through other students like
him. Enclosed is my gift of:

__ $25 __ $50 __ $75 __ $100 __ Other $____
```

3. OFFER A PREMIUM FOR A HIGHER GIVING LEVEL.

This is similar to the range with the exception you offer some incentive for giving at one of the higher suggested levels. When you make an offer of this type, the cost of the premium has to be factored into your analysis of results. A premium may increase the giving level, but do you end up with higher *net income*? That's the key question. Here's how to do it:

```
__ Please renew my membership as a member in the
category checked below:

__ $100 __ $50 __ $25

We greatly appreciate your support as an
Associate member at $25 this past year. Your mem-
bership identifies you as one of the special few
who know that _____ will endure only
with your support. It is my hope that you will
consider advancing your membership level in the
_____ by joining an inner circle of _____
members with a contribution of $50. At this
level, you will have additional privileges to
enhance your enjoyment . . . "
```

4. MAKE A BILLING-ONLY OPTION.

This offer is considered one of the strongest in direct mail. It is most often used when a publication of some sort is sent to donors. In this offer you don't require the donor to send money up-front . . . only the acceptance of being billed later. This type of offer will give the highest up-front response, but the important point is to evaluate the net paid results after the results from the subsequent billing series are in. Again, the cost of billing has to be factored into the analysis to get a true picture of how successful this offer really is. Here's a sample of the bill-me only offer:

```
SEND NO MONEY

Introductory Reservation Form

Please send me my first issue of _____ free. If
I like it, I'll receive the next eleven issues
for only $ ____. If I don't wish to be a mem-
ber, I'll return your invoice within two weeks
marked "Cancel" without further obligation or
commitment. In any case, the first issue is
mine—FREE!
```

5. CASH PLUS BILL-ME OPTION.

This one combines the option of sending payment up-front or requesting to be billed later. While the bill-me only offer is attractive and appeals to a lot of donors, there is a group of donors who want to make their gifts only by cash. This offer allows for both groups to be satisfied. Here's a sample of the cash plus bill-me option offer:

```
____ YES! I accept your invitation to join _____.
Please enter my subscription to the _____, send
me my membership card and all the other benefits
of membership.

__ Individual $25 __ Family $35

Check One:

__ Payment Enclosed __ Please Bill Me Later
```

6. FREE PREMIUM FOR PROSPECT TO KEEP REGARDLESS OF DECISION ON MAIN OFFER.

This is similar to the previous offer but is used with one-time premiums that are featured in the promotion. The prospect is told that he or she will receive a free gift for joining or subscribing and that they can keep the gift even if they decide not to pay the subsequent bill. Here's how this option works:

    __ YES! Send me a FREE copy of _____. If I
    choose to continue my membership I'll return your
    invoice with my payment of $_____. If I choose not
    to continue, I'll write "cancel" on the invoice
    you send me and keep the first issue of my members
    magazine free. I understand you will also send me
    a FREE copy of _____, which is mine to keep
    regardless of my decision on the membership.

7. OFFER THE CREDIT CARD OPTION.

With the almost universal use of credit cards these days, an offer that includes an option of charging to a credit card can add to the response. To make this type of offer arrangements must be made with credit card companies. And you must plan for some additional administrative expense to process the contributions. Here is what you add to the gift response form for the credit card option:

    __ Check enclosed

    __ Charge to my

    __ VISA

    __ MasterCard

    Account # ____ ____ ____ ____

    Signature _____ Exp. Date _____

8. ALLOW AN 800 NUMBER RESPONSE OPTION.

This is an option that definitely should be tested before adoption. In it you allow the potential donor to call a toll-free number that you have set up to process gifts. It can be counterproductive if you have an inbound telemarketing service that receives calls only during a limited number of hours. To be successful you will have to consider contracting with an 800 number service that provides around-the-clock service and a capacity for taking a large number of calls. If you are promoting through television, an 800 number is essential. In direct mail, its use is limited pretty much to catalogs. However, for fund-raisers there is an application if you have an emergency appeal and need the funds almost overnight. Here's a sample of the copy to use for an 800 number on a direct mail response form:

```
For faster service, call toll free:

1-800-____ - _____

Please have your member number and your credit
card number handy when you renew by phone.
```

9. INTRODUCTORY DISCOUNT OFFER.

Organizations that promote membership can utilize this offer in which the prospect is given a discount off the regular one-year membership rate. Here's a sample of this type of offer:

```
__ YES, send me the _____! I'm enclosing
$24.95 (crossed out, and $19.95 inserted in script
with message: Special introductory offer), which I
understand entitles me to an introductory member-
ship including 12 issues of the magazine _____
and all the other benefits of membership.
```

10. YES-NO OFFERS.

To induce maximum response the yes-no option can be used. In this offer the fund-raiser incorporates a nonmoney response in the response form. It's an involvement technique to boost overall response and, it is hoped, at the same time increase the paid response. Many prospects find when they get right down to the ordering part they back off from the "No" response. Yet this is an attractive offer to get maximum response. Here's how a yes-no offer looks on a fund-raising mailing:

```
__ YES, I am with you in your plan to expand the
_____ research program. I have enclosed my gift
```

```
to support this and other _____ programs to find
a cure for _____. Please send me my gift copy
of _____.
```

```
__ $15 __$25 __$50 __Other $___
```

```
__ NO, I don't believe that _____ should expand
its _____ research program at this time.
```

11. CANCELLATION OR REFUND PRIVILEGE.

To minimize objections in the initial sale, fund-raisers will make money-back or refund offers. This is typically done with offers that include merchandise and/or magazine subscriptions. If a prospect is on the borderline of ordering it helps to suggest they can get their money back if not satisfied. Here's the statement to add to your order form for this offer:

```
Money Back Guarantee: I understand that if I am
not completely satisfied I may cancel my member-
ship and receive a refund (full or for the unful-
filled term of my membership).
```

12. TRIAL OFFER.

The trial offer is effective in breaking down initial price resistance. In cases where the annual membership or subscription fee is significant, it helps to attract new donors by offering a three- or six-month trial. This type of offer is used when a publication (newsletter or magazine) is a central part of the benefits. Here's the way to outline the trial offer:

```
__ YES, I would like to receive a special 3-month
trial membership to _____ for only $____.
This entitles me to all the benefits of member-
ship, including three copies of _____
Magazine. At the conclusion of my trial period I
understand you will bill me for a one-year mem-
bership at the special rate of $_____. If I am
not completely satisfied I may return the invoice
you send me later on marked CANCEL and be under
no further obligation.
```

13. AUTOMATIC FUNDS TRANSFER OFFER.

This offer encourages regular, systematic giving over a longer period of time. Here is the copy to use for the automatic funds transfer option.

Join ____'s Convenient Giving Plan.

If you take advantage of ____'s Convenient Giving Plan, each month your gift is automatically transferred from your checking account to _____. A record of your contribution appears on your monthly banking statement as well as your _____ statement.

I hereby authorize my bank to charge my account each month and pay to ____ the amount shown below, in accordance with the terms and conditions shown on this form. I have enclosed a check for my first month's gift.

My authorization to charge my account at the bank shall be the same as if I had personally signed a check to _____. This authorization shall remain in effect until I notify my bank or _____ in writing that I wish to end this agreement and my bank or _____ has had reasonable time to act on it; or until my bank or _____ has sent me 10 days' written notice that they will end this agreement. A record of each charge will be included in my regular bank statement and will serve as my receipt. In the event of an error, I have the right to instruct my bank to reverse any charge. I understand that this must be done by written notice within 15 days of the date of the bank statement or within 45 days after the charge was made.

14. MEMORIAL GIFTS.

In certain types of cases there is an extremely strong motivation to give gifts "in memory of" or "in honor of" of a particular named individual. This applies to health or disease organizations especially. If a loved one or close friend has died of the particular disease the nonprofit does research in, people will be very receptive to giving in memory of the deceased. But this type of giving applies to other types of fund-raising organizations as well. If you have a core group of members who are very deeply associated with your organization, then offering the "in memory" gift is a wise idea. For example, fraternal groups and educational institutions can make this offer effectively as well. Here's how to work the copy on your gift form for this type of a gift:

```
The enclosed gift is in memory/in honor (circle
one) of:

(Please indicate name) _____

Please notify the following person(s) of this
gift:

(Space for name and address)
```

Of course, several of these offers can be combined into one. For example, the bill-me option and/or charge option can be added to the cash option. It's important that the offer be compelling and easy to understand. There should be no confusion or possible misinterpretation on the offer. After all, you don't have a sales representative standing by to answer questions. In other words there should be no questions. Otherwise your mailing will be DOA (dead on arrival)!

22

Designing Your Direct Mail Package

Typically when people think of graphic techniques or design as applied to a direct mail fund-raising package (e.g., outer envelope, letter, gift response form, return envelope, and other enclosures), they tend to think first of large four-color pieces on glossy stock; in other words, "design" conveys lots of eye-catching material, die-cuts, and unusual graphics. As a matter of fact, good direct mail fund-raising design techniques have a different objective, namely, to heighten the personal one-on-one communication look and to convey an emergency appearance. You do not want to look "expensive" in a fund-raising mailing. This could easily convey that the contribution will be used primarily for further direct mail efforts. The design should look right for a fund-raising appeal. In this chapter we'll review some of the more common techniques used by direct mail fund-raisers to achieve designs that are effective in highlighting the fund-raising message.

How to Achieve the Personal Look on the Outer Envelope

Personalization in direct mail does not simply mean the use of the prospect's name and address in the letter and/or order form. Personalization can be more broadly defined as all the techniques used to make the mailing conform to a personal one-on-one communication. Fund-raising personalization starts with the outer envelope.

The best outer envelope is a closed-face (nonwindow) envelope that has the recipient's name and address in a typewriter type. If the closed-face envelope carries a first-class stamp, you have the ultimate in the personal-ized look. It may also include an organizational logo, name of sending orga-nization, and address. This is a one-on-one personal communication—regardless of the total number of pieces sent out. Never denigrate your effort by saying or thinking it is a mass appeal. It is read by only one per-son at a time. The message from beginning to end should strive to sound personal. There's one thing for sure. If, in the designing process, you think this is a mass appeal, it will look that way! Always try to design the mailing as if it were being received by only one person.

The goal of a fund-raising design is to make your mailing look as close to a personal communication as possible. It's possible to simulate the first class look with the only change being a live third-class nonprofit stamp. It has the same look as a first-class mailing with a live stamp, even though the stamp is at the nonprofit rate. Most people do not study the postage stamp all that carefully so you get a first class appearance for the lower third-class nonprofit rates.

There are other ways to pay the postage to simulate the first-class appearance. These include third-class metered postage or a simulated rub-ber stamp of the nonprofit third-class indicia.

The least preferred way to pay for the postage is the printed third-class nonprofit indicia. This is a dead give-away that the mailing is bulk mail. However, there are times when you're not trying to come through as a fully personalized letter enclosure so you can go with the lower cost (in mail house charges) of the nonprofit indicia. This does not diminish the personal nature of the message. It simply means that the clear-cut promotional purpose of the mailing is evident on the outer envelope.

How the Fund-Raising Letter Should Be Designed

The central piece in any mailing is the letter. This is the document in which the sender clearly states the case for a gift. It is the *raison d'être* of the mail-ing. In this book you have seen a number of different types of letters that can be employed. In this section we look at the graphic techniques to employ in the letter so it has the best possible chance of being read. The overall rule is this: Every technique employed should enhance the impor-tance and readership of the printed message. As a first rule, always use a typeface in the letter itself that looks like it has come directly from the type-writer or word processor. Avoid in most instances typeset type. This is a step removed in terms of the personal look. Also consider using underlinings and brackets and other emphasis lines in the margins. Hand-ruled under-linings and marginal "squiggles" can make a plain printed letter look much more enticing and easy to read. This is not gimmicky. It is a way to help the reader stop at important points. And it is a good way to entice readership from individuals who only plan to take a quick glance at the letter. If you can arrest a person's eyes long enough to read a sentence or two you stand a better chance of getting full readership and action on your request.

Another way to improve readership of the letter is to use "call-outs." A "call-out" is material that is printed in the margins of the letter—usually brief handscript statements—to call attention to something within the text that's important. Don't overlook doing this on the assumption that "nobody is fooled." You aren't fooling anybody—you are simply calling attention to a key part of the message. If you've ever received a printed family newslet-ter that is tucked in with some folks' holiday greeting cards, you know that the very first part of the message you look at is the added hand-written message in the margins if there is any. We do this because we realize the handscript has some interesting little personalized tidbit of interest. Call-outs in direct mail letters are doing the same thing. Here are some margin-al call-out statements that you can use:

Important

Big savings

Free gift

Please help

Special price

Your extra benefit

Thanks for your help

Good news

Print Letters on Both Sides of the Sheet

Because success in direct mail fund-raising depends heavily on economical mailing packages, in most cases you will probably want to print your letters on the front and reverse side of the same sheet. Most people are used to this, and with today's environmental concerns, it carries another subliminal message—you care about the environment. However, there are times when it's important to print the letter only on one side of the sheet because you are trying to develop a fully personalized look in a mailing to a high-level donor. In these cases you've spent money on all the other elements to make the package look first class, so it's wise to follow through with the letter and print on only one side of the sheet.

Why Long Fund-Raising Letters Usually Do Best

How long should your letter be? The quick answer is—long enough to get a contribution response. Writers who are effective in getting top response in direct mail usually find that longer letters do better than shorter ones. If your cause is the Salvation Army, the Jerry Lewis Muscular Dystrophy Association Telethon, or the American Red Cross, you can probably get by with very short copy. Most people are very familiar with these organizations. However, this is usually not the case with most fund-raisers. Even if the fund-raising organization is well known it may be promoting for a special need that requires a fair amount of copy to explain. Here's the guideline: Make the letter long enough to cover all the major reasons why a person should contribute.

Check Your Letters for Readability Before Mailing

In this book we have concentrated on the written message. We've considered a number of different types of letters that can be used. Before printing and mailing your letter, sit back and look at it simply from a visual point of view. Does it invite readership? Is it reader-friendly? Here's what you should look for: short words, sentences, and paragraphs; lots of underlinings; a sprinkling of indented paragraphs. The average paragraph length should be no more than four lines. The first page should have a fair amount of white space so the reader is enticed to begin reading. And on the page breaks, split the copy in the middle of a thought to tease interest to the next page. It doesn't make sense to spend a lot of time and money on writing a solid message only to "clothe" it in a letter that appears hard to read. Evaluate your letters from this reader-friendly appearance and pretty soon you'll begin to see how all these slight techniques help in clearly presenting your message.

How to Design the Gift Response Form

The design of the gift response form (the form with the donor's name and address and check-off blocks on gift amounts) is critical to the success of the mailing. Your letter may motivate someone to give. But if that prospective donor looks at the gift response form and is confused or unsure as to how to respond all the good effort on the letter is lost. There are three important guidelines to follow in creating the design for the gift response form. *First,* it should be absolutely crystal-clear on what you are asking the prospect to do. And the gift "ask" stated in the letter must be the same as that in the letter. Any discrepancy here is bound to confuse the prospect. *Second,* the gift response form should look easy to use. If it appears long and complicated, you've got a problem. Many fund-raisers laser-print the name and address on the gift response form or at least affix a label to the gift response form. This makes it easier for the donor to respond, and it allows the fund-raiser to key or code the labels so the mailing package and list source of the gift can be tracked. A *third* rule in designing gift response forms is not to print information that the recipient may want to retain. Your prospect may hesitate to send in a gift if he or she feels they are also losing some type of information that they would like to keep. Determine what information is necessary for the response and what information you prefer to have the prospect retain. The latter information can be printed on a perforated stub. The donor keeps this vital information and returns only the necessary data on the larger portion. Generally speaking, it is good not to print any copy on the reverse side of the gift response form other than, "Complete the gift response form on the reverse side and mail it today. Thanks." This way it's clear no matter what side of the form your prospect looks at first, he or she realizes that this is the piece that gets returned with the gift. Also it is good practice to utilize a separate enclosure for the gift response form. When you do this the piece stands out and is less likely to be overlooked. If you also enclose a brochure consider a coupon gift response form as a secondary gift-making form. In these cases you include the following copy by the coupon:

- Use the separate gift response form to send your gift. If lost—or if you want to share this message with a friend—use the coupon below.

When to Use a Brochure in Addition to a Letter

Don't assume that every mailing should also have a brochure enclosure. As a general rule, don't enclose a brochure unless you have some information that can only be conveyed in this extra enclosure. Usually the reasoning is done the wrong way around: "Let's enclose a brochure . . . what should we put in it?"

There are some valid reasons for enclosing a brochure in a fund-raising mailing. There may be vital information or illustrative material essential to your message that would clutter up the letter and make it sound less personal. You may want to illustrate a premium offer and/or membership benefits. Sometimes fund-raisers print a number of testimonies from people who have either been helped by their organization or testimonies from people who have a positive feeling in connection with making a gift. Or you may want to illustrate a project for which you are asking for a gift. When you do use a brochure keep clearly in mind that this also is a fund-raising piece. That is, the need for funds and a direct ask should appear in the brochure as well. As is the case with the gift response form some prospects will look first at the brochure, so it's important to reach them with the central point of your mailing. Here's a sampling of cover headlines from different fund-raising brochures to illustrate their purposes:

- 12 Good Reasons Why You Should Consider Membership in _____

- Join today and we'll send you this FREE _____

- You can make these children's dreams come true

- Hear what enthusiastic donors have to say about _____

- Read what these leading newspapers say about _____

Other Enclosures That Work in Fund-Raising Mailings

In Chapter 3 we looked at some front-end premium enclosures that work in direct mail. In addition to these premium enclosures, you may want to enclose such items as a newspaper clipping or a photo. The newspaper clipping should carry an overprinted script message that tells the importance of the clipping <u>and</u> makes another gift request. Here is a script statement that can be printed at the top of the reprint:

- (Name of newspaper) reports on the success of _____'s program to _____. But you can see the battle is far from won. That's why your gift today can make a big difference. Thanks for your help.

Photo reprints have been effectively used as enclosures in fund-raising mailings for years. Photos tend to convey a sense of immediacy and personalization to the mailing. It's as if the letter-writer took a picture and enclosed it to illustrate some point in the letter. When photos are used, it's important to include a copy message on the reverse side of the photo reprint. Make the point that the photo illustrates and then add a line that, in effect, says "this is why we need your support." Here's an example of a script statement on the reverse side of a photo:

- I thought you would like to see the results of our work in (country). 100 families now get fresh clear water from this well. But there are so many more desperately needy families that need a well in their local community. A gift of only $25 will help—when combined with gifts from other concerned citizens. Thanks for your support.

How to Improve Results with a "Lift Letter"

A standard fixture in direct mail today is what is known as the "lift letter." This enclosure began some years ago in magazine mailings that made a free sample copy offer. It was initially known as a publisher's letter (it was a second short letter in addition to the main letter), and the copy read along these lines, "If you've decided to turn down this offer please read this . . .". The letter simply went on to repeat the offer and state that "you really have nothing to lose, you can return the invoice we send you later marked 'Cancel' if you don't want to continue and you'll owe nothing . . .". Because this short additional letter enclosure worked so well in magazine mailings, all kinds of mailers—including fund-raisers—began to employ this type of an extra enclosure. It works well because it generally answers an objection, or it gives one strong emotional selling point. People are attracted to it (as they are for a P.S. statement) probably because it is short, engaging, and provocative. Fund-raisers use it to repeat the offer, to give special testimonies, or to recap excerpts from letters written by recipients of aid.

The lift letter samples that follow illustrate different ways that this effective enclosure can be used. It is a simple item to create and can be easily tested in your acquisition mailings.

LIFT LETTER—
NATIONAL WILDLIFE FEDERATION

IF YOU'VE DECIDED TO TURN DOWN OUR <u>FREE</u> OFFER, PLEASE READ THIS MEMO FROM OUR EXECUTIVE VICE-PRESIDENT . . .

I understand quite well why people are skeptical about answering mail that offers to send them something FREE. There are very few things in this world that are FREE—with no strings attached. But the National Wildlife Federation's offer to send you a copy of NWF's WILDLIFE magazine, at no charge to you, <u>IS VALID</u>! And the FREE copy has actually been reserved for you.

Why? We are anxious for you to see and read this beautiful publication, primarily because we know you're going to find it informative and visually exciting. And once you see it, we're betting that you'll want to keep getting it. Unfortunately, you can't—unless you're a member of the National Wildlife Federation.

Aha, you say . . . there's the catch. No catch, really. The National Wildlife Federation is a nonprofit, nongovernmental conservation group made up of people like yourself, who recognize the urgency of today's conservation crisis. When you think of the multitude of challenges facing us—the pollution of our waters, the dwindling numbers of some of our wildlife, the overdevelopment causing damage to our environment—you realize how many memberships it will take to make some lasting gains. It gives you some idea of why we encourage you to join the National Wildlife Federation.

That's why we're hoping that you find NWF's WILDLIFE magazines and all the other benefits of membership tempting enough to stay with us. Whether or

Reprinted with permission, National Wildlife Federation.

not you decide to continue, the lovely issue we send
you is yours to keep and enjoy.
    No strings . . . just the National Wildlife
Federation trying to introduce you to a great magazine and a worthwhile organization that deserves your
support.

                        Sincerely,

                        Thomas L. Kimball
                        Executive Vice-President

    Here's a typical lift-letter approach. It was mailed some years ago, but
it beautifully illustrates all you need to know about an effective lift letter.
This organization is making a special free examination offer on its magazine. The lift note features the offer. It deals with the natural skepticism that
people have and very persuasively makes a pitch for the prospect to at least
see one copy of the member's magazine.

LIFT LETTER—
THE NATIONAL WILDFLOWER RESEARCH CENTER

Dear Friend,

Wildflowers occupy center stage in my life these days . . . they claim my heart. Perhaps you, too, share a love for the native flowers, grasses, trees, and shrubs that adorn our landscapes. If so, I hope you will become a Member of the National Wildflower Research Center.

As a member of the Center, you will learn much about the beautiful plants we've neglected for so long—and you will enjoy their special place in your own garden. When you begin to use native plants—whether it's two pots on a terrace or a multi-acre spread—I hope you will experience some of the pleasure I feel when I walk among the brilliant wildflowers at the LBJ Ranch. It's a special exhilaration, a feeling of peace in the heart and of union with the natural world.

When I founded the National Wildflower Research Center in December 1982 to encourage and enable the increased joyous use and protection of our beautiful heritage of native plants, grasses, wildflowers, I fulfilled a dream I'd had for many years. Won't you share that dream by joining the Center today? It would give me pleasure to welcome you to our membership.

Sincerely,

Lady Bird Johnson /s/
Mrs. Lyndon B. Johnson

Reprinted with permission, The National Wildflower Research Center.

Here's another basic use of the lift letter. This organization was founded by a well-known person, Lady Bird Johnson. She has been identified with wildflowers for most of her public life. Here she simply puts her love and passion in writing and urges the prospect to join her as a member of the Center she founded.

The Value of a Video Enclosure

One of the strongest enclosures used today in fund-raising mailings is a video presentation. A 12- to 15-minute video presentation can be used effectively to generate high-level contributions for a special effort or to renew active or lapsed members. The powerful emotional and personal impact that can be made by a video enclosure is hard to match. Today many organizations are utilizing TV—either spot commercials or long-form infomercials—and a natural spin-off from the TV production is a shorter video tape that can be enclosed with a mailing to donors.

VIDEO ENCLOSURE RENEWAL LETTER—
WORLD WILDLIFE FUND

Dear World Wildlife Member,

I'm writing you today to thank you for your generous past support and to urge you to renew your membership in World Wildlife Fund . . .

You, and every other member of World Wildlife Fund, play a vital role in our programs—from emergency wildlife rescue projects to habitat protection to park establishment—and much more.

That's why we're counting on your renewed support.

To show you how important your continued support of WWF is, I've sent you the enclosed visual tribute.

This 10-minute presentation was made possible for two reasons. First, because most of the photographs used were taken by WWF staff in the field, costs were kept to a minimum. Second, and more importantly, the pictures reflect the conservation victories your support has made possible.

In fact, this presentation is dedicated to you and all the members of WWF. When you watch it, you'll see that your commitment to WWF does indeed make a difference.

(Ensuing copy talks about projects of WWF that need support.)

When you joined, I promised you action on behalf of wildlife. And I kept my promise.

The action I take in the year ahead depends now on your renewed commitment to winning the many critical battles that lie ahead of us.

Please let me hear from you soon.

Sincerely,

Kathryn S. Fuller
President

P.S. After you've watched the enclosed presentation—and perhaps shared it with a friend or colleague—
please return it to us by affixing the enclosed label
to this packaging. We can then send it to others who
might also wish to support our projects.

Here's how to use a video in a renewal letter. It mentions the low cost
of producing. It also requests that the video be returned with an enclosed
label. An appropriate way for a nonprofit to use a video in its mailings.

Test the Use of Enclosures

In Chapter 24 you'll see some of the critical elements that should be tested in fund-raising mailings. One of those elements is the use of an extra enclosure—whether it's a brochure, news clip, or photo reprint. Do a test with and without the particular additional piece. If the test shows that the enclosure helps response enough to pay for its cost, then continue using it in future mailings. If not, you can save expense by not printing it. In fund-raising each enclosure in the mailing needs to produce more in revenue than it costs in printing and inserting. A simple "with versus without" test will give you the answer.

Improving Results with a Return Envelope

Why enclose a reply envelope and why pay the return postage through the use of a business reply permit? The only reason you do this is to increase the total number of gifts by making it easier for the prospect to respond. If your prospect doesn't have to scurry around to locate an envelope and/or a stamp, it is easier to respond. Some fund-raising mailers have found through testing that a regular return envelope (non-business reply permit) works just as well as the business reply. However, without doing your own testing, it is wiser to mail with a business reply envelope.

In addition to the postage question, there are promotional factors to take into account on the return envelope. If you have an important or well-known letter signer asking for the gift it's not a bad idea to incorporate that name somewhere on the return envelope. People like to feel they're being recognized for doing the right thing. This is a simple way to give that recognition. While this is subtle, it tends to convey that the important person asking for a gift just may see and recognize the donor's support.

Some fund-raisers also print a simulated rubber stamp message on the return envelope to heighten its importance. Statements like the following tend to give the return envelope a little bit of extra sales impact.

```
Please expedite—for the XYZ emergency fund . . .

Your first-class stamp on this envelope will save
funds needed to save the _____
```

The Importance of the Emergency Style

If your message is one of extreme urgency—and the more urgent it can rightfully sound, the better—you may want to consider using any number of different "Emergency Formats." But it's critical that your written message in fact be urgent. It's counterproductive to scream emergency in the graphic design and have a laid-back flavor to your copy.

23

Producing Cost-Effective Mailings

The cost of mailing your direct mail package is a critical factor in determining the success of your efforts. In this chapter we'll look at ways to get the most efficient direct mail components printed and mailed.

Early in the writing stage you should have an idea of what the final end product will look like. If you wait until the creatives are done and then start to think about production details, you most likely will end up with costly mailings. And worse, you'll have mailings that are difficult to process from a mail-shop point of view.

How to Develop Printing and Mailing Specifications

An important first step is to think through how many pieces you will have in the mailing. For example, you might plan a mailing that includes an outer envelope, a letter, a gift response form, and a return envelope. Ask yourself if it will help to have additional enclosures. (See Chapter 22 for guidance on when to use extra enclosures.) Also determine in your own mind approximately how long the copy will be for each component in the mailing. In this early planning stage you will want to consider the size of the outer envelope that will carry all the components of your mailing. As you consider these factors here are the printing specifications to keep in mind.

1. USE STANDARD ENVELOPE AND PRINT SIZES.

Here is a list of the most common—and hence economical—size envelopes:

Style #6 1/4 Size 3 1/2 in. × 6 in.

Style #6 3/4 Size 3 5/8 in. × 6 1/2 in.

Style #7 Size 3 3/4 in. × 6 3/4 in.

Style #7 3/4 Size 3 7/8 in. × 7 1/2 in.

Data Card Size 3 1/2 in. × 7 5/8 in.

Check Style Size 3 5/8 in. × 8 5/8 in.

Style #9 Size 3 7/8 in. × 8 7/8 in.

Style #10 Size 4 1/8 in. × 9 1/2 in.

Style #11 Size 4 1/2 in. × 10 3/8 in.

Style #12 Size 4 3/4 in. × 11 in.

Unless you have some very specific reason not to go with one of these sizes, I strongly recommend that you pick an envelope size from this chart. There is also one other size envelope that is standard and is readily available—the 6 in. × 9 in. envelope. Mailings that are machine-processed require the flaps to be open side or what is called booklet-style envelopes. The #10 style envelope is by far the most common envelope used today. That's why you should consider selecting another standard style so your outer envelope stands out from all the rest in the mail shuffle.

If you plan any windows (i.e., openings in either the front or back of the envelope for name and address to show through or some other enclosure element to be displayed) on your outer envelope, it is also important that you pick standard window dimensions. If you select a nonstandard window size, you will pay extra charges to have a special die made by the envelope manufacturer.

The standard window size is 7/8 in. × 4 1/2 in., positioned 7/8ths inches from the left edge of the envelope and 1/2 in. from the bottom edge of the envelope.

As you consider the pieces in your mailing, discuss with your production department and/or your printers the most economical size for them in printing. These will be sizes that involve a minimum of waste paper in the printing process or, conversely, pieces that get maximum press coverage. For letters, the standard sheet size is 8 1/2 in. × 11 in. The point is to develop creatives that can be accommodated by these standard sizes.

2. SPECIFY THE PAPER STOCK FOR PRINTING.

The more standard papers (e.g., those that printers have in inventory) will naturally be the most economical. If you or your designer want a particular color or special type of paper stock, try to find the closest one that your printer has readily available. Specifying a unique paper stock that is hard to get will add considerably to your costs and the time it takes to do your job. It is possible to get different colors by laying a tint screen of an ink color on a standard white stock. This is an economical way to get paper stock colors.

3. USE RECYCLED PAPERS.

In today's environmentally conscious market it is important to use recycled papers and inks that cause the least waste-disposal problem. Many nonprofit mailers today find that soy inks fill this specification. When you use recycled paper you can convey this important point to your prospects by having the recycled logo printed on each piece that is printed on recycled stock. While this imprint is important, it shouldn't be in so prominent a position as to detract from your main fund-raising message.

4. BE CAUTIOUS IN USING EXTRA COLORS.

The least expensive mailings are done in one color, black. Generally as you add additional colors to the printed pieces, the costs usually go up. Some presses can accommodate several ink colors simultaneously, so that the additional colors do not add that much to the job in these cases.

But there is another consideration for fund-raisers—and that is the *appearance of costly inserts*. Bear in mind that you are asking for a gift for a particular cause and that you don't want your prospects to feel that their gifts are going for costly printing jobs. There should be a considered reason for using additional colors. For example, if you want hand underlinings to look personal, have them printed in blue ink. Or if you are raising funds for a wildlife organization and you want to illustrate a particular kind of animal that is endangered—color really brings the image home. The general rule is to keep the number of colors to a minimum and use additional colors sparingly and only with a good reason.

5. USE SELF-MAILERS

There are different readily available formats from various manufacturers that give you a completely self-contained prepackaged mailing piece that only requires the affixing of a label to mail it. If your print quantity is large enough and if you feel your message can be adequately represented in the preset format of the self-mailer, this is a route to consider. The problem with self-mailers is their impersonal look. They do have that mass-mailer look to them. If you can convert one of your standard packages to an economical self-mailer, it might be worth testing.

6. ISSUE MAIL SHOP INSTRUCTIONS THAT ARE CRYSTAL CLEAR.

Mail shops that process large mailings have their own requirements for efficient processing. It is important to consult with your mail shop representative before printing the pieces to make sure the mailing you ask them to process can be handled. Generally speaking, mail shops require inserts that have a 1/2-in. clearance left to right and 1/4-in. clearance top to bottom in the carrying envelope. The bulkier your inserts, the greater these clearance specifications must be.

The way pieces are folded can also create mail shop problems. The open panels of a Z-fold should be avoided if at all possible. This type of folded piece can be handled by certain types of inserting machines, but for many mail shops, this adds to the time of processing and the expense. The most common wrap-around folds are the best. The inserting machines typically pull inserts into the envelope and work most efficiently with wrap-around folded pieces. Also allow plenty of space for the label area. Know the size of the labels you are using and make sure there's enough clearance around the position for addressing. Otherwise you may find that the name and address label covers some of the copy on the gift response form. Also be aware of the fact that certain inserting machines can handle a limited number of inserts. You should know these limitations as you plan the print specifications of your package. It is always a good practice to show your mail shop dummy samples of the planned mailing *before it is printed*. This way you'll debug the package at that critical early stage. Then, when it is processed by the mail shop, there'll be no complications that hinder the efficient processing of your mailing.

Utilize Different Methods of Paying the Outgoing Postage

Mailings that contain an emergency appeal, or ones that have a close deadline for response, are usually mailed first class by a live stamp. However, most nonprofit fund-raising mailings are mailed at the preferential third-class rates. And there are many different ways that you can pay for the third-class postage. Let's look at some of the more common ways. From a mail shop processing standpoint, the least expensive way is to use a third-class nonprofit indicia bulk imprint that looks like this:

```
         Non-Profit Org.
          U.S. Postage
              PAID
        Permit No. _____
           City, State
```

To mail with such a permit you have to apply with your post office. If the mailer holds a permit in two or more post offices the last two lines (Permit No., City, and State) may be replaced with the name of the non-profit organization. There are other methods of paying the postage that can be used. A live third-class nonprofit stamp can be affixed or you may have your mail shop utilize a meter imprint.

If your mailing is going by first class, it's important to use a live first-class stamp, or if it's a first-class meter, print the phrase FIRST CLASS on the outer envelope in a simulated rubber stamp.

Because of the preferential postage rates for nonprofit organizations, their mailings usually go third class at the special nonprofit rate. There are times, however, when the emergency nature of the appeal requires faster delivery. That's one time when first-class postage can be justified. On new donor acquisition mailings, it is important to test the class of postage that is most cost effective and the method of paying for the postage (e.g., live stamp, meter, indicia).

How to Correct Your Address File

If you are mailing to your own list of prospects, it is important to up-date the addresses periodically. (Note: The overall population change of address rate is estimated at 20% a year.) A first-class mailing will get forwarded if the recipient's forwarding instructions to the local post office are still in effect. While this will get you maximum deliverability, it will not help you clean your file. The best way to do this is to mail third class and print the following statement on the outer envelope:

```
ADDRESS CORRECTION REQUESTED
```

In these cases, if the post office has an active change of address on file for the intended recipient, you will receive back from the post office a card that informs you of the new address. This should only be done on mailings to a list that you maintain and want updated because they perform well for you.

Use the All-Important Business Reply Envelope.

Many mailers will pay the return postage on their mailings by using what is called a Business Reply Permit.

You need to apply to your local post office to get such a permit, and then you will have to maintain a balance of funds at the post office to which it can charge the mailer with the return postage. This charge is at the first-class rate plus a fee per piece for processing.

You can use the following statement—or a variation of it—on your business reply envelopes to save some of the return postage costs:

```
Your first-class stamp on this envelope helps
even more. Thanks.
```

It is important to test the method of paying the return postage. If you find that you can get the same return without using a Business Reply Permit, then you will save all the return postage costs. In this case you would simply use a return envelope that has your name and address printed on it and a ruled-line box where the donor affixes a postage stamp.

Labeling or Imprinting Name and Address on the Return Piece

Consider labeling one of the return pieces—either the back of the return envelope or the gift response form that you want returned. Why? If that name and address is on your file, you will be able to find the name more easily and update it correctly. Typically names on a database have a match code that expedites the computer look-up processing time. Otherwise (if recipient has to fill in name and address), you may get back a variation on the name and address in your file and inadvertently create a duplication. It is also considered to be effective promotionally to require as little as possible on the part of the recipient in making a contribution. The name and address label also can carry the source code of the mailing so you will be able to trace results to a particular package mailed to a particular list. Being able to "source" your contributions is essential.

24

Testing: Learning from Your Own Winners and Losers

It's important to review the information you gather as a result of various mailings you have made, whether the results are good or bad. Either way you can learn valuable things to guide you in developing future creatives.

In this chapter we'll consider what items are worth testing and what items are best left to your judgment. We conclude with a final checklist of questions to ask yourself before you print and mail your fund-raising package.

Keep Good Records

Keep a sample book of your mailings along with the results achieved. Occasionally you may want to test or retest an important feature in your mailing package, and you lose the value of testing if you do not keep accurate records. (You are bound to repeat your past mistakes if you don't record results from all your mailings.)

How to Find the Best Themes for Your Mailings

If you keep accurate records of results, you will begin to build a fund of knowledge regarding which themes work for you and which ones don't. When you see a certain topic working over and over again in your various mailings, you should be very careful about switching to entirely new and different themes for your mailings. The new donor acquisition mailing is not the place where donors are to get the complete scope of what you do as a nonprofit organization. If you find one specialized theme that works best on new donor mailings, keep mailing it until the returns fall off. The new donors will eventually get a better understanding of your work through subsequent newsletters, appeals, and annual reports that they will receive as long as they are active on your file. Resist the temptation to try and convey the "full picture" on your new donor acquisition mailings. The first order of business is to acquire the donor. Then the education process starts and donors will get a greater understanding of your group as the months roll by.

Learn from Others

Important creative guidance can come to you from other organizations. When you hear test results that appear valid, it helps to keep this information in your own record of tests. Benefiting from the experience of others is a way to keep your own test costs down. And if you see a package by someone in your field or a related field mailed over and over again, look at it closely. Keep these samples and determine their essential features. You, in effect, are getting valuable test results delivered to your own mail box!

Develop Your Own Success Formula

I recommend you study your winners and losers in the mail. Look carefully at the key components of these mailings. Pretty soon you will begin to see that there is a certain promotional approach that works best for you. This approach or approaches are the ones you will want to duplicate one way or another in your mailings. Sometimes mailers feel they should inject a lot of variety in their different efforts and not necessarily follow their winning formula. This can be dangerous. It is important to remember that your prospects see your mailings possibly months apart and that they have received a lot of other mail in that intervening period. They don't keep a personal record of mail received and check it every time they get a mailing from you. Make changes to your successful packages only when the market tells you it is no longer interested. You will get bored of your approach long before your prospects do!

What Items Should Be Tested?

There are important things to test in fund-raising mailings—and there are things that your own judgment can evaluate that don't need to be tested. Let's first take a look at items that every mailer should consider testing at some point in time. Then we'll review areas that fall within your own judgment and aren't worth the expense to test.

Seven Important Features Every Mailer Should Test

1. THE LIST.

The responsiveness of the list you're mailing is one of the most important factors influencing results. A regular program of testing new lists is an essential for any direct mail fund-raising program. Test different lists and different selections from these lists such as the recency of the contribution, the frequency of the gift, and the amount of the gift.

2. THE OFFER.

This is the second most important test item. In Chapters 20 and 21 we reviewed different money amount asks and different offers. The offer is a relatively easy item to test in a mailing, and it is a factor that has great influence on the results. For example, you might want to test a $15 minimum ask level versus a $25 minimum ask level. Or you might want to test the improvement you get in results by offering a premium for an upgrade gift amount. These are much easier tests to set up than a completely new letter, brochure, or package. So take time to review all the ways you can structure your offer and test the most powerful ones against each other.

3. THE COPY.

Different types of letters can get dramatically different results. It is worth testing to find out just what theme or slant to the copy works best for you. It's important when testing copy or any other specific item that you test only one variable at a time. This way you'll be able to isolate the reason for the variation. If you test two different letters, for example, that make different offers, you won't know the relative influence of the two factors in the test results. The rule is to test one variable at a time.

4. LONG COPY VERSUS SHORT COPY.

Many fund-raisers find that the longer copy approaches work better. This is something you need to confirm for yourself. If you can get by with shorter copy, your pieces will cost less and you will be more effective. When evaluating results take the long term into consideration. One piece of copy may get exceptional up-front returns but poor subsequent performance. You want to go with copy that gives you the best results over the long-term.

5. ADDITIONAL INSERTS.

An additional insert such as a brochure, a photo reprint, or a news clip doesn't always improve response. If your additional enclosure is costly, then you should find out by testing with and without the enclosure if it's worth it.

6. LETTER-SIGNER OR SPOKESPERSON.

Some mailers find that using well-known celebrities to sign their letters improves results. The celebrity may sign the main letter or a lift letter in which they give a strong testimonial for your cause. Political fund-raisers, for example, know that the name of the person who signs the letter is one of the key variables in determining response.

7. OUTER ENVELOPE TEASER COPY.

Probably the most critical copy in the mailing is that message that you print on the outer envelope to get the prospect to open your envelope and read your enclosed message. Outer envelope teaser variations are relatively easy to do and have an important bearing on results. Some mailers who have used a control package for years retain all the inserts intact but vary the outer envelope teaser copy to freshen up the appearance. You may find that just this little amount of variety will give your mailings longer life.

Things Not Worth Testing—Avoid the "Blue-Green" Tests

Most mailers have limited budgets and must use their available test funds judiciously. This means there are certain items on which you should use your own judgment. Is it worth testing two different second colors on a printed piece? Does green pull better than blue? A test might provide an answer, but would test information really make any difference? Should you test indented paragraphs versus nonindented paragraphs? If it was my money you were spending, the answer is "no." The bottom-line question to ask is this: Once I get an answer on a test, how significant will the results be in projections of future mailings? If you find out that blue beats green by 3 percent, is that really significant? Probably not. Next time, green might beat blue by 3 percent! Avoid the "blue-green" tests!

Nine Critical Questions to Ask Before You Print and Mail

You've done your creative work. Your letter, gift response form, and other inserts are finished. The copy and the artwork are done. You are now ready to hand it over to your printers and then a mail shop for that all-important scheduled mail date. But wait! Before you take that final step, take just a few minutes more to review your mailing with these nine questions. You just may catch a fatal flaw before you deliver your tender mailing plant into the jaws of the monolithic mail system. Here they are:

1. ARE THE CROSS-REFERENCES TO THE ENCLOSURES CORRECT?

Make sure the entire mailing hangs together. If you refer to a particular enclosure in the letter, is it included? If you say "postage-paid" envelope, are you, in fact, using a business reply envelope? Review the mailing to make sure all the internal references are correct.

2. DID YOU ASK FOR A GIFT IN EVERY PIECE?

Give your mailing this test. Take one item alone and see if there is enough information in order to solicit a gift. This is what I call the "Did I ask" test. Your mailing has one overriding purpose: to raise funds. Make sure you consistently ask for a contribution, no matter where someone starts looking at it.

3. IS IT A "READER-FRIENDLY" MAILING?

From a visual point of view, is the mailing inviting? Or does it look imposing and heavy? You want it to be attractive and look as if it's going to be an enjoyable experience to spend a little time with it. Give it an overall review from the "reader-friendly" look.

4. CAN AN IMPARTIAL READER GET THE POINT?

You probably have lived with this package for months. Good bits of the copy are firmly entrenched in your mind. And that's just the problem. Give it to some disinterested person (someone representative of a person on the list you're mailing) and ask that person to read it for the first time. This check is mainly to see if the offer is crystal-clear. If your fresh reader doesn't get the point easily, rewrite until it is clear.

5. DO THE ENCLOSURES FIT?

This is where the rubber meets the road. Make sure you have sufficient clearances for the inserts fitting in the carrier envelope and the return document fitting in the return envelope. Also check to make sure the address correctly matches the window if you have a window envelope. Your mail shop person can give you guidance on all these nitty-gritty questions. Much better to get this guidance *before* the pieces are printed than *after*!

6. DID YOU KEY OR CODE THE MAILING PROPERLY?

Are there list codes and package codes? If you are planning to measure the response, make sure that you have precoded the mailing. Otherwise, your results may get merged in the incoming mail stream and you won't have a clue as to how it performed. One other important point: Make sure to run the package by the people who open and process your return mail. Let them know in advance what to be looking for and how you want the results recorded. Discuss with them any special fulfillment requirements such as preparing labels to mail an offered premium.

7. DOES YOUR LETTER PASS THE FUND-RAISING COPY TEST?

Look at your letter copy. Then ask these questions: Did you ask for a specific size gift? Did you tell the prospect what you planned to do with the gift? Does the need sound urgent? Was the introductory copy provocative? Was there a P.S.? Will the recipient learn something new and interesting by taking time to read your letter?

8. DOES THE GIFT RESPONSE FORM STAND OUT?

A gift response form must not be hidden in the mailing. Next to the letter, this is the most important enclosure. You want it to pop out, just begging to be returned.

9. DOES EVERY PIECE IN THE MAILING ADD TO THE FUND-RAISING MESSAGE?

Take a long hard long look at each piece and ask the difficult question: Is this piece necessary? Would anything be lost if it weren't included?

A Final Word

Now you're ready to print and mail your letter. And when the results start coming in, make sure to keep accurate records for at least eight weeks of returns. And then—whether the results are good, bad, or just average—I urge you to analyze the numbers with as much care as you took to prepare the mailing in the first place. I've observed a strange phenomenon over the years: Unless a mailing has blockbuster results, mailers tend to give short-shrift to carefully considering what the results teach. That's tragic. There's just a wealth of information to be gleaned from comparing the mailing itself with the results. So my concluding wish to you in this book on writing good fund-raising letters is that you learn everything you can from each and every mailing you send out. The worthiness of the good work you're doing demands it. And you'll be the better fund-raiser for exercising this important discipline.

Index